BEYOND *the* MUSIC

An insight into the heavenly
realm when we worship God

MARGARET PICKSTONE-DARK

Ark House Press
arkhousepress.com

© 2024 Margaret Pickstone-Dark

All rights reserved. Apart from any fair dealing for the purpose of study, research, criticism, or review, as permitted under the Copyright Act, no part may be reproduced by any process without written permission.

Some scriptures taken from the New King James Version®. Copyright © 1982 by Thomas Nelson. Used by permission. All rights reserved.

Some scripture quotations are taken from the Holy Bible, New International Version®, NIV®. Copyright © 1973, 1978, 1984, 2011 by Biblica, Inc.™ Used by permission of Zondervan. All rights reserved worldwide. www.zondervan.comThe "NIV" and "New International Version" are trademarks registered in the United States Patent and Trademark Office by Biblica, Inc.™

Cataloguing in Publication Data:
Title: Beyond the Music
ISBN: 978-0-6457741-7-7 (pbk)
Subjects: REL013000 [RELIGION / Christianity / Literature & the Arts]; REL055020 [RELIGION / Christian Rituals & Practice / Worship & Liturgy]; REL012120 [RELIGION / Christian Living / Spiritual Growth]

Other Authors/Contributors: Pickstone-Dark, Margaret

Design by initiateagency.com

Dedication

I dedicate this book to my dear sister, Lorraine, who had always been my support in my spiritual journey, and through her insight gave me understanding of the supernatural realm.

I also dedicate this book to my dear husband, Peter. He has encouraged me all the way offering his wealth of history and biblical knowledge.

CONTENTS

Acknowledgements...5
Ministry Endorsements 7
Foreword..9
Preface..11
Introduction..17
Chapter 1:   O give thanks to the Lord 19
Chapter 2:   Change the Climate..30
Chapter 3:   The Presence of the Lord.................................39
Chapter 4:   Knowing God 51
Chapter 5:   Why we Worship God 64
Chapter 6:   Why we Worship God 80
Chapter 7:   Earth – First heaven 100
Chapter 8:   Atmosphere Around the Earth – Second heaven 113
Chapter 9:   Heaven – Third Heaven 131
Chapter 10: Music and Worship in the Beginning............139

Chapter 11: The Temple of the Lord 158
Chapter 12: The Temple of the Holy Spirit 174
Chapter 13: The Holy Spirit 190
Chapter 14: Prayer for all Nations 199
Chapter 15: House of Prayer 219
Chapter 16: The Watchman 241
Chapter 17: The Prayer of Faith 250
Chapter 18: Power of Unity 263
Chapter 19: The Coming of the King 276
ABOUT THE AUTHOR 291

ACKNOWLEDGEMENTS

There are so many people in my life who have shaped, encouraged and led me in my journey throughout the years. First of all I would like to thank my Heavenly Father for saving me and surrounding me with such beautiful people. My deepest gratitude to all those who have taught me the truths of God's word over the years to establish me in the ministry of music and prayer. I would like to thank all my fellow prayer partners from Branxton and around the Hunter Valley who many times laid aside their own agendas to flow where the Holy Spirit was leading us. Many have already gone home to meet Jesus face to face.

To my dear friends, Nina and Warwick Wheatley, I thank for opening their home to regular prayer meetings for over twenty years, and also for spontaneous meetings during times of local or world disasters. And dear Jennifer and Stuart Anderson, who were always available to help with practical needs that arose, I am forever grateful.

Many thanks to Elizabeth Phillips who has been a solid rock and a listening ear for many years. Her prophetic anointing and counselling insight, has spurred me on in the Lord, time and time again.

To my precious friend, Ellice, whose gentle nudge steered the course of my life into making a big decision which has brought so much blessing to my life, a huge thank you.

A big thank you to all those extra special, praying people who have encouraged me in leading worship and the writing of this book. I sincerely thank all my loyal friends at Morpeth Prayer fellowship, Nick and Heather for their love and support in everything. I am forever grateful to dear Robin, who has not only opened her house each week for prayer meetings, but has offered her knowledge with editing issues. I will always be thankful to Michael Lorraine for his encouragement and patient help with proofreading Beyond the Music.

My deepest appreciation to my dear sister, Bev, and her husband, Hilton, for supporting us and enabling us to live in a place surrounded by their beautiful garden—a touch of paradise on earth to inspire any writer, artist or musician.

To Matthew, my brother, I thank for being an inspiration in boldness and showing me that we are all called to do amazing things through the power of the Holy Spirit. Also a big thanks for setting the example of fervency in prayer and not giving up when the going gets tough.

And my nephew, Lucas, I thank for his endless patience and help with his digital expertise, to make the completion of this book possible.

MINISTRY ENDORSEMENTS

I have known my friend Margaret for over 30 years and she has proven to be a faithful and loyal friend. We have laughed together, cried together and shared a lot of fun together. We have sung, played music, prayed and worshipped together. We have prayed up and down the Hunter Valley together meeting up with praying people along the way. She has lived her life for her Lord Jesus. This book will be a must read for anyone serious about prayer and worship.

Nina Wheatley, *Former Assistant Prayer Co-ordinator, Mount Shammah Prayer Network.*

It is my absolute pleasure to recommend this book to you. Margaret is an exceptional writer who conveys her passion for prayer and believing for the amazing things God can do in the beautiful Hunter Valley region and beyond.

Julie Charman, *Secretary/Treasurer Aglow, Maitland; Hunter Regional Leader of Victorious Ministry through Christ, (VMTC).*

Margaret over many years has shown to be gifted with heavenly visions of our God's glorious, Heavenly Kingdom which we believers will occupy for eternity.

Nick Smith, *Prayer ministry, Morpeth.*

As a friend and prayer partner I know that Margaret has been gifted to lead with authority from the throne of God. She brings release from heaven with her praise and worship to see the captives set free.

Pastor Christine Yeomans, *Hunter Christian Life Centre.*

For over 30 year years Margaret has been involved in Prayer and Praise Ministry throughout the Hunter Valley in New South Wales and has brought a wealth of valuable prophetic insight and wisdom to her ministry endeavours.

Di McDonald, *Founder of Singleton Kingdom Catalysts.*

FOREWORD

It has been my joy and delight to know Margie (Margaret) as a friend since 1982. Over the years we've spent hours together in prayer, worship, travel and evangelism. We've laughed and danced; wept and groaned in intercession. We've sung God's praises and bowed down in holy awe in His Presence.

I was overjoyed when Margie and Peter married and I saw the union of two lovely hearts who made a great team for God. Now I'm excited and thrilled as she "births" her books which have been conceived in the Holy Place during her intimate communion with her Lord and carried in her heart for a long time. Margie is a prophetic watchman and worshipper who has always lifted up the sword of the Spirit in one hand and with the other played songs of Heaven which breaks the darkness and brings the glory.

She has been a forerunner in worship, spiritual warfare, teaching, imparting, inspiring and discipling. Margie has brought Heaven's sounds to people and places as diverse as outback Australia and to the churches and streets of other nations.

May these written words of hers within this book continue to sound forth Heaven's voice in many hearts and lands for the glory of God.

Elizabeth Phillips —*Fellow worshipper and reaper in the harvest field.*

PREFACE

I have always been one to look for something more than my natural eye could see. If I sit on a rock looking out to sea, I wonder about the countries beyond the vast, blue ocean. Sitting and relaxing on our property at Mount Royal, I gaze at the misty-blue, forested hills wondering what, and who, is on the other side of the mountains. When I lived in suburbia many years ago, I would sit on our front patio with a cup of coffee and watch the cars go by. *Who were in them and where are they going?* I wondered. I began to pray for the occupants of the cars. This started me early in life, praying for those around me.

Even as a little girl, I wasn't satisfied with just looking on the outside of my dollies or playing with them, I needed to find out what was on the inside and how they worked. How did its head, arms and legs move? I had to take it apart and find out. One particular doll said, *"Mama."* That intrigued me so I took off its head looking for the reason it spoke. My mother said when I was a baby, and old enough to sit up and crawl, she would put me on a blanket outside near the clothesline while she hung out the washing. I always seemed contented with only a few baby things to play with but many times I would just sit and stare. What would I have been seeing or thinking?

I have seen a lot of children just staring into space, or so it seems, and they are usually accused of day-dreaming. Is it just day-dreaming, or are they seeing beyond what the natural eyes see? Jesus said the Kingdom of Heaven belongs to little children. After pestering my parents for years, they finally bought me a piano. It was re-conditioned and sounded beautiful. I mastered hymns using both hands by midnight the first night and would have kept going until my father sent me to bed. The next day was to be exciting as I had planned to see on the inside of the piano and how it sounded with the front casing off.

I am like that with God. I love the Lord, but I am never satisfied with just a knowledge of Him. I not only want to see His glory, but also feel and touch Him. Yes, I accept Him by faith, but there is more to a relationship of love than just believing by faith. As the scriptures tell us, I want to live in the heavenly place far above all principalities and powers of this earth. It is through prayer and worship we can enter straight into the throne room of God. My passion, while I still have time on this earth is to take others where I go—into the heavenly place through song and prayer.

We live in a high place overlooking a valley. Beyond the open valley, the roofs of the retirement village shine white like tents in the sunlight. This brings me into intercession for homeless, stateless, refugees living in war-torn countries. Far into the distance the blue hills are visible on a clear day but when they are hazy, the eyes of my spirit see miles of barren hills in the deserts of the Middle East and Africa where the hardships of villagers are overwhelming. The view from our dwelling is spectacular and I constantly soak it in, but the needs of the nations often break into my thoughts and my spirit quietly prays in empathy.

PREFACE

There is so much hidden from our view that God wants us to see, as we open ourselves to His Spirit. We begin to hear and see what He hears and sees. He trusts us with His burden, not to bog us down, because His burden is light and His yoke is easy. The joy comes after we are obedient to His leading in prayer.

God sees all who need Him. He sees the one lost sheep and goes to any length to rescue him. God has His generals and famous people to do mighty things in His kingdom. We all admire them and many want to be like them; others are just content to soak in their ministry without putting their knowledge to use. God sees beyond what we see. He sees those who are downtrodden and insignificant in this world. The big names have their praise from those who see their works. But God sees those who faithfully serve Him night and day behind the scenes.

When I first settled in the small town of Branxton and started a prayer network, I was told by a local friend who had lived there all her life, that a hawker about fifty to sixty years before, used to walk from one country town to another selling his wares. People used to think he was strange because he would kneel in the paddocks and pray with his hands raised to heaven. There were only a few streets with houses in those days, but many years later new housing developments sprang up in many areas where he had prayed. We also found out that he used to kneel in the property where our prayer fellowship was held about sixty years later. He was one of the unseen workers in God's field. If he was alive today, he would be amazed how his prayers from that place had spread around the world. One day I will meet this man in heaven and witness him receiving his reward for his faithfulness and obedience to God.

There is a story I would like to share taken from Ecclesiastes 9:14-16: *'There was once a small city with only a few people in it. And a powerful king came against it, surrounded it and built huge siege works against it. Now there lived in that city a poor man but wise, and he saved the city by his wisdom. But nobody remembered that poor man. So I said, "Wisdom is better than strength." But the poor man's wisdom is despised, and his words are no longer heeded.'*

I liken the poor man to someone who prays and intercedes for towns, cities and nations. They are usually hidden away in the background and no-one knows how their prayers have changed the course of nations, averted calamities, and even opened ways for highways to be built. Prayer births and enables a situation to happen in the unseen realm. When the answered prayers become reality, the ones who receives the glory or recognition, are those who get the job done because everyone sees the results.

How wonderful God is. He sees and rewards according to the prayer warriors' perseverance and faithfulness. Their rewards are the blessings of eternity. It is in the secret place where God reveals His plans, (Amos 3:7; John 15:15).

I have always been shy and reluctant to step forward to do anything that required public recognition. I had trouble reading out loud at school and my knees would tremble when asked to. Years ago, an elderly lady at our church approached me one day and said that God desired me to write down His oracles. I hardly knew what she had meant until I began to hear God's voice in my quiet times with Him and started to write down what He impressed upon my heart. My mornings with God became longer and revelation of scripture became stronger. When I was given the role as music director at the church I had attended, I was so nervous of speaking to our team, I wrote down inspirational reports each week for them to read. Praying out loud was still the most terrifying thing I had to do. The scripture: "Open your mouth and I will fill it," has motivated me throughout my life and God has never let me down.

It is always a faith walk what we can do through God. God enlarges small beginnings into enormous projects through His anointing. I began

PREFACE

writing "Beyond the Music," in 2004. For many years I had just let it rest as other cares in life were pressing on me. After a well-known evangelist came to town and was selling and handing out his books, I looked for the publishers and saw Ark House Press.

I had written many books before but I had not persisted in publishing. Ark House was very prompt in response to my enquiries and treated me with respect and kindness, so now I have launched a new ministry.

May God open your eyes to see beyond the natural and into the wonderful realm of His Spirit. If you are a musician or singer, may your fingers play and your voice sing glorious songs of the Lord to break open the heavens. And if you do not class yourself in this category, be open for God to do the miraculous.

INTRODUCTION

The world has taken the wonderful God-given, gift of music and made it something that is pursued for self-glory and money. We are living in a world of extremities. To be successful in this industry you must be the best, sometimes not so much in talent, but presentation for show production. Everyone wants to be a somebody—to be noticed in their field of interest. There is no competition in the kingdom of God. Every one is accepted for who they are. God created all things beautiful and has given everyone of us gifts and talents to be used in worship to Him and to bless others. Striving to please the world's standards often brings stress, disappointment and discouragement. Everyone is born to worship God and nothing can compare with the joy He brings.

This book is about what pleases God and how to achieve His purpose for our lives. God never disappoints. He has so much for each of us in our daily lives that lasts for ever. There is an unseen world of beauty and action we can enter into which brings true satisfaction. How? You may ask. It begins with sitting at the feet of Jesus and allowing our love for God to flow from our inner-most being. Sometimes there are no words. Just a release of a never-ending, river of worship and prayer, inter- changing with the melodies of our heart.

You may not consider yourself gifted in the music scene. Be ready, for God is not limited. You may be the best candidate for God to shine His glory through and a testament of God's refining release from the natural abilities, to the spiritual abilities.

In the Old Testament every musician and singer who served the Lord was meticulously recorded by name. That is how important their function was. As you read this book you will realise the power that we carry as worshippers of God. We live in days leading up to Jesus' return. He is leading us far beyond the music and into His anointing where the blessings happen.

The heavenly realm is more real than the earthly sphere that we are so caught up in. There is a realm we can enter into that we can feel, taste and see through the eyes of our spirit which is in union with the Holy Spirit. This Heavenly Kingdom is *eternal*. Our heavenly home is there.

The question to ask is: *What happens in this spiritual realm when we pray and worship God?*

"Beyond the Music" is inspirational about prayer and worship to create a balance between earth and heaven. It is not meant to teach separate subjects with points and formulas to observe. These I have intertwined together to inspire a deeper relationship with God. This book is designed to encourage every reader to consecrate their lives to Christ and walk in holiness as a weapon against the enemy of our souls. Chapter One begins with the dramatisation of scripture to stimulate insight of what goes on 'backstage.'

Before reading this book open up the Bible to **2 Chronicles 20:1-27**.

(NIV translation is used)

CHAPTER 1

O give thanks to the Lord

2 Chronicles 20:1-27

> 'A vast army is coming against you from Edom, from the other side of the sea. It is already in En Gedi.'

At the news-bearer's urgent message, Jehoshaphat, king of Judah, froze—face ashen. He knew what that meant! These armies were not fooling around! His own skilled and valiant fighters—about one million all told, were no match for the strength of the Edomites, Ammonites and Moabites who had joined forces against them. He had to act—fast!

There was only one option—the mercy of God!

Quickly calling his judges, other officials and troops, they urged all the people from every town in Judah to gather together in Jerusalem without delay.

The horses hooves thundered on the desert floor. With muscles rippling, foam dripping, manes flying, they galloped on with driving intention at the tough hand of their riders. They came across the desert from the east like myriad swarms of giant locusts. Thick clouds of white dust enshrouded the sun. The eerie clatter of the chariots' wheels, excited the feral instincts of each rider. They were after blood—Judah's blood! They swept on with seething fervour.

God had promised Judah that if they ever were overwhelmed by an army too powerful for them, seek Him and He would deliver them. Jehoshaphat remembered this. He hurried into the temple of God and raised his face and hands towards heaven.

It was not only the armies of the three attacking nations that were to be feared but the unseen realm. The atmosphere was alive with hordes and hordes of demon spirits. The blackened orb was thickening. Like vultures to a carcass, they swarmed upon the riders and clung to their backs. Digging in their leathery claws they twisted the minds of the riders. 'Judah must be wiped out from the face of the earth!'

'O God! Power and might are in Your hand...!'

Suddenly, at the cry of GOD, the atmosphere exploded into brilliant light. Magnificent angels touched down and surrounded the temple.

The demon spirits momentarily shrank back from the blinding light. At the furious shriek of command from their captain they snapped into line and doggedly came on.

The angelic sentries, commissioned by the Lord of Hosts, adopted their positions and waited. They were vigilant, braced for conflict; their massive hands over the swords still in their sheaths by their sides.

The men of Moab and Ammon thought nothing of the slaughter of innocent people. They were experienced at that. They were even oblivious to the screams of terror when their own children were sacrificed in the fire to the evil gods, Molech and Chemosh. They were hardened to pain and suffering.

They were well practised in listening to the demons they worshipped. They delighted in leading the Israelites astray to follow the gods of the nations.

They let out a whoop of triumph when Edomites from the south joined their ranks. These men were also tough and fierce. Their forefathers had barred Moses from crossing their land and nothing was going to stop them now. They were rock dwellers. Many lived among the natural fortresses of Edom. They were used to the smell of blood. To them the tribe of Judah was like the poisonous snakes they battled with in the desert. Their vendetta against Judah possessed them to carry on with their evil mission. Heading west they melded with the other armies as a united front. They could smell the stench of death. They loved it! It spurred them on!

> '**...We will stand in Your presence O God, before this temple that bears Your name and will cry out to You in our distress, and You will hear us and save us...**'

The drumming of the armies came closer and closer. They were nearly there! Beads of sweat dripped from the bronze faces of the men. Adrenaline raced like never before. The horses' muscles bulged under their lathered coats. They sensed the thrill of war and their hooves hardly touched the ground.

> '**...Men from Ammon, Moab and Mount Seir, are coming to drive us out of the land You gave us...**'

White dust infiltrated the atmosphere surrounding the land of Judah. Victory was assured! There was no doubt about that. The enemies of Judah were the conquerors! This was going to be easy. Yet . . . ? They were puzzled. Where was the resistance? None? Unbelievable!

Nevertheless, the riders' hearts drummed wildly like war drums in excited-anticipation of the kill.

Suddenly, with united precision, the angels of light snapped to attention and whipped out their swords. There was a great flash and their beings emanated the glory of God. They stood alert, their eyes blazing and fixed on the black mass zooming their way. Yet it was not time for action. Their job was not to fight, just defend. There had been no command from the Throne Room.

'...We have no power to face this vast army that is about to attack us. We don't know what to do but our eyes are on You!'

There was no time to call up a popular seer or prophet to give them a word from God. Prophets were wanderers anyway. Who knows where to find one? No, they needed immediate help!

All of Judah were there—men, women and children, standing before the Lord rather than trying to escape the pending onslaught. They had no choice but to throw themselves on the mercy of the God of Abraham, Isaac and Jacob. He alone was able to deliver them from the hand of their enemies. David and his mighty men were long in their graves. Who else could save them? No one but the Lord God Almighty!

It takes a strong man, a bold one to stand up before such a crowd and offer hope. It was not the time for a war on flesh and blood—the battle was too great for that. No, the battle needed to be fought by spiritual means to combat the powers of darkness confronting them. They needed air troopers to prepare the atmosphere! The Lord of Hosts had the right man for the job!

Like snarling, feral beasts, the spirits of darkness plunged forward to smash through the heavenly, containment lines. With lightning speed the angelic warriors fused their flaming swords together barring the demons' entrance. Whips of blue fluorescent light scintillated up and down the lengths of the angels' swords. The first demons to hit shrieked in agony and they were flung through the air like rag dolls.

It was still not time to fight, just to defend. The angels' eyes glistened in amusement. Those demons were sent to irritate, stir up trouble among the people of God—to grip them with fear and weaken their faith. They were there to stop the word of the Lord from being uttered. The angels knew the worst was yet to come. They had seen Satan fall like lightning from heaven but also knew his power was not to be meddled with by the weak. It was the scorning and hatred of God's chosen people that really riled them. But, they also knew that the Lord of Hosts would carry out His promise to deliver Judah.

They continued to hold up their blazing swords forming a band of fire around the people of God. Radiant, glory pulsated through their beings. They waited for the message from the Throne Room. Ready to obey the instant they received their orders.

God raised up His man to be His voice!

'The Spirit of the Lord came upon Jahaziel (son of Zechariah, the son of Benaiah, the son of Jeiel, Mattaniah, a Levite descendant of Asaph) as he stood in the assembly.'

Who would have thought of it! Yet ... of course! Good choice.

Jahaziel! He was a musician, a singer from the line of musicians and singers trained in Solomon's temple. A man of praise and worship before the Lord. A man trained to prophesy with the harp and well versed in the prophetic song. He was a man who could see beyond the music and into the spiritual realm. Like his forefathers' mentor, David, his music was powerful. He could see the battle waging in the heavenly realm between the two spiritual forces well before any ground trooper needed to go out and fight. He was highly respected before Judah.

Jehoshaphat was not new to this sort of thing. He had worked with the prophet Elisha before this, and if it was good enough for Elisha to have musical background while prophesying, why should not that mantle be passed on to other prophets and musicians?

Hope soared!

> **'Listen, all you of Judah and you inhabitants of Jerusalem, and you king Jehoshaphat!'**

There was power and authority in that voice and it came across loud and clear to the hundreds of thousands gathered.

All eyes turned to Jahaziel then quickly to the ground. Even the army bowed their heads in reverence before God and waited. They were hardened by war—tough, sinewy, magnificent hunks of manhood. They had known victory many times over. They were trained for action; had tested their strength to the limit, but this was a battle of another kind— strength of another kind—not with muscle power or brawn, but the power of God. They stood in humility to hear the word of the Lord.

> **'Listen, King Jehoshaphat and all you who live in Judah and Jerusalem! You will not have to fight in this battle. Take up your positions; stand firm and see the deliverance the Lord will give you, O Judah and Jerusalem...'**

Phew! Jehoshaphat heaved a heavy sigh of relief and mopped his sopping brow. He was held responsible before God for these people. If he disobeyed God in any way their blood would have been on his shoulders.

> **'Jehoshaphat bowed with face to the ground and all the people of Judah and Jerusalem fell down in worship before the Lord. Then some Levites from the Kohathites and Korahites stood up and praised the Lord, the God of Israel, with very loud voices.'**

Flares of brilliant light waves illuminated the atmosphere in shafts of glory. The demons screeched in agony. They hated the praises of God! Covering their ears from the resonating sound, they plunged out of the range of the blinding light. In rabid fury their captain roared out his orders to bring them into ranks.

Jehoshaphat once again took up his command as king and said:

> **'Listen to me, O Judah and the people of Jerusalem! Have faith in the Lord your God, and you will be upheld; have faith in His prophets, and you will be successful.'**

When he had consulted with the people, Jehoshaphat appointed men to sing to the Lord, to praise Him for the splendour of His holiness, as they went out before the army, saying:

> **'O GIVE THANKS TO THE LORD FOR HIS LOVE ENDURES!'**

"NOOoo!" The lesser-ranking demons wailed in protest. They loathed the love. There was too much power in that word. They could feel their beings disintegrating. It was the heat of the light emanating from the praises causing all this—they hated the light as much as the love. They had to get out of

there pronto. They shrank back into oblivion leaving behind a puff of burning sulphur.

"EEEAAGH!" The captain of darkness swooped down with hordes and hordes of his minions. These were the best. The most powerful. Tenacious like crazed bears, they smashed through the effulgence and flooded in as a tidal wave. To their surprise, they could only see a few visitors from heaven; it was hardly a challenge.

'O GIVE THANKS TO THE LORD FOR HIS LOVE ENDURES'

The captain of darkness was losing power. "Love ...love ...love ..."

It rang in his ears over and over again like the needle stuck in a groove on an old record. He had to shake it off. In wild delirium he plunged at the captain of the sentry angels.

WHAM! Their swords smashed together. A million, fiery sparks spattered the sky. Again and again they struck. One to one, strength to strength—one powerful dominion against the other. One side fighting to the death with his own agenda, the other defending lives of the people of God.

Love ... love ... love ... *The captain of darkness' face contorted with rage. Of love he knew nothing. Hate he was more comfortable with. This was his territory. Was it not he who incited and deceived the nations surrounding to worship his master, Satan?*

'... ENDURES FOREVER!'

LOVE FOR ETERNITY! The very thought sent violent tremors through his writhing being. With dogged determination, he advanced again for the slaughter.

Thousands of voices lifted up in exultation resounded over and over, louder and louder until the whole heavenly atmosphere was filled with the presence of Almighty God. There was the sound of war—the sound of praise and it began to form a rhythmic pounding as of a battering ram. The glory grew heavier and brighter.

"*NOT THE GLORY!*" *screeched a million spirits. They began to shrivel and melt like candle wax into nothingness.*

The Edomites, Moabites and the Ammonites came to an abrupt halt. Something was not quite right...

What was that sound ...? You've got to be joking!

What were those ridiculous people of Judah doing this time?

They stealthily crept forward on foot, muscles taut, minds focused, bows drawn and ready for action.

Suddenly, a tumultuous fanfare detonated the universe. The heavenly, troop of trumpeters had joined the praises of Judah. There was a mighty roar of jubilation as thousands of angels began to sing praises to God. It was the sound of rapturous victory!

'The chariots of God!' shrieked the remaining spirits of torment. 'Look the chariots of God! screamed the captain of darkness to his cohorts. They had to get out of there–now!

'O GIVE THANKS TO THE LORD FOR HIS LOVE ENDURES!'

The chariots swept in like the fury of a whirlwind. The mighty warriors of God extended their powerful arms and crossed over their flaming swords with their companions. An explosion of light and energy erupted like a volcano shattering the little darkness that was left.

Blinding light struck the last of the demons and they bolted the scene. In their frenetic haste, they floundered around tripping over one another. Chaos broke loose among their ranks and they lashed out at anything within reach. The captain of darkness fought his way through in frenzied fury. Never mind *killing off Judah, it took all his wits to fight off his own kind. One demon after another came at him, irritated by his promise of victory—look where he has led them!*

He shot one venomous glare at the warriors of God. "I'll be back," he hissed and dissipated in a black, puff of foul-smelling smoke.

'VICTORY BELONGS TO THE LORD!' Announced the heavenly herald.

It was finished. All of Judah stood silent before the Lord. They were exhausted but elated.

What happened?

'When the men of Judah came to the place that overlooks the desert and looked toward the vast army, they saw only dead bodies lying on the ground; no one had escaped. Then led by Jehoshaphat, all the men of Judah and Jerusalem returned joyfully to Jerusalem, for the Lord had given them cause to rejoice over their enemies. They entered Jerusalem and went to the temple of the Lord with harps, lutes and trumpets.'

Fact or fiction?

Reading scriptures like the above does make you wonder what is happening in the heavenly realm when we praise the Lord. There are many dramatic passages in the scriptures where God had saved His people when they cried out to Him. As we explore God, man, and the unseen, heavenly realm in between, let our eyes be open to the probable.

This world that we live in will pass away but God has set eternity in the hearts of mankind. As we read earlier, Satan is still inciting hordes of demons to wipe out God's people—first the Jews then the true believers in Christ. Why? What can we do? What has this got to do with music? Plenty. It has nothing to do with professionalism in music and worship, but God and His divine, creative power working through His surrendered servants. Are we ready to take a journey that will mean laying down our lives, achievements, gifts, performances and self emulation upon the altar of sacrifice for God's cleansing fire to consume.

OUCH! Might hurt? Could well do!

CHAPTER 2

Change the Climate

'But who can endure the day of [His] coming? Who can stand when [He] appears? For [He] will be like a refiner's fire or a launderer's soap. He will sit as a refiner and purifier of silver; He will purify the Levites and refine them like gold and silver. Then the Lord will have men who will bring offerings in righteousness, and the offerings of Judah and Jerusalem will be acceptable to the Lord, as in days gone by, as in former years,' (Malachi 3:2-4).

God is seeking pure-hearted worshippers whose offerings of praise are from refined hearts. The above scripture gives a clear picture of God, as the refiner, sitting before the fire—His eyes intently studying the furnace during the refining process so the precious metal will not be ruined. If you ask any refiner how they know when the gold or silver is finished being refined, the answer would be: "When I see my own reflection in the shining metal."

If we yield to Him, God continues the refining process until He sees the reflection of Christ shining from our lives. When each worshipper is finely tuned into the orchestra of heaven, Christ's glorious presence is manifested in ways far greater than our human understanding of music could ever imagine.

The above passage says the Lord will purify the 'Levites'. The Levites were descendants from Levi, the son of Jacob. Moses was having a wonderful, mountain-top experience with the Lord on Mount Sinai but when he came back down among the Israelites, he found they had made a golden calf and was worshipping it. In righteous anger, Moses called out: "Who is on the Lord's side? Let him come to me!" The sons of Levi came and stood with him, (Exodus 32:26-29). They chose the Lord and not the world.

From then on the Levites were consecrated for ministry in the house of the Lord—first in Moses' tabernacle, then in Solomon's temple. They were chosen to become doorkeepers, musicians and singers. Before they entered upon any service they were thoroughly cleansed and consecrated. They did not own houses or lands like the rest of the tribes of Israel because their inheritance was the Lord Himself, (Duet. 18:1-8), and they lived to serve Him night and day in the temple, (2 Chronicles 5:12-14).

The Levites had a very high calling in God and they are typical of all Christians who are redeemed, cleansed, set apart in ministry to the Lord and belong in heavenly places rather than clinging to earthly ties. We will study more of their function in a later chapter.

Are we ready to let go and let God in on our music and worship? To feel the pulse and music of God's very own heart? Are we ready to fight the spiritual battles presiding over our towns with the sound of war? This is for the whole body of Christ. Not just musicians, singers and leaders.

Praise and worship can be so much more than just singing a few sweet or rousing songs in our services. I am not saying this is wrong, for sometimes that is how the Holy Spirit is leading. Music and singing can be used for so many different purposes, but for the spiritually bold and the adventurous, there is a completely different realm that we can delve into. A special area which requires total surrender to the Lord. We have the God-given power to change the spiritual climate of our place of worship, work, church, home or community. Let us face it: How many people come to church with so many problems yet go away at the end of a service without any real life changes—still weighed down, the devil still whispering in their ears.

God has given us the power to change the atmosphere!

One time, as an intercessory prayer group, we were invited to join other praying people prior to a tent crusade organised by a well-known church about an hour's drive from where we lived. As visitors to the church, we had planned to subdue our praying style—not wanting to shock anyone, but it seemed God had other ideas.

The visiting preacher was an American from the Full Gospel Business Men's organisation and was moving in the freedom of the Holy Spirit. The first meeting held was a Friday morning and only a handful of people attended.

Suddenly, during the time of worship, the sound of voices grew louder and louder. I was enjoying the presence of the Lord at the time with my eyes closed. At length, it registered with me that the members of our group were the strongest singers gathered, and this magnificent choir was not us. Not everyone present heard the worship of heaven, but the preacher was excited and mentioned the visitation when he rose to speak.

And there is more! On the last night of the crusade, the speaker encouraged us to worship the Lord with our spirit throughout the whole meeting—through his preaching and ministry at the altar.

The atmosphere of that town had so changed that angels were seen coming in and out of the tent. I did not see them with my natural eyes as others had witnessed, but I certainly felt the presence of the Lord.

A small child had wandered outside the tent and was brought back in by an angel whom she described as a nice man, though the parents could not see him when she tried to show them. A man thought the chair alongside of him was empty until the speaker pointed to it and said: 'There's an angel sitting next to you, sir!' Then there was the incident when a group of angels were seen walking up the aisle and when they passed by, people fell down before the Lord.

By this time, the members of our prayer group were the only ones strong enough to keep the worship flowing, (most of the congregation were unfamiliar with this type of singing). When we would begin to weaken, the speaker would exhort us to continue. What a night! We went home exhausted but exhilarated that the Lord had touched and changed the lives of so many people.

Why was there such a strong representation from heaven that weekend? We do not really know, but my thoughts are: God would love to interact with us more but we are not open to His Spirit. In our flesh and ego, we do not want what we have planned for our services to be interrupted—even by God Himself. I would say that prior to this crusade and during the crusade, a prayer chain from the speaker's own home church would have been busy in non-stop prayer and worship. Combined with the local prayer group and our team, it released power from on high and God wanted to bless us.

Genesis 28:10-13 gives an account of Jacob's dream in which he saw a stairway reaching from earth up to heaven. Angels of God were ascending and descending on it and there above stood the Lord and He spoke to Jacob.

In John 1:51, Jesus says to Nathaniel: *'I tell you the truth, you shall see heaven open, and the angels of God ascending and descending on the Son of Man.'*

Jesus is the ladder that connects between earth and heaven and there is so much more He wants to show us in the heavenly realm if only we would take off our religious glasses.

You may have heard the popular saying that musicians are temperamental—half temper, half mental. In other words—*moody*. Often that is so: it is something I had to deal with long ago in my own life. An angry person could play music in a way that jars the spirit and can change the whole mood of a gathering by wrecking how the Holy Spirit is moving. On the other hand, an over-passive or lay-back person can bring a false peace into a situation quenching action where it is needed—again, missing out entirely what the Spirit of God is saying.

God has given musicians a sensitivity that comes with the creative gift and if channelled the right way, this sensitivity can be used as a powerful tool by the Holy Spirit to lead God's people in the direction God wants. This is all part of the refining process that God takes us through if we are genuine in yielding to Him. We need to be able to hear what the Holy Spirit is saying for every occasion.

'There is a time for everything, and a season for every activity under the heaven ... a time of war and a time of peace,' (Ecclesiastes 3:1-8).

A time of war

We are living in tough times where there is no peace on earth at an international level—wars and rumours of war; terrorists' attacks; anti-God laws passed or on the agenda in our own nation; false religions and the occult to seduce our children. Humanistic teaching to put self first. Their aim is to destroy God's perfect design and confuse young ones into believing they are not the gender they were born with.

All these things are a threat to our Christian heritage. Are we going to sit back and allow this to happen? Or are we ready to lead the people into aggressive praise that will scatter every demon in our area into confusion. The devil is not inhibited and loves to show off. As we noticed in chapter one, the people of Judah knew how to have a praise party with just a simple line of:

'O give thanks to the Lord for His love endures!'

To change the spiritual climate of our towns and nation would be the rewards of true worship; not a public performance or entertainment that is perfect and makes us feel good. This does not always glorify God and break through into the heavenly realm.

Music is a powerful tool. That is why it is so important to hear what God is saying and play and sing according to HIS voice. Christians in the music department need to be praying people and have a backing of intercessors if they can.

Music tells the story of what in going on behind the scenes in the spiritual realm

As the devil always tries to block what God is doing, often there is a battle between the spiritual forces. Many times over the years, when I have led worship in churches and prayer groups, my spiritual eyes have been opened to see the action behind the scenes. During these times I knew what direction to take and flowed into the scene to bring about a change in the atmosphere. As we noticed in the opening chapter, music and worship can determine whether we win or the devil wins. It is only the anointing of God's Spirit that we can move with this kind of insight. To be a worship leader, it is so important to operate in the discerning of spirits—human or spiritual. It takes experience and much waiting on God. We will go into more depth later on.

Many times I have come to a meeting with a list of songs chosen for the service but God soon made it apparent He had something else in mind—completely different in fact. Why? Because of the devil trying to take a foothold to disturb the attitudes of those gathered. But this is not always the way, and God also blesses preparation beforehand, which is the usual the way to work in a team. To be able to tune into God's Spirit is the greatest gift for every prayer warrior, worship leader and musician.

Once I was playing the keyboard during a prayer meeting and suddenly felt to stop midway through a song. Thinking I had misunderstood the leading of the Holy Spirit, I did not respond to His voice and kept playing. God fixed that—the keyboard supernaturally cut off and came on again at an acceptable time. I do not know why this happened, but God should be able to intervene when He sees fit to do so.

Let God have His way in His Church!

Going by experience, I find the Holy Spirit flows in waves. The music can be loud and aggressive to encourage the mighty warriors to wake up, or can create an ambience to comfort and heal. Letting go of all of ourselves and letting God take over brings such freedom to both the praise team and the rest of the body of Christ. Let our worship rise to greater heights in glory, beyond our own hangups and feelings. As we lift up our hearts in worship, with everything we have within us, let it rise as incense, an unseen yet tangible substance. That is true worship.

Okay, you may be thinking: How do I get to that point in knowing what God wants to do? You may be feeling a little discouraged and confused. Nevertheless, read on!

A time of peace

What brings peace to our body, soul and spirit? Jesus does! Jesus says in John 14:27:

'Peace I leave with you; [My] peace I give to you, I do not give as the world gives. Do not let your hearts be troubled and do not be afraid.'

At times the world cries out PEACE! Especially after the twin towers attack in September 2001. During this time demonstrators, including churches, raised up their banners emblazoned with the 'peace sign': ignorant of the fact that the very sign of 'so-called peace' means quite the opposite. It is an emblem the occult identify with – the cross of Nero, a Roman emperor notorious for his cruelty and corruption. This depicts an inverted and broken cross, sending the message to defeat Christianity. It was resurrected during the hippies era.

Christians do not know what they are doing! They follow humanistic ways, thinking they are doing God a service, not realising they are doing just the opposite by fighting against truth. We must seek truth! Copying what seems good and popular by the world's standards is not good enough for us until we have checked out the roots, or the hidden agenda behind each situation or movement.

'For unto us a [Child] is born and unto us a [Son] is given, and the government will be on [His] shoulders. And [He] will be called Wonderful, Counsellor, Mighty God, Everlasting Father, Prince of Peace,' (Isaiah 9:6).

So really, the message that the peace rallies brings is: "We can do it our way—we do not need a Saviour!"

Does it work? Take Jesus, the Prince of Peace, out of our lives, family and government, we will be left with the devil as our companion, giving him rights to take over our nation.

No! Our peace comes from God alone! His peace is much deeper. His peace is everlasting, the world's peace is false and temporary.

How do we tap into the Lord's peace? By hungering and thirsting for His presence and His word.

CHAPTER 3

The Presence of the Lord

Eternity

Imagine coming before a massive curtain separating heaven and earth—God and man. You tug on the curtain crying out "Father I want to come in!" You know He is behind that barrier but your cries go unheard and unanswered. The curtain is too thick. You are desperate and pound the floor outside in devastation.

Suddenly, a loud cry shatters the stillness around you. "IT IS FINISHED!" At the sound of the voice there is a mighty explosion. The earth shakes, rocks shatter and darkness enshrouds you like a blanket. Then with a tremendous roar, the curtain before you rips open from the top to bottom. The way is open! Radiant glory floods over you. It is hard to see because of the blinding light but you are drawn by what seems like a magnetic force.

"What do you see? What do you see?" the crowds pressing against you call out. "I see ..." Your words fade, for standing in the glory with arms outstretched and nailed-pierced hands is the One more brilliant than the sun, more beautiful beyond description. His face is resplendent with joy. With arms wide open, He urges:

"Welcome into the presence of our Father! Come on in and let's worship Him together! If you have seen Me, you have seen the Father!"

What an invitation! What a celebration! This is Eternity. Ecclesiastes 3:11 says that God has set eternity in the hearts of men. The word of God tells us in Hebrews 12:22: *'You have come to Mount Zion, to the heavenly Jerusalem, the city of the Living God. You have come to thousands upon thousands of angels in joyful assembly, to the church of the firstborn...'*

Eternity is where Christ is—seated at the right hand of the Father; far above every principality, power and dominion in the heavenly places and on earth. When Jesus asked His disciples whether they would leave Him, Peter said, *'where would we go, You have the words of eternal life.'* And these words are the same words that are engraved within our hearts. The word of God is for ever! It is powerful, sharper than any two-edged sword! Jesus is the Word. He became flesh and lives among us.

In a later chapter we will take a look at the 'river of life.' This is an eternal river flowing from the throne room of God and through our lives. When we receive Christ, we become partakers of His divine nature—the nature of eternity, (2 Peter 1:3-4).

Music is a gift that is eternal. It never ends. It keeps flowing like the river of eternity. A gift we use forever as we worship God. A flowing river is never fragmented. All water molecules work together. Water can divide but still flows in the same direction as a united force. Seek those things that are above—eternal treasures.

THE PRESENCE OF THE LORD

Matthew 6:19-20 says: *'Do not store up for yourselves treasures on earth, where moths and rust destroy, and where thieves break in and steal. But store up for yourselves treasures in heaven, where moths and rust do not destroy, and where thieves do not break in and steal. For where your treasure is, there your heart will be also.'*

Jesus wants to share all those glorious heavenly treasures with us. To seek those things that are eternal. He would have been overwhelmed with joy when He opened the way for us to enter the presence of the Father. It is like Christmas morning when children open up their presents. It gives the parents great pleasure to see the delight on their faces. When we have guests from overseas, we love to show them outstanding beauty sites of our region—those areas that we ourselves enjoy and admire.

Several years ago a young, teenage boy I was teaching phoned me just as I was finishing piano lessons for the evening. Excitement was in his voice and he urged me to go outside and look at the sunset. It was breathtaking! His parents were not home and he said he could not enjoy what he was experiencing on his own, but had to share it with someone. I came to his mind. What a privilege to share God's awesomeness with him. I, in turn rang Matthew, my brother, who already was outside enjoying the sky and my nephew, Lucas, was up on the roof of their house taking photos.

Imagine Jesus wanting to share the glories of heaven with us. His heart must be bursting with eagerness, but because He is a gentleman, He does not force us. We have been given a free will and unfortunately, we allow the heavy curtain in our hearts to remain intact, still separating us off from the presence of God. We allow obstacles to block our view.

Some time ago I travelled with my niece and nephew past a beautiful lake. I stopped at a high place overlooking the lake so they could have a clear view of the spectacular scenery to take photos. I was disappointed that trees had grown up since my last visit and long grass was also obscuring the view. Knowing that around the corner and further along the road would be a better spot, I called out to come on. They were so engrossed and happy in what they could see, my suggestion did not register with them. I was a little impatient to move on in anticipation of their pleasure with the open panoramic view that we would encounter.

God has so much more He wants to show us. So much more of Himself He would love to reveal. Are we just satisfied with the little we have—to stay on the outside? Are we hungry for more of what He has to offer?

An artist and a photographer see things through the creative perspective which opens up a whole, different world of observation and possibilities. A blade of grass can become an object of beauty with light and shade giving it form and dimension. We are living in a colourful world of variety designed by a Master Creator. I had a friend whose soul was bound up with the hurts and trauma of the past. She came to live with me for a season. Within a week God released her of her pain, and for once she became aware of the beauty around her. She reacted in delight like a child would have responded to the vibrant colours in the garden and the blue sky above. Her world before lacked colour and everything seemed grey. She began to express herself in writing and other talents came to the surface as she worshipped God.

A musician's world is also a colourful world of sound. Blending of notes creates melodies, harmonies and rhythms all working together to form something for us to enjoy. Musicians and composers can hear and feel music within their beings that is not audible to others around them. They can conduct orchestras inwardly bringing in the different instruments at the precise moment. What goes on inside of creative people is exciting but invisible and inaudible to the physical world.

Creativity develops first in the heart of a person. So much more when we become worshippers—the heavenly world opens up to the awesome presence of God. And this is where it all begins.

Worship is a lifestyle of devotion to the Lord. Often we have commented to each other after a church service: *"Wasn't the worship awesome!"* Perhaps it was—but to whom? Which part of it was awesome? Was it when the drummer let loose before the preacher came to the pulpit? Perhaps it was the *sound* of worship that gave us goose bumps.

When was the worship of God to ever become a means of entertainment, or having admiration for the sound of people worshipping in singing and music? Worship invites God's presence and that is what we love and enjoy.

We should not be bound in the style of the worship but rather committed to a lifestyle of worship.

We need to look at what impresses God. The sound of worship may be appealing to man but God looks at a heart that is constantly surrendered and humble before Him. Too many times we hear leadership call the congregation to, 'let's worship the Lord,' or 'who feels like worshipping?' giving the impression that worship begins at the time of singing songs and not the preparation beforehand.

I love big orchestral and choir sounds; pomp and ceremony; the pounding drums and clashing cymbals: the grandeur of royal weddings when the sound of the fanfare-trumpets herald the arrival of the dignitaries. Love it all!

It excites me and moves me to tears. This stirring of my emotions is not the real deal and only temporal. It can never be compared to the anointed worship that brings lasting cleansing, healing and life-changing ministry. Music is a tool to draw us closer to God. When we truly enter His presence we leave all behind and go beyond the music into His throne room.

While I was editing this section of writing my brother, Matthew, phoned to say he had been going up to Mt Sugarloaf (a high lookout) alone to pray at night. As he worshipped the Lord, God's presence had been so glorious. This excited me, because for several months he had been bombarded with multiple sources of pain and discomfort which has baffled the medical professionals at times. This has been a huge setback for him. Yet through all his struggles, Matthew never once blamed God but praised Him all the more. He is a missionary to Indonesia and has a heart to train others in evangelism, healing the sick and deliverance.

He understands that without the love of God in his life he cannot use the grace and power of God. This can only come through many hours in God's presence, and his favourite place is the quiet, high lookout close to where he lives.

'As a deer pants for streams of water so my soul pants for [You] O God.' (Psalm 42:1)

This psalm was written when the writer's spirit was low. Like Matthew, he had a choice to wallow in his misery or seek God. The psalmist chose the best option—to enter the presence of the Lord. There are times when, especially in constant pain, we tend to wallow in the circumstances but we do not need to stay there. If we seek God He will lift us up out of ourselves.

'How lovely is [Your] dwelling place, O Lord Almighty! My soul yearns, even faints for the courts of the Lord; my heart and my flesh cry out for the living God,' (Psalm 84:1-2).

Again, this psalm was written by the same psalmist. He obviously knew the presence of the Lord and loved Him with all his heart and whole being. I know personally what it is like to long so much for the presence of God.

THE PRESENCE OF THE LORD

At times I have felt as if the river of life inside of me had dried up. In my desperation, I have literally panted after God making quick breathless sounds. It is like your heart is throbbing or aching for more and more of the Lord. Sometimes there seems to be a deep, bottomless, chasm inside that can never be filled up.

Jesus says in Matthew 5:6: *'Blessed are those who hunger and thirst for righteousness, for they will be filled.'*

There is so much truth in that song we used to sing: *'When the music fades.'* It speaks of coming back to the heart of worship—laying down our lives, not just singing a song, because it is not about us but about Jesus.

Worship is all about God and His overwhelming love for us, and our love and devoted response to Him. Anyone can sing songs and words, but not everyone is a worshipper.

We will always remember the words of Jesus: *'Martha, Martha, you are worried and upset about many things, but only one thing is needed. Mary has chosen what is better, and it will not be taken away from her,'* (Luke 10:41-42).

It seems a bit unfair to Martha but it is not about her but what pleases Jesus. He knows what is best for us in every situation. Sometimes we are so stressed out in the preparation of entertaining, we find we have no time to spend with our guests. We can get so caught up in the organisation of our *worship service* that we do not have time to spend with our very special guest, Jesus, who is to be loved and adored. God is desiring something much deeper than our preparations and our lip service.

An example of this in my own life was the time when we invited a guest speaker to come and share with our intercessory, prayer group at the small country town where I had lived. As we travelled out of town to church on Sundays, we met in homes to worship and pray during the week. When we held special meetings and invited others, we would hire the local RSL hall to accommodate a larger gathering of people. Because the hall was a little drab, we would beautify it with colourful flags, banners, pot plants and flowers to bring the finishing touches.

For this particular occasion, I was to take my new, digital piano and was rather apprehensive whether it would be suitable in the hall as we lacked amplification. One night prior to this special event, I had a dream as follows:

In the dream we were in the hall. The chairs were set out in order and people were quietly filing in and sitting down. There was a silent awe in the atmosphere. I looked around the hall, and was shocked to find that nothing had been prepared. There were no banners, no pot plants and even my piano was not there. Instead, an old, battered, conventional piano stood in its place and the lid was closed. I was to lead the worship yet I could not respond to lift up the lid of the piano.

I just stood there facing the people. There was a look of expectation on their faces, waiting for something to happen. I was supposed to be in charge but still seemed to be glued to the spot. My heart was thumping with anxiety wondering what I was suppose to do, but still made no effort to do anything.

Suddenly, the most glorious sound came through the door—the sound of a heavenly, solo singer, singing: "Hallelujah!" over and over again. The singer came up the aisle towards me yet I could not see him, just heard the penetrating voice and sensed his strong presence. As the singer reached me, the whole room exploded with angelic voices singing harmonies beyond my earthly comprehension.

The singing pulsated through my being and the atmosphere came out of a dream into reality. As in a trance, I got out of bed and headed to my new piano in the lounge room. I adjusted the settings to choir and vibraphone and without any thought of key or notes, I played and sang with the heavenly choir in perfect pitch.

Gradually, the sound faded to my human ears but I kept playing and singing. Finally I was aware of my natural surroundings and I glanced at the clock—it was 2.00 am. We used to sing a song: 'Heaven came down and glory flooded my soul'. It sure did in the early hours that morning and I will never forget that visitation from heaven—or to be more accurate, I had entered another dimension in worship led by the angels.

The heavenly realm is real

I had learned through this experience that when the presence of God floods our house, church, streets and town, nothing else matters. No one was going to notice whether the RSL hall was attractive or not, because all eyes would turn to the One who is more brighter than the sun, more beautiful beyond anything we could describe.

A few weeks later after that experience, the time came to decorate the hall for the special event. After setting up, and before anyone had arrived, our team of six, joined hands and began to worship God. We realised God had already entered the building and His presence was so powerful throughout the whole day. We had a good-sized crowd and some of the visitors from Sydney testified that they had first sensed the presence of God as soon as they entered the Hunter Valley region. Others said they felt the presence of angels during the worship and others had heard them! We tend to say things like: "Praise God for showing up!" God is always there with us. We need to tune in to Him and throw off our cares and inhibitions.

Worship is all about God wanting us to enter His realm

God is wanting us to enter the heavenly realm where there is love, peace and joy. We tend to think that heaven is up or far beyond our reach. Heaven is just another dimension we can step into when our hearts are right before God. I often hear preachers lead new believers in the 'sinner's prayer' and repeat: 'Lord Jesus, come into my world.' Jesus has already done that and paid the price. We expect God to come down to our level. Why? What have we got that He has not already given to us? I guess it is okay for new believers with limited knowledge of God, but for mature Christians, we need to see the bigger picture and enter more into the *fullness* and wonder of the kingdom of God that is eternal.

Jesus said to the Samaritan woman in John 4:23-24:

'A time is coming and has now come when the true worshippers will worship the Father in spirit and truth, for they are the kind of worshippers the Father seeks. God is spirit, and [His] worshippers must worship in spirit and in truth.'

How many times during a worship service have we appeared to be worshipping—maybe knees bent, noses to the floor or singing songs of devotion with hands raised heavenward in surrender, yet our minds are far away. We could be wondering whether we have left the stove or iron on, what to have for lunch, or fretting about what someone had said or done to us. By appearance, we are fronting up to church in an outward way by conforming to whatever everyone else is doing. Oops, we have all been there!

Would this be the kind of worship Jesus is talking about? Hardly. This type of worship is not in spirit and truth but a show before man and is not pleasing to God.

God is searching for truth and sincerity—a heart that is yearning for a deeper relationship with Him. A classic example of Jesus seeking for truth is in John 21:15-21. Simon Peter had denied the Lord three times on the night of Jesus' crucifixion, yet Jesus looked beyond that when He asked Peter three times:

'Simon, son of John, do you truly love [Me]?' And Peter answered with a strange answer. *'Yes Lord, [You] know that I love [You].'*

THE PRESENCE OF THE LORD

What! Imagine, if anyone held a gun to your head and a close friend said: "Nope ... never seen him before," to save his own skin and then afterwards when the crisis was over said: "What are you on about? You know very well I love you and will always stick by you.

I do not think I would buy that one and the friend would not expect me to. Nothing could be hidden from Jesus. He knew Peter and the work He had invested in him. Jesus looked beyond his weakness. Peter had passed the test. Jesus was satisfied with his answer. He already had great plans for Peter knowing full well the power of His Spirit will completely transform Peter from timidity to fearlessness.

It had to be established between them. Peter needed to confess his love for Jesus for each time he had denied Him, to set him free of his own guilt and pain. Peter's love for the Lord had to be deeper than just an act of Peter's will or intellect, but p*hileo* love, which is love of the heart—an attachment beyond human ability, in order for him to feed the flock of God.

Jesus is still asking us all that same question: "Do you love Me?"

A penetrating question. If our answer is yes, then we need to yield to His will and hear His instruction: "Lead my people into my love?"

1 John 4:18 says: *'There is no fear in love. But perfect love drives out fear.'*

2 Timothy 1:6 says: *'... fan into flame the gift of God that is in you through the laying on of my hands. For God did not give us a spirit of timidity but a spirit of power, of love and of self-discipline.'*

God's agape love is powerful. We all need it especially when we are working among crowds. Many times we do not go to places, stand up to sing or speak because of fear of what people may think of us. In the first chapter of this book I have likened love to that of a battering ram. It became a weapon against the enemies of Judah.

Sometimes we create an impenetrable wall around ourselves like the fortresses we see in old movies. The only way in through the giant, heavy doors, was to use many men with a battering ram in rhythmic persistence. God's love can break through those walls of resistance to set us free to be what He has chosen us to be.

CHAPTER 4

Knowing God

Jeremiah 9:23-24 says: *'This is what the Lord says: "Let not the wise man boast of his wisdom or the strong man boast of his strength or the rich man boast of his riches, but let him who boasts boast about this: that he understands and knows [Me], that I am the Lord, who exercises kindness, justice and righteousness on earth, for in these I delight, declares the Lord."'*

Worship is about love and devotion to someone we know. How can we worship someone we do not know? The wonderful thing about our God, is that He *wants* us to know Him. He is calling us to have an intimate relationship with Him—more intimate than a friend, sister, brother, parent or even more intimate than a lover. It is not good enough to worship Him because we *have* to, it has to be much deeper than that.

Matthew 15:8 says: *'These people honour [Me] with their lips but their hearts are far from [Me].'*

Then how well do we know God? What is our mental image of Him? Is He the great controller and awesome inhabitant of the universe who is aloof? Or do we think He recoils in shock every time we fail in meeting His standards. Some of us no doubt, who have been brought up in hard-line religious systems, have had to work through the notion that God is not out to punish us, but really does love us.

Then again, some of us may think of Him as a marshmallow God—soft and easily manipulated into meeting our demands and whims: or a passive God who has nothing better to do than listen to our grumbling, yet does nothing to fix our problems.

Yes, God knows everything about us as we read in Psalm 139:13. He is the God by whom we are *'fearfully and wonderfully made.'* Let us find out who He *really* is and about His character.

The word of God teaches that God is big and extravagant! He has proven that many times with His provision and blessings, (Psalm 65). He is the same yesterday, today and for ever. The world sees Him as 'old fashioned' and want to change Him to suit their own humanistic ideas. Those who love Him see Him as eternal. In the book of Genesis He is the God of the universe—the great Creator. In Exodus He is the great I AM. In the book of Revelation, He is the ALPHA and OMEGA—the Beginning and the End. He is the God of glory, splendour, magnificence, wealth and honour. He is all powerful. He is the God of eternity. God of our existence!

All our springs of life are in Him. Psalm 36:9 says: *'For with [You] is the fountain of life. In [Your] light we see light.'* Jesus is the Light of the world.

God is our Father, Deliverer, Provider, Protector, Healer, Comforter and our Shepherd. He is our Counsellor, the Truth, Way and Mighty God. He is the Christ, Messiah, Saviour, Redeemer, Emmanuel, Lamb of God, Prince of Peace, Lord of Lords, King of Kings. God is love and He is faithful. The list goes on and on! Who else do we need? Who can compare with such a great God?

And to think that this ruler of the universe is our Father and our friend! When Christians are struggling in their walk with Jesus, it is common to hear others say: "If only they knew who *they* are in Christ." My response to that would be that first they need to *know* Christ.

Hunger for Him and He will reveal Himself—then you begin to think like Him. The apostle Paul wrote a beautiful prayer to the Ephesian church that we still pray today over our friends and family. It is found in Ephesians 3:16-19:

'I pray that out of [His] glorious riches [He] may strengthen you with power through [His] Spirit in your inner being, so that Christ may dwell in your hearts through faith. And I pray that you, being rooted and established in love, may have power, together with all the saints, to grasp how wide and long and high and deep is the love of Christ, and to know this love that surpasses knowledge— you may be filled to the measure of all the fullness of God.'

This should be our ultimate desire to be filled up and overflowing with the Lord. To fully know and understand His love would be the greatest joy in the whole universe. To become like Him and love as He loves, see as He sees, and touch others as He touches our lives. To know God more can only come as we spend time in His presence, reading and absorbing His word.

Isaiah gives us a picture of the Lord in Isaiah 6:1-5:

'In the year that King Uzziah died, I saw the Lord seated on a throne, high and exalted, and the train of [His] robe filled the temple. Above [Him] were seraphs, each with six wings: With two wings they covered their faces, with two they covered their feet, and with two they were flying. And they were calling to one another: "Holy, holy, holy is the Lord Almighty; the whole earth is full of [His] glory." At the sound of their voices the doorposts and thresholds shook and the temple filled with smoke. "Woe is me!" I cried, "I am ruined! For I am

a man of unclean lips, and I live among a people of unclean lips, and my eyes have seen the King, the Lord Almighty.'

With meeting the Lord, Isaiah saw Him highly exalted, seated upon a throne. The heavenly setting was full of splendour and holiness. The seraphs covered their faces with two of their wings in worship and two wings covered their feet in reverence, and the other two wings were used for active service.

They were crying holy, holy, holy, is the Lord of the whole earth. Isaiah could immediately see his own unclean state as well as those around him. He knew he could not survive in God's holiness without his sins atoned for. Interesting, his lips had to be purified and a seraph touched his mouth with a live coal in order for him to speak the unadulterated word of God. Isaiah does not mention the uncleanness of his heart but his lips. Scripture does say that 'out of our heart our mouth speaks'. It is an example for us to curb our tongue and not speak or sing words that do not glorify the Lord. God must receive all the glory in our lives.

My dear husband Peter is always quoting from Psalm 19:14, *'Let the words of my mouth and the meditation of my heart be acceptable in [Your] sight oh Lord, my Rock and my Redeemer.'* And that is how he lives—not a cross or nasty word to anyone or about anyone.

The apostle Paul says in Philippians 3:7-10:

'But whatever was to my profit I now consider loss for the sake of Christ. What is more, I consider everything a loss compared to the surpassing greatness of knowing Christ Jesus my Lord, for whose sake I have lost all things. I consider them rubbish, that I may gain Christ and be found in [Him], not having a righteousness of my own that comes from the law, but that which is through faith in in Christ—the righteousness that comes from God and is by faith. I want to know Christ and the power of [His] resurrection and the fellowship of

sharing in [His] sufferings, becoming like [Him] in[His] death, and so somehow, to attain to the resurrection of the dead.'

Paul was prepared to give up everything he once put his trust in and was proud of, to gain Christ. Once receiving Christ all else seemed like rubbish with no value. The high calling of God was his prize. He wanted to know Christ and become like Him. Whatever Jesus suffered he also wanted to suffer even to the point of dying. He wanted to know the power of the resurrection working through his own life.

In this world we are surrounded by high achievers whether it is sporting heroes or music and singing stars. They have so much glory, so much fame: elevated and worshipped beyond practical reasoning just for kicking and hitting a ball, or singing a song. We must be the best! We must win! Such glamour with the screaming and pushing multitude of fans. The question for Christians should be: What pleases God's heart who is the giver of all the wonderful gifts? However, there are times when God does make His people famous, and if they follow Jesus' example as in Philippians 2:6-11, they will succeed and are able to bless others.

'Who, being in very nature God, did not consider equality with God, something to be grasped, but made Himself nothing, taking the very nature of a servant, being made in human likeness. And being found in appearance as a man, He humbled Himself and became obedient to death—even death on a cross.'

As God exalted Christ to the highest place in His heavenly kingdom, He raises up His servants and gives them honour for a job well done. But the key is verse 3 and 4 of the same chapter.

'Do nothing out of selfish ambition or vain conceit, but in humility consider others better than yourselves. Each of you should look not only to your own interests, but also to the interests of others.

Praise God He looks at the heart and interprets unspoken thoughts and attitudes. Years ago I was staying alone in a hut in the mountains. My parents were in another cabin across the road. It was pitch black outside the hut, and except for the open fireplace with the fire blazing cheerily inside, it was lonely and scary. I had a little recorder with me. I had not played this little instrument since schooldays, but nevertheless, I needed to express myself with music. At first I produced a few squeaks and squawks but it was not long before I could play familiar tunes. In that little hut that night I had an overwhelming sense of God's pleasure in what I had offered up to Him in worship. He interpreted music from my heart and I understood from that moment on I could worship Him with music. To anyone listening outside it would have been pathetic but to God it was beautiful.

Who is God? What pleases Him? Isaiah 57:15 says it all.

'For this is what the high and lofty One says—[He] who lives forever, whose name is holy: "I live in a high and holy place, but also with him who is contrite and lowly in spirit, to revive the spirit of the lowly and to revive the heart of the contrite."'

God is music

We have looked at who God is and how important it is to know Him and what pleases His heart. We have all had different experiences with Him that shapes our understanding of Him. If He has provided for us in amazing ways we will know Him as our provider. If He has healed us of injury or diseases, we know Him as our healer. If He has led us through dark times we know Him as our shepherd. We could go through all scripture and study the names of God realising that God is everything we need for life. He is El Shaddai, the all-sufficient one.

I have encountered God through heavenly music and singing, so I know God as music. Music begins in the heart of God. I would find it difficult to separate God from music and singing. He *is* music. He sings, (Psalm 32:7; Zephaniah 3:17). The whole creation resounds, pulsates and is alive with harmonic sounds and rhythms that sometimes our human ears cannot hear. Scientists have developed technology, which confirms the word of God, and are able to record sounds coming from inanimate objects. I have a property in the mountains and often on a still night I can hear a deep droning sound, similar to that of a bulldozer working all night. I believe it is a sound coming from the earth.

All of creation is expected to praise God. We read in the scriptures that the heavens, stars, valleys, mountains, hills, waste places, trees and birds sing for joy. The sea roars in praise and Jesus said that even the stones will cry out if we do not praise God, (Luke 19:40). Someone once said, don't let us be out done by stones! But we are stones—living stones!

1 Peter 2:4 says: *'As you come to [Him], the Living Stone—rejected by men but chosen by God and precious to [Him]—you also, like living stones, are being built into a spiritual house to be a holy priesthood, offering spiritual sacrifices acceptable to God through Jesus Christ.'*

If you do not believe that all creation worships the Lord, try singing in front of canaries. I had a pet canary whose whistle was insufferably shrill for sensitive ears. I used to have to put him in the garage while I was teaching music because he would be too overpowering from the moment the music and singing would start. I have had magpies turn up to join me while worshipping the Lord outdoors alone. They have sat on my picnic table or the low branches of the trees nearby and their song was pure and harmonious. We have had kangaroos stop in their tracks and line up to listen while we worshipped the Lord outdoors and would hop away when we had finished. At one time when our *shofar blower blew strongly over the paddocks bordering a town, a herd of cattle from across the hill came running toward us and stood in a line along the fence. It was a clear day without wind, yet suddenly at the sound of the blast, the long, dry grass of the paddock swayed towards the sound.

We were invited to a horse stud to pray and once again when our team member blew his shofar, the horses in the distance galloped down to join us. The manager of the stud said she had never seen them come all at once like that even when she sounded the car horn for their attention.

All of creation responds to the call of our Creator!

No gift is too poor or too small if it is given in love. Isaiah 29:13 says: *'The Lord says: "They honour [Me] with their lips, but their hearts are far from [Me]. Their worship of [Me] is made up only of rules taught by men."'*

Worship starts with the heart not with the lips, words or songs. God looks at the heart not outward show or displays. Words are not the way to get God's attention but the feelings of the heart. Why? Some people are more eloquent than others. They have the right words but not necessarily the right words of the heart—a hunger for God.

Every created thing has a language given by God. God understands every language—of man and every created living thing. Romans 8:22 says the whole creation is groaning. The whole creation expresses its need of redemption.

Psalm 19:4 says: *'The heavens declares the glory of God the skies proclaim the work of [His] hands. Day after day they pour forth speech. Night after night they display knowledge. There is no speech or language where their voice is not heard. Their voice goes out into all the earth: their words to the end of the world.'*

Language is far beyond our spoken words to each other. It is a oneness with all created things—a universal communication with our Creator. Animals and birds can communicate to one another even of different species. They express their needs and appreciation to us. My canary used to tweet loudly when he wanted me to give him fresh bath water. I understood what he wanted and enjoyed seeing him splash around in his bath. My dog used to ask me to take her for a walk. She would communicate in the way all dogs do and I would understand. She was always sensitive to how I was feeling and would bring support and comfort, even howl when I was led into travailing prayer. Plant life communicates their need by drooping branches and leaves when needing water, and discolouring of foliage is a tell-tale sign if the composites in the soil are not suitable for them.

We have a language of our heart that only God can understand. Romans 8:26-27 says: '… *But the Spirit [Himself] intercedes for us with groans that words cannot express. And He who searches our hearts knows the mind of the Spirit because the Spirit intercedes for the saints in accordance with God's will.*'

Music is also a language that can be expressed

When I was young and was upset or angry over something, I would always go to the piano and play to escape the situation. I had a choice of playing music that would identify with my feelings or soothing music to deflect away from my anger. I usually chose something that was highly technical and was soon lost in concentration to deflect away from what had just occurred. The incident that caused my frustration became insignificant and unimportant in comparison to the pleasure stimulated from the music I was focused on.

In Revelation 2:29 we read: '*He who has an ear, let him hear what the Spirit is saying to the churches.*' Musicians must be always alert to what God is saying and respond accordingly. Music can accompany God's word whether it is read or delivered through a word of prophecy. More on that in a later chapter.

Take background music out of movies and documentaries and see the results. Music emphasises the 'wow factor'—builds up the suspense and action. It stirs up our emotions, awakens our senses and gives, as dramatic fiction writers put it—"my heart leapt-to-my-throat" feeling.

Just picture the opening scene of creation: *"In the beginning God created the heavens and the earth!"* The first verse written in the word of God could be opened with incredible musical background! Even— "In the beginning GOD!" could explode into an incredible fanfare of sounds. Could our human imperfection and abilities match that splendorous event?

In Job 38:4-7, God describes this enormous and grandiose happening then adding: *'While the morning stars sang together and all the angels shouted for joy!'* Imagine the tremendous sound of joy in heaven. Praise accompanied God's action! Everyone and everything participates in joyous harmony and unity. Another incredible occasion was at the birth of the Saviour of mankind!

Luke 2:13-15 describes the scene: *'Suddenly a great company of the heavenly host appeared with the angel, praising God and saying: "Glory to God in the highest and on earth peace to men on whom [His] favour rests."'*

What a glorious, heavenly show for the shepherds! Who else would have seen it? We are only told about the shepherds. Shepherds were the ones who attended the new born lambs for the daily sacrifice. It would be only fitting that they would be there to identify the Lamb of God who was to be the eternal and final sacrifice to atone for the sins of all mankind. Some translations say the angels sang, but the key word here is 'praise'. Praise once again accompanied God's announcement to mankind. Matthew 2 gives the account of the Magi from the east following the star of the birth of the King of the Jews. It must have been a brilliant and distinct star to lead them straight to the house in Bethlehem where Jesus and His parents were living. This was an amazing fulfilment of prophecy from Micah 5:2.

What a contrast to the account of the crucifixion of Jesus portrayed in Matthew 27:45-55. There was no triumphant fanfare, no wonderful singing of angels—even though they were there waiting and expecting. Jesus said earlier that twelve legions of angels were at His disposal. Matthew still describes a dramatic event. God got the attention of the world. Darkness came over all the land.

As the Son of God, the light of the world, hung dying on the cross the sun lost its light and the blackness of sin and all the depravity of Satan was heaped upon Jesus.

He bore all the wickedness of mankind and the punishment of His Father and cried out *"Father, Father, why have you forsaken [Me]!"* The agony He bore would have been unimaginable—far above anything mankind could endure. It was not only the physical pain and suffering but all of hell's fury cutting Him off from Father God and heavenly glory. It was all about the world, sin and darkness: Jesus dying for it all with no intervention or comfort from heaven. All seemed to be in suspense— watching and waiting for the right moment. There was no place for singing and rejoicing.

That was to come later throughout eternity!

The scene slowly changed. The son of man breathed His last and His spirit left His body. Then the dramatic happens! The curtain in the temple tore from top to bottom: the earth shook; the rocks split; the graves of many righteous people opened and they rose to life and appeared in the city of Jerusalem. No mention of music: no mention of praise and worship. No pomp and ceremony of a funeral procession; no obituary where those who knew and loved the deceased spoke of the wonderful deeds He had done. There was not even a place prepared to lay His body. Instead, a man named Joseph asked Pilate for his body, wrapped it in a cloth and placed it in his own new tomb. But this Jesus was no ordinary man. He was the Lamb of God offered up as a ransom for all of mankind. God had a bigger plan and once again summoned His power by shaking the heavens and the earth. The way for His glory to flood His temple was through the death and resurrection of Christ. The whole earth was affected. God again got the attention of mankind!

We read in Haggai 2:6-9:

'In a little while I will once more shake the heavens and the earth, the sea and the dry land. I will shake all nations, and the Desired of all nations will come, and I will fill this house with glory, says the Lord Almighty.'

This has happened! Through Jesus making a way and ascending to heaven, the Holy Spirit descended upon us and has flooded us with His glory. We are the spiritual temples of the Holy Spirit knitted together to form one house—one temple.

Jesus is coming again!

We are told that the second coming of the Lord will be announced *'with a loud command, the voice of the archangel and with the trumpet call of God...'* (1 Thessalonians 4:16*).*

Another good way to get a crowd's attention is to give a signal blast or call on a trumpet. What a glorious event we will bear witness to. We will be there! We will rise to meet Him in the clouds of glory— the Desire of all nations!

When Jesus comes as King of kings and Lord of lords, riding a white horse to set up His kingdom on earth for a thousand years' reign, we will be involved! After this dispensation, can you imagine the sound produced when the new heaven and the new earth comes down out of heaven, when the old will pass away. Revelation 21:3 says:

'And I heard a loud voice from the throne saying, "Now the dwelling of God is with men, and [He] will live with them. They will be [His] people, and God [Himself] will be with them and be their God.'

This is eternity! Our future glory! To rule, reign and worship Christ forever!

We have been looking at the wonderful use of music and singing when God announces something new. However when we read in Isaiah 30 from verse 30, a graphic and different picture is created when background music is used when God pours out His punishment on rebellious nations:

'The Lord will cause men to hear [His] majestic voice and will make them see [His] arm coming down with raging anger and consuming fire, with cloudburst, thunderstorm and hail. The voice of the Lord will shatter Assyria; with [His] sceptre [He] will strike them down. Every stroke the Lord lays on them with [His] punishing rod will be to the music of tambourines and harps as [He] fights them in battle with the blows of his arm.'

*A shofar is the horn of a ram or antelope, used by the Jews to call the people to worship and to break open the spiritual realm in war. It can have a powerful effect on a situation or community.

CHAPTER 5

Why we Worship God

Part A

Isaiah 9:6 declares: '*For to us a [Child] is born and to us a [Son] is given, and the government will be on [His] shoulders, And [He] will be called Wonderful, Counsellor, Mighty God, Everlasting Father, Prince of Peace.*'

Lucifer, puffed up with pride, rebelled against God's sovereign rule and along with a third of the angels was cast from heaven like lightning— (Luke 10:18). The whole universe was disrupted! Satan like a savage lion is out to destroy earth's response of worship heavenward. His aim is to shut the mouths of those who honour the Living God and to seduce mankind into destructive worship and glorification of anything but the One who is worthy to sit on the throne. There needed to be a mediator between heaven and earth to restore harmony between God and man.

'Glory to God in the Highest! Peace on earth and goodwill to all men!'

The famous declaration of the angel to announce
the birth of the Saviour of the world!

'Who being in the very nature of God, did not consider equality with God something to be grasped, but made [Himself] nothing, taking the very nature of a servant, being made in human likeness. And being found in appearance as a man, [He] humbled [Himself] and became obedient to death—even death on a cross! Therefore God exalted [Him] to the highest place and gave [Him] the name that is above every name, that at the name of Jesus every knee should bow, in heaven and on earth and under the earth, and every tongue confess that Jesus Christ is Lord, to the glory of God the Father, (Philippians 2:6-11).

Jesus is not coming back again as a baby or a lamb to the slaughter, but as the Conquering One! King of kings! Lord of lords! Righteous Judge! Jesus is the ONE and HE ALONE is worthy to be worshipped!

Heaven responded to the pitiful groans and cries of the whole earth and in His mercy and great love, God sent His only begotten Son to reconcile man back to God. For a happy and healthy existence, the whole earth needs to respond to the blessings and goodness of the Lord. It is essential to enter into the flow of Creator God to bring harmony and peace on earth. That is why we worship the Lord of lords—to set a wheel of response in motion, bringing order and harmony to this chaotic world.

We worship God because He is WORTHY. He is supreme in majesty: all goodness, wisdom and power belongs to him.

Revelation 4:11 says: *'You are worthy, our Lord and God, to receive glory and honour and power, for [You] created all things, and by [Your]will they were created and have their being.'*

Just seeing the universe with all its planets, sun, moon, constellation of stars and billions of undiscovered galaxies—all things on earth, under the earth and the magnificent world under the sea, gives us reason to acknowledge and admire the glorious Being who made them all and governs them.

God requires us to worship Him.

It is the first commandment, Exodus 34:14: *'Do not worship any other god, for the Lord, whose name is Jealous, is a jealous God.'*

In other words, Creator God is passionate about our worship and claims absolute loyalty and devotion. He is also particular how we worship Him. Our worship must be from an undivided heart.

We have two options—give glory to God or give glory to the devil. I told someone that several years ago and she said she does not worship anything. Not true. She was deceived. Everyone worships something. In her case, SELF was the object of her devotion. She thought she did not need God. In her rebellion, she put herself above God, like most people on this planet do—a trick of the devil to take us away from God. Fortunately, this lady repented of her sins, and forgave everyone who had hurt her throughout her life before she died.

To express love and devotion

To worship God is the reason for our existence. There are many benefits in worshipping God! When I was very young I could never understand why God needed to be worshipped. No-one had ever told me why. I somehow developed the impression that God was on an ego trip and wanted a lot of attention. Even with this wrong concept, my heart was crying out for Him. The built-in drive to belong in His heart was strong within me at an early age. I felt an emptiness inside of me that needed to be filled.

No religious experience or theological knowledge could satisfy the ache inside. I was more or less brought up to look pure by outward standards: dress right, do and say the right thing, read the Bible, say my prayers and obey parents, while all the time neglecting what God would call acceptable to him—a love relationship of intimacy with my Saviour.

My life was transformed the day I had a revelation or a vision—I have never been quite sure which:

I was looking upon the scene of the crucifixion. I saw a small, black figure crouched at the foot of a rough, wooden cross. I knew beyond doubt I was that person. Jesus was hanging on the cross. He was dying in agony carrying on His body the burden of my sin. His blood flowed freely down and immersed me. As it did, I turned into glistening white. I rose from a state of death to life. It was the beginning of a deeper love relationship with the Lord.

Philippians 3:10 says: *'I want to know Christ and the power of [His] resurrection, and the fellowship of sharing in [His] sufferings, becoming like [Him] in [His] death, and so, somehow to attain to the resurrection from the dead.'*

Until we go through the death to self experience and know the power of His resurrection, we can never truly worship Him from the depth of our heart for what He has done for us. Too often we want the material blessing—the froth and bubbles without the deep work of the cross which leads to a risen life in Christ. God is looking for broken vessels, those yielded and fully surrendered to Him.

'The sacrifices of God are a broken spirit; a broken spirit and contrite heart, O God [You] will not despise,' (Psalm 51:17).

We read in Amos 5:21 how God despises religious feasts of the rebellious and ungodly. He will not accept sacrifices or offerings from hearts that are not truly surrendered to Him. Verse 23-24 says: *'Away with your noise of your songs! I will not listen to the music of your harps.'*

Jesus said, "take up your cross and follow Me." This means to run after Him, throwing off everything else that hinders us from achieving the goal of entering His presence. It is giving our lives totally over to the Lord no matter what the cost may be. **That is when worship becomes the overflow of our hearts!**

Unfortunately, mankind has cluttered his heart with the garbage of this world leaving no room for God. Imagine having a nice clean home and someone comes and dumps a truck load of rubbish through the front door and it fills up the entry. A visitor knocks on the door, and if you are used to callers like I am, you'll call out, 'Come in!' The visitor will soon respond: 'I can't—you've got a pile of garbage blocking the way!'

My sister, Bev, had visitors ringing the doorbell one day and she called out, "come in!" "We would," they answered, "but you have a snake behind the door!" Yes, it could be a bit of a deterrent I guess.

When the Lord knocks on the door of our heart, can He find a way through, or is our entrance blocked by the rubbish the devil wants to dump on us?

Because of the fallen state of mankind, he has changed his object of worship to fill the vacuum inside. People need to worship God whether they know it or not. The heart of man is desperate to feed his bottomless cravings. He yearns for power and wealth, feverishly striving to achieve recognition from his fellow man. The more he gets the more the hunger grows. His drives, lusts and cravings swirl around in the vortex of his soul, leaving him more dissatisfied and empty than ever before. Without Christ to fill the dark, deep, hole within our hearts, life is as futile as chasing the wind.

Worship draws us into intimacy with God

Mankind has cut himself off from communicating with God. He has turned his back on his Creator and revels in the idols of his own hands. When we think of idols we often think: 'Nope, I'm safe. I don't worship golden calves or stick up asherah poles to Baal like the disobedient Israelites had done in the Old Testament.

What about our homes, material dreams? What about our sport heroes, pop and rock stars, social media and video games? Of course there are the popular Christian singers, music bands, popular preachers and other personalities? Even our own ministries! Oops!

'But that's Christian stuff!' SO?

Idols are anything that comes between us and the Lord. Anything that takes first place in our lives apart from the Lord. Music in today's Christian world has become such a draw card for the young people that they are in danger of losing their focus of worship. Idols can consume us to the point of being obsessions in our lives. God is not like that. He does not force or coerce us. He waits to be invited into our lives.

It is not only the youth, most contemporary churches are adopting a certain style that is a copy of a major church which is successful in the music industry. It seems that if you do not keep up this trend, you are not acceptable as a musician or singer. This type of hype is just creating clones—sound the same, dress the same and move the same. There is no true beauty or diversity in that.

In an orchestra there are many different instruments with their own unique sounds and their own parts to play. If they play in unison, each playing the same part, it is okay but boring. When harmony is introduced it creates a much more full, rich and beautiful sound. It is also the same with a choir of human voices. Harmony brings the stirring of the soul.

The body of Christ needs to be heard—every individual voice is important. Singing in a choir we are trained to listen to the singers next to us and blend in—not one louder than the other. If you cannot hear the person next to you your voice is too loud. Then there is a connection, blending in with all around you. It is such an exhilarating feeling to be in unity with the whole choir.

We have lost that togetherness in many of our churches. It is hard to hear those around us because the spotlight is on those leading and the amplification for them is adjusted so loud. Many places you cannot see each other as the lights are turned off. People come out of darkness and into the light when they come to Jesus. They are taken to a church into darkness again with everything painted black. Personally I have issues with that. I love to see the glory of God on each face around me—people enjoying the presence of God. 1 Thessalonians 5:5 says:

'You are all sons of the light and sons of the day. We do not belong to the night or to the darkness...'

Let us be free in our Saturday or Sunday worship times. We go to church to enjoy God and also fellowship with one another. Study the children how free they are in the presence of God. My three-year-old, great-nephew and his little sister brought joy to many people who could see them at Church. While we were worshipping God with music and singing they came out to the front where there was room and their movements were extraordinary—freestyle expression of pure little hearts before Jesus. It makes our spirits soar and challenges us to be more passionate in singing praises.

When the second world war ended in 1945 celebrations flooded the streets of Sydney. A man was so joyful he danced, he leapt, he twirled around while waving his hat in the air. Joy brings freedom and he knew how to express himself without inhibitions. Why can we not express our joy in *God's* presence by dancing and leaping.

WHY WE WORSHIP GOD

Palm 8:2 says: *'From the lips of infants and children [You] have ordained praise, because of your enemies, to silence the avenger and the foe.'*

When my sister, Bev, was a little girl, my father could hear her chatting to someone in the lounge room. He poked his head around the door to see who it was. There was no one in the room only Bev but he sensed the sweet presence of God surrounding her and knew she was talking to Jesus, or an angel.

My young, seven-year-old, step-granddaughter was listening to a lady who was working through some issues in her life and the child advised her to read Psalm 100—a wonderful psalm of praise and thanksgiving. It is so important to bring up the little ones in the house of the Lord and with the word of God.

Jesus also says in Matthew 18:3: *"I tell you the truth, unless you change and become like little children, you will never enter the kingdom of heaven. Therefore whoever humbles himself like this child is the greatest in the kingdom of heaven."*

Jesus does not mean for us to behave in a childish manner or surround our life with childish things, but to have a heart that is pure before Him: to be humble and trusting. Let us not lose our simplicity and individuality as churches. Copying others and how they do things can be idolatry: the style of music is worshipped. Many people cannot enter into worshipping the Lord unless the music conforms to the style they are used to. That is not true worship. Worship is about pouring out our love to Jesus, not the music. It is only a tool to lead us deeper into heavenly places.

God has not made us clones but individuals to have the freedom to express our love to him. If the music we listen to or play does not spur us, or others, on to worship God and long for a deeper relationship with Him, it has no place within the church. The platform at church is not meant for a means of entertainment. I am not referring to new musicians in the ministry who are still trying to find their way, but experienced people in the music field.

It takes a lot of hard work and practice to develop a freedom in the Lord and sensitivity to His voice, so be encouraged if you are just starting out in this area.

As a music teacher, I appreciate all styles because music ministers to different emotional needs and moods bringing balance into my life. But I have found more satisfaction in just sitting at the piano and allowing my heart and hands to create worship to the Lord that flows from my spirit. During these times all my needs are met and I am able to rise above my circumstances.

Music is meant to lift us out of ourselves and into the Lord

I am not saying it is not good to have mentors, because it is a good thing to have godly mentors, or even people to learn from who are skilful in their craft even though they are not Christians. That is how we learn— they are there as examples to teach us technique and inflame a passion to do better. But do not be satisfied with their level when God has given us the wealth of His kingdom.

There is so much to discover in the world of music and worship and the Holy Spirit is the greatest teacher. Creativity comes from drawing near to God and allowing Him to play or sing through us. When we do this we bring lasting change to our own lives and others.

Idols can be anything we trust or place our security in instead of trusting God with our lives.

Today's media is creating fear within our nation. We must flow with the tide and trends—sign up for medical insurance, buy your home now while the interests rates are low. Have you a retirement plan? Have you invested in a funeral plan? Sell while the market's good—buy, sell, buy sell! Buy now before the GST gets in and hits you hard, was the cry many years ago: the country will go down the tube if this tax takes over. GST came in and hit many hard but life goes on. I remember the fear before the new millennia came in—end of the world!

Then it was the hew and cry about the work-place reforms, global warming now changed to 'climate change'—big political issues. Next it was Covid 19; closure of banks. That will go as well and something else will replace it. As Christians, we do not need to trust in man's ways that bring fear and insecurity.

King David says in Psalm 11:1: *'In the Lord I take refuge, How then can you say to me: Flee like a bird to your mountain.'*

There is always someone to drag you into their net of fear. It makes no difference to God what is happening. He is still reigning on the throne and looking after us. God does not panic; He is not depressed. He is not worried about global warming, climate change or Covid 19.

Okay, I am not saying these things are not to be concerned with, but what I am saying is: as Christians, are we beginning to bow down entirely to the world's system of security for our future? They can be Satan's devices to cause panic and take us from worshipping God and giving all of ourselves over to him.

Fear is having faith in the devil

What did the tribe of Judah do when they were surrounded by their enemies? PRAISED GOD! Their declarations of God's love and mercy echoed around the universe.

If you are older you would remember the days before television and social media—before the world's negativity and pressure invaded our homes. What bliss!

Jesus said in Matthew 4:10: *'Away from me Satan! It is written: Worship the Lord your God, and serve [Him] only.'*

Maybe it is time to get tough with the devil, and all his demons, and tell him to flee like Jesus had done when tempted by Satan in the desert. God is our future. He is our source of living. His power is in us to overcome the world, not to succumb to it!

Take a look at what Romans 12:1 says:

'Therefore, I urge you brothers, in view of God's mercy, to offer your bodies as living sacrifices, holy and pleasing to God—this is your spiritual worship. Do not conform any longer to the pattern of this world, but be transformed by the renewing of your mind. Then you will be able to test and approve what God's will is—[His] good, pleasing and perfect will.'

It is good to ask ourselves regularly this question: What, or to whom do I devote my energies, physical, mental and spiritual? Of course we have to live in this world full of people so most of our time is taken up trying to keep the peace and order in our family life, school or work. The question is aimed at the areas of our lives that do not particularly emanate the glory of God or those things that we waste precious time on. Most of us can use our own initiative on that one.

It is time to get the world out of us and let God into us!

Once my sister, Lorraine, was sharing with a lady on spiritual things when the lady said: "You've just scared the hell out of me." Lorraine flashed back, "Good, maybe now you've got room for heaven to get into you!"

There is a popular saying among Christians: "Some Christians are too heavenly minded to do any earthly good." Maybe so, but from my observation, I find many Christians are too earthly minded to do any heavenly good. In other words, their weapons against the powers of darkness are weak because of clinging to the things of this world, with its cares, attractions and false securities. Colossians 3:2-4 puts it into a nutshell:

'Since then, you have been raised with Christ, set your hearts on things above, where Christ is seated at the right hand of God. Set your minds on things above, not on earthly things ... When Christ, who is your life, appears, then you also will appear with [Him] in glory.'

There are rich treasures and joy in heavenly places that we can tap into now. Our real life is in this realm—all eternity in fact! This natural life is too short to please ourselves. The kingdom of God is for EVER and EVER! It is best to invest wisely into eternal things that reap eternal benefits. If we were to invest in building a new house we would put every effort in researching the details of the plans. We would carefully choose the builder, materials to use and colour schemes while bearing in mind the costs. Yet this life is only short compared to eternity. Should not our eternal home be more important?

Because I enjoy God's presence and able to maintain His joy in my life, I have had Christians tell me I need to live in the *real* world. Nonsense! What is this real world? Why would I want to live in the devil's world that he has corrupted to become a replica of hell? The heavenly realm is much more real than this decaying, physical world that we are just passing through. This world will be destroyed, but heaven is eternity and was around before we humans came into being. To invest into eternity and the kingdom of God is wisdom and life. This *is* the real world where true worshippers of God live and will inherit as we see in Revelation 11:15:

'The kingdom of this world has become the kingdom of our Lord and of [His] Christ and [He] will reign for ever and ever.'

How glorious is our future and our inheritance! Ironically, those who have abandoned themselves in worship, and intercessors who stand in the gap on behalf of the community, are more likely to reach out to others than those who criticise them. Why? They hear from God and are more sensitive to the needs of people around them and more able to stand in the midst of trials. Also, if you have got something good going that you are crazy about, you will want to share it with everyone!

Every thought, action and emotion can become an act of true worship. Worship just does not happen overnight. It is a progressive walk with the Lord incorporated into our daily lifestyle.

Worship begins with our personal relationship with Jesus Christ. His Spirit woos us into intimacy with Him. When Christ washes away our sin by His blood and we die with Him through water baptism to cleanse us from the effects of the world, He has made provision to enter into the very presence of God. Worship comes from a deep hunger to be like someone bigger and greater than ourselves. It is not just singing a few songs on Sunday at church when the song-leader says to.

We become like the one we worship

Why do we worship God? Because we become like the person we worship. Worship is for our own benefit! If we trust in a dead thing, we will become just that—dead. There are many states of 'deadness' in our body, soul and spirit.

Let us take a look at Psalm 135:15: *'The idols of the nations are silver and gold, made by the hands of men. They have ears, but cannot hear, nor is there breath in their mouths. Those who make them will be like them, and so will all who trust in them.'*

Praise God Jesus is living!

All honour belongs to Jesus! All glory belongs to Him! And as we are to be fellow-partakers of that divine glory (2 Peter 1:4), yearn for the best, do not be satisfied with just a dry old experience: go for the higher calling—entering the very throne room of God.

One of my mentors in worship and singing was a dear prophetess to the nations. She used to encourage hours of worship in spontaneous singing by urging, "keep singing until the glory comes." And it sure had done. I used to love her meetings.

She had a loud voice, not harsh just powerful. When people commented: it was alright for her because her voice was loud, she would respond: "How do you think I got this voice?" Vocal cords are like any other muscle, the more you use them the stronger they become.

Someone told me some time ago, "I see you like a little dog clinging to a big bone and will not let go." Believe me, if that bone was hard, and dry and someone offered me a juicy, meaty leg of roast lamb garnished with a hint of rosemary or mint gravy, I'm sure I would drop that dry bone like a red-hot poker and grab the best offered to me.

It is like God saying: "Hey, I have so much more to offer you. My very presence is yours to keep. I offer you love, light and power. My comfort is everlasting. Do not be satisfied with just sitting on the outskirts, but come right into my heart where satisfaction will saturate your whole being. I will show you great and wonderful things."

Back to the *sinner's* prayer again. How often have we led new converts to say: "Come into my heart, Lord Jesus?" Perhaps it is time to say: "Lord, I come into *Your* heart. Wrap me in *You*. Saturate me with *Yourself.*" I love that old hymn that was used in evangelism crusades in the past, "Just as I am." Each verse ends with "I come." It stirs the will and emotions to respond to Jesus. 1 John 3:2 says: *'Dear friends, now we are children of God,* and what we will be has not yet been made known. But we know that when [He] appears, we shall be like [Him] for we shall see [Him] as [He] is.'

This is exciting! If only we could grasp that there is satisfaction of dying to selfish ambitions and the worldly attractions. The benefits are to rise up in the likeness of Jesus. Matthew 5:8 says: *'Blessed are the pure in heart for they will see God.'*

David, the psalmist, had the same revelation before the work of the cross. I love his words in Psalm 17:15: *'As for me I will see [Your] face in righteousness; I shall be satisfied when I awake in [Your] likeness.'*

I remember the day this verse first touched my spirit—the knowledge that one day I will be like my Saviour—pure and holy. I cried for months. Tears spring to my eyes still.

I remember as a child and, even though I was brought up in a strict, religious fellowship, I knew the difference between the man-made rules and real worship. There used to be a brother in the Lord whose face shone with God's glory when he prayed. I was fascinated. Even at a young age I yearned to touch heaven like this man had done. To know God more deeply has been my goal ever since. Only in recent years have I learned that the scripture above was written on this servant of God's grave. He is forever beholding the face of His Saviour.

King David was a worshipper, first as a shepherd boy, then as a king of Israel. He knew the presence of the Lord. With all his wealth and victory, he knew they were only temporal in comparison to the glory and satisfaction ahead—meeting his Redeemer face to face. He knew that his inheritance was God Himself and had confidence in His saving grace. He constantly stirred his spirit in worship and praise. The more distressed he was—enemies wanting him dead, the more he worshipped God. He said to the Lord—*'In your presence is fullness of joy and at your right hand are pleasures forever more.'* David knew this by experiencing God, and because of this we have the privilege of meditating on the wonderful psalms he had written.

If you are in a dry place at the moment and clinging to a dry, dead thing, cry out to the Lord to open your eyes to see something better. God has promised to— *pour out water on him who is thirsty and floods on the dry ground'*, (Isaiah 44:3).

CHAPTER 6

Why we Worship God

Part B

So far we have looked at several good reasons why we worship God and now we will continue with that theme.

For our protection and deliverance

Loving worship to the Lord is an act of surrender to Him. Psalm 91:1 says: *'He who dwells in the shelter of the Most High will rest in the shadow of the Almighty. I will say of the Lord, [He] is my refuge and my fortress; [My] God in whom I trust.'*

The whole of Psalm 91 speaks of the protection of the Lord for those who trust in Him. Trust can only develop out of a relationship with Him. In chapter one of this book, we saw how the tribe of Judah chose to enter the presence of the Lord in His temple. It was here in this shelter that God spoke comfort and direction to their hearts.

As I mentioned before, King David sought after God with all his heart. He trusted in God's mercy rather than put his trust in human fortresses and strongholds. He says in Psalm 32:7: '*You are my hiding place; [You] will protect me from trouble and surround me with songs of deliverance.*'

It is interesting how music and singing is mentioned in relation to God's deliverance. In Zephaniah 3:17 we read: "*The Lord your God in your midst is mighty. The Mighty One, will save; He will rejoice over you with gladness, He will quiet you with His love, He will rejoice over you with singing.*" (NKJ)

One of my favourite psalms is Psalm 27. Written below is from verse one to verse six:

> *The Lord is my light and my salvation*
> *whom shall I fear?*
> *The Lord is the stronghold of my*
> *life – of whom shall I be afraid?*
> *When evil men advance against*
> *me to devour my flesh, when my*
> *enemies and my foes attack me,*
> *they will stumble and fall.*
> *Though an army besiege*
> *me, my heart will not fear;*
> *though war break out against*
> *me, even then will I be confident.*
> *One thing I ask of the*
> *Lord, this is what I seek:*
> *That I may dwell in the*
> *house of the Lord all the days*

*of my life,
to gaze upon the beauty of the
Lord and seek [Him] in [His]
temple.
For in the day of trouble [He] will
keep me safe in [His] dwelling;
He will hide me in the shelter
of [His] tabernacle
and set me high upon a rock.
Then my head will be exalted
above the enemies who surround
me;
at [His] tabernacle will I
sacrifice with shouts of joy.
I will sing and make music to the Lord.'*

What an example David was to Israel in times of trouble! And not only Israel but to us. This confidence in God can only come through relationship with Him, and experiencing His help and deliverance.

When I was young and did not own a car, I had to walk a couple of kilometres home from teaching music. Sometimes it was dark and every silhouette of trees, posts or garbage bins became objects waiting to pounce. To overcome my fear, I used to sing the wonderful hymn, 'Lord Thou art with me whom shall I fear.' It did not take long to drive away the fear and joy would bubble up. I would walk with confidence knowing God was surrounding me with His angels.

If we would only remember to seek Him in hard times—to hear what He is saying, help and direction would come so much sooner. To seek the presence of the Lord by choosing to worship Him with joy, we are lifted up out of our circumstances. Many problems seem to melt away when we worship God, or if troubles pursue us, He gives us strength and wisdom to face them. If we live a life continuously in praise and song, Holy Spirit will draw upon that in times of trouble. We have a deep well within our spirits which will burst free like a fountain as we release a song during times of stress, danger and devastation.

I have been tested many times in the area of trusting God through dangerous situations on a forest road leading to our property in a mountain area. One incident of many that stands out was when we were driving through horrendous, gale-force winds. We could hear the crashing of trees coming down around us—back of the car, front of the car and the sides of the car. The whole time the song I mentioned earlier was going around and around in my head. I changed the words from "whom shall I fear" to "what shall I fear". It worked! God saved the day. Not one tree fell on the car and what did fall on the road in front was easily removed with the saw my father had in the car. God is a God of the miraculous. He is bigger than us. His angels are there to protect us. Singing prepares the heart for the miracle.

Worshipping in song gives us strength and comfort

Singing through the night

We hear of many persecuted Christians who sing through the night hours. Through the darkest hours of their lives they offer up praises to the Lord. It ministers to their spirit and soul bringing strength and joy.

When I was about eleven years old, my mother went through a time of emotional breakdown. She was pressured by the religious group we were involved in. They brain-washed her into thinking that she would be lost by the wayside if she did not give up all associations with members of her family who did not belong to this group. This was a big issue for her. Not only did this include her parents, nine siblings and their families, but her own husband and oldest daughter who refused to join this group. In our mother's depression, fear and confusion, my sister, Bev, a young teenager at the time, sat in the hallway of our house and sang hymns to her.

Over sixty years later, I can still still hear her young, sweet voice singing, "Sing aloud to God our strength". My mother also sang with her lifting her from the ashes. How important the ministry of song is! As a child I was ministered to by the words of the hymn Bev sang and in times of trouble throughout my life the words still spring to mind. If we fill our minds and spirits with verses of scripture and songs from very early in our Christian walk, there is a deep well within us that the Holy Spirit draws upon in the troubled times of life. Sometimes I find myself singing songs learned during childhood, still bringing comfort when needed. We often think, *where did that come from?* I believe that songs are some of the treasures we have invested in heaven bringing everlasting rewards.

My sister, Lorraine, had not sung when she was a child. I do not know why as Bev and I always had. Lorraine's life changed dramatically when she was filled with the Holy Spirit and began singing with her spirit. It was beautiful. All her married life she had not had the freedom to sing out loud when she wanted to. Her release came during her latter life while she suffered with dementia. She became as free as a little child. She sang, she whistled and danced. One day we took Lorraine into a local Chinese restaurant and when introduced to the owner's relative, who could not speak English, Lorraine took the lady's hands and danced and sang with her. What a change of atmosphere!

It came time to place her into care. It was a sad day for us. She struggled at first but it was not long before her freedom was apparent and there were no restrictions placed on her at the nursing home. It was amazing. Many of the staff would turn up with their mobile phones to take videos. Others would come and try to sing with her but she sang in the language of the Holy Spirit. The presence of God was so strong during those times and we could see heaven was unveiled to her.

It it so important to invest into heavenly things and build up our spirits while we are able so that if we do lose our capacity to function through confusion and memory loss, our inner man takes over. There were times of sorrow and depression but when the joy came it was hilarious. Jesus took Lorraine home in 2022 and I can imagine her worshipping around the throne of God. It brings such comfort to those left behind who know the Lord.

Not so long ago, I underwent surgery on my shoulder. The twenty four hours post-surgery was agonising. I was attached to so many tubes and things I could not move, let alone get up and walk around. Worst of all I had to lay half sitting in one position with my back on the bed. The problem with that was, I kept slipping down and where my waist and back should have been, my neck and shoulders were in the fold of the back of the bed. It seemed I was trapped and in prison. It was a long, miserable and sleepless night. I remembered my husband, Peter, telling me when we were courting that if he could not sleep at night he would sing through his whole repertoire. I was not in a position to sing out loud but I sang in my mind and what a difference it made. My situation did not change but peace came through allowing the words of the songs to minister to my soul and body. God is so good and has given all of us songs to sing through the hard times.

After my mother passed away with a brain tumour I was devastated. I was single at the time and lived with her and was able to bring the care she needed. Before this happened my mother was so strong in believing God's healing power, that it would never have entered my mind she would die of such a disease. I was hurt and confused. My good friend, Nina, phoned me to see how I was and I poured out my grievances to her. In the time of grief it is hard for anyone to know what to say and she had the grace to listen in quietness. After we ended our phone call I was walking to the door to go outside and I began to sing an old song about the mercy and goodness of God. My mind wanted to grumble but my spirit rejoiced in God. I was surprised and wondered where the song had come from.

This can only happen by what we feed our soul and spirit. The Holy Spirit had something to draw from to bring comfort and healing in my hour of need. In scripture there is a clear example of music used to bring temporary relief from an evil spirit troubling King Saul. We read of it in 1 Samuel 16:23: *'Whenever the spirit from God came upon Saul, David would take his harp and play. Then relief would come to Saul; he would feel better, and the evil spirit would leave him.'*

Music has the capacity to bring healing in times of trouble. David's preparation to become king of Israel was in the fields looking after the sheep. The Psalms are full of his worship songs. Because of his devotion to the Lord he grew strong, even to protecting his father's sheep by killing a lion and a bear with his bare hands, (1 Samuel 17:34-37).

In the foyer of a major public hospital in the Hunter Valley, a baby grand piano is placed strategically so its sound can be heard throughout the hospital. Anyone is allowed to play the piano but volunteers are encouraged to not make it an opportunity for performance but rather for therapy. The following notice on top of the piano gives the reasons why. Quote: *'Music washes away the dust of everyday life.'* Red Auerbach

Also this: Quote: *'Playing live music to hospital patients can help to lower their blood pressure and reduce depression and anxiety. Research at Chelsea Westminster Hospital, London suggests: "In this busy place where people may be feeling stressed and anxious we offer times when live music is played. Talented staff members in their break or after work, our volunteers, wandering minstrels,*

Conservatorium students, will play for you to ease the burden of your day. We thank them for their generosity.' End of Quote.

The medical field has always recognised the value of music to the soul. How much more can Christians, with the anointing of God, have to offer to bring lasting healing and deliverance from depression and other problems.

Hebrews 13:15 says: *'Through Jesus therefore, let us continually offer to God a sacrifice of praise—the fruit of lips that confess [His] name. And do not forget to do good and to share with others, for with such sacrifices God is pleased.'* My husband is a good example of this as he continually has a song for every occasion. In fact I call him my singing tree. He is so happy and sees most things as blessings. He takes the word of God literally, especially the proverbs and psalms, which speak of happiness and joy. God loves a cheerful giver and accepts that which He ordains and is freely given from a surrendered heart. For us living under the New Covenant through Jesus' death and resurrection we offer up praise, worship and intercession.

Most of us do not live in close proximity of a church building to seek God every time we need to, so it is vital to have that special, secret corner to be alone with God in our homes or any place we are comfortable with.

I like to worship God outdoors as much as possible. As I can be very loud at times, having been trained in voice projection, when I am singing or praying, I go somewhere so I do not disturb my neighbours. Several years ago, I made it a practice to go to the local park for children and playing fields where I could let loose without alarming anyone—or so I thought.

Four-thirty in the morning seemed a reasonable time in the park, so one particular morning while it was still dark though I could see in the moonlight, I took my freedom seriously and I let rip full steam. My voice rose higher and higher ... then it happened—I was in the glory! All kinds of things happen when I reach that level: I laugh, I clap and dance with the

Lord! Following the joy comes the strength to war and on this occasion I did not hold back on my cries for the town to repent!

Suddenly, the unexpected happened. A dark figure emerged from behind the storage building and grabbing his push bike leaning against the wall, could not hit the dust fast enough. He had obviously bedded down for the night under the shelter of the building, so I can imagine the shock of being disturbed in the wee hours by such a racket from a crazy woman only about ten metres away. I still wonder what his side of the story would have been. Has he repented yet?

This was not the first encounter I have had at this hour—the first time, two people emerged from sleeping bags in the middle of the oval and took off post haste. Since these two experiences, I have made it a practice to wait until the sky reflects the colour of dawn before going to a public place. This has cramped my style somewhat, but Proverbs 27:14 says that if a man blesses his neighbour early in the morning it will be taken as a curse. It could also apply if you shout, "Repent!" as well.

Many times God has led me to go on prophetic prayer assignments by myself before taking a team along. I have been to the most wilderness, high places around the Hunter Valley, where you may not see another person for days. I have had Christians comment that I should not go alone as I would be an easy target for the devil to attack. Why? The safest place to be is in the will of God. The key to God's protection is obedience which does not bring fear but confidence. My faith is not in what the devil can do to me but what God can do through me.

On these assignments, the presence of God had been so strong around me—like being enclosed in a canopy of glory. One time I was on a high ridge overlooking the infinity of mountains and valleys and my spirit and voice soared in worship to God. I had a strong sense that this natural, panoramic beauty was the cathedral of the Lord. This was not a building made with human hands but of the magnificent, handiwork of the Creator who loved me. I felt like Jacob when he awoke from his dream at Bethel and said: *'Surely the Lord is in this place ... How awesome is this place! This is none other than the house of God; this is the gate to heaven,'* (Genesis 28:16-17). I felt secure, protected like a chicken under the shelter of its mother's wings.

There are so many benefits to acquire if only we would worship Jesus more passionately. Why are we so afraid of passion in worship and prayer? We give ourselves permission to be passionate about everything in life but to express our devotion to the Lord or share about Him, causes us to freeze.

Someone complained to a minister of a church where I had attended many years ago that Margaret spoils the prayer meeting because she is too loud. My pastor laughed and said he was used to that type of passion having come from overseas. People complained because the prayer and praise was too loud in a prayer meeting my brother was leading. Yet extremely loud, amplified music drowning out the congregation's voices, is accepted. This is accepted in the churches but not loud prayer and praise. Why can we not show emotion in worshipping the most precious Person to us? Emotion comes with love. Countries where there is a real move of God are very demonstrative in their services. The devil is out to quench the voice of heart-felt worship and prayer.

My sister, Lorraine, had a wonderful dream of devotion to the Lord.

Below are some excerpts from this dream written in her words:

Quote: "...Suddenly there was the most compassionate, loving face—one could not imagine such a face. He was smiling at me with pleasure and delight. I saw only the face of my Teacher. I saw no other part of Him, but felt His bodily form—His loving presence pouring into me. As He took me by the hand, He said: "Come with Me." He hugged me close to His side so that I leaned against Him ... There was such security, incredible stability, trustworthiness; all wisdom, all-faithfulness, all-knowing; everlasting assurance of eternal love. A warmth and glow flowed through me like the river of life, bringing such wonderful healing and joy! I was so comforted, so comfortable, so attracted to the One at my side—so attached, nothing and nobody could separate me from His love. I wanted to stay under His shadow, yet I didn't see any shadows; everything was glorious, bright and glistening within His immediate presence.

I was surrounded by multitudes, yet they were indistinct to me. My whole attention was fixed upon that glorious, beautiful, pure and holy face. I delighted in Him alone, all else was unclear. All else did not matter.

I never ever wanted to leave Him. I wanted to abide in Him and He in me forever. I loved and adored Him. The love I had for Him was exactly the same as He had for me, for I had absorbed His character that flowed through His presence into me. It was a natural attraction: no striving, no compromise, no working. I did nothing and could do nothing—just received, just rested in that unconditional love ...

I have just made an attempt to explain the emotional side of my dream, but still not adequately. My focus and absorption was the Groom. Now He said: "Come with Me My bride. I will show you what I am preparing for you." I thought at the time the words were strange, but only for a fleeting moment. I was just enraptured by the specialised attention. So much love and adoration for this beautiful One!

The multitudes also looked on with delight and adoration for the glorious One. I knew the multitudes were there but still could not see them distinctly. They also smiled approvingly at me and said, "The Groom loves His bride." Everywhere, they called Him the "Groom". I didn't speak throughout the entire dream, just trusted—never questioned, just accepted everything that was happening as a natural course of things." End of Quote.

This experience was between the Groom, the Lord Jesus Christ, and His bride—the true believing and devoted members of the body of Christ. The Groom is to be adored and the bride is so cherished by the Groom.

In the rest of the dream, Lorraine goes on to describe in detail as she enters the banqueting hall in heaven. Afterwards the Groom then takes her to the nasty side of life on earth but because she clung to Him, His love protected her.

We worship the Lord, because of His great drawing and magnetic love to us. God is preparing us in love to be made fit and ready to become the bride of His dear Son, Jesus. He will go to the extremities to protect and deliver His children from the hand of the evil one but it can only come through our loving response and trust.

Read Psalm 18

What a song! God is passionate about His children as we read in the above Psalm. David had tremendous insight into what went on behind the scenes when he cried out to God. We need to be passionate about a fiery God. He is zealous for those who love Him. When we cry to Him, His protective anger shakes the earth; bows the heavens; rides the cherub; flies upon the wind, sends clouds of darkness with hailstones; coals of fire and lightning while puffing out smoke and fire at the thunder of H i s voice. Then He parts the water ... *'He also brought me out into a spacious place; He rescued me because [He] delighted in me,'* (verse 19).

Wow! God will go to all that trouble for those who love Him? What a relationship David had with the Lord! He knew the enormity of God's power and yet in verse 35, in other translations of scripture, he says of the Lord that His *'gentleness had made me great'.*

With our limited insight, we may be thinking that David was over- exaggerating triggered by his vivid imagination, but we must take into account that he was speaking to God when this song was sung. His father- in-law, Saul, was after his blood so David simply cried out to God and was saved. He showed his appreciation in this graphic description of how God had done it. God did not rebuke him for getting carried away with the details. A person could only speak like that under the power of the Holy Spirit. There is a battle going on in the heavenly realm that we do not always see. This Psalm is also a picture of the horrendous torture that Jesus suffered on the cross and the darkness surrounding Him. He went to the grave and into Hades to preach to the righteous imprisoned there. God reached down and brought Him up from the grave. Praise God, He conquered death! He is seated at the right hand of the Father and holds the keys to death and hell so we do not have to go there when we trust in Him.

If God goes to all that extremity to answer our prayers, there is hope yet!

There are so many incidents in scripture where God's people cried out to the Lord in their distress. Then in Jonah 2:9 he says: *"But I, with a song of thanksgiving, will sacrifice to [You]. What I have vowed I will make good. Salvation comes from the Lord."* Then we read after this that the Lord caused the fish to vomit Jonah up onto dry land. Jonah obeyed the Lord and travelled to Ninevah.

Then there is the wonderful example of Paul and Silas having a praise party in prison—a good place to start no doubt.

'About midnight Paul and Silas were praying and singing hymns to God, and the other prisoners were listening to them. Suddenly there was such a violent earthquake that the foundations of the prison were shaken. At once all the prison doors flew open, and everybody's chains came loose.'

In Acts 16:24-33, Paul and Silas and the other prisoners could have walked free at that time but they chose to obey God which resulted in the salvation of the jailer and his household, and perhaps other prisoners. Their release came soon after they sang praises to the Lord. I call that a response to prayer and praise straight from the Father Himself.

During times of worship people can be set free of demonic strongholds and ministered to by bringing a touch from the Lord. This can happen anywhere, even in the market place. The key is listening to God, denying self and acting in obedience.

I remember one time when a friend and I were visiting a town during a prayer assignment. We had just finished praying together and planning to go to our car when the Holy Spirit directed me to kneel on the pavement where I was, raise my hands and worship the Lord in the Spirit with singing. *Oh boy!* Every bit of pride screamed out! Loudly. I was outside the Council Chambers, a court house, local police station and opposite a busy round-a-bout—traffic non-stop. But I had to obey and I did.

Something had broken in the atmosphere—I could feel it. After I had finished, we climbed into the car ready to get out of there pronto, when a lady tapped on the car window wanting to know what I was doing. Immediately, the Holy Spirit told me her problems and through her tears, we were able to minister to her. The time and place to worship God seemed inappropriate to us but if we are willing to give all over to the Lord, He will do outstanding things through us.

During the days following the 9/11, twin towers attack, God gave me a dream. I knew I had to gather a team of praising, prayer warriors and head for Sydney, Australia. I phoned around and most of our core team could go—others more distant agreed to pray. Our target was to go to the Opera House. There was an urgency, almost desperation to get there and the drive had taken two hours from the Hunter Valley. We caught a ferry to the Opera House and was surrounded by foreigners so we prayed loudly all the way in tongues without drawing any attention.

At the Opera House, the Holy Spirit led us to lay hands on every entrance into the building. No one was there on guard to stop us. Afterwards, we felt to stand on the steps leading up to the Opera House and with eyes closed, hands raised, we worshipped God by singing in the Spirit. The presence of God was so powerful. By this time a group of foreign tourists had gathered to listen. It was time to go home. We were to leave the results to God after that, wondering what was the actual significance of what we had done through the Spirit of God.

We were soon to find out on the news that night. Intelligence got wind of an impending terrorists' attack on Sydney Opera House that afternoon! The police had swarmed in after we left. They were not needed, God had already alerted His prayer warriors, not only us, but many other praying people across Australia that day as we had heard later. We felt humbled that God had sent us to be used on site.

It is so important that whatever we do, do it GOD'S WAY! I could tell of many other occasions where God had led us by His Spirit to bring miraculous results. But the point is: that the time and place to worship God may seem inappropriate to us but if we are willing to give all over to the Lord, He will do outstanding things through us.

I believe God wants us to have a big picture of Him—enlarge our vision and not limit Him to our puny thinking of who He is. It is like He is champing at the bit, rearing to go, but has to restrain Himself because of our lack of knowledge of Him. We tend to receive His gentleness readily enough, but overlook His incredible passionate love to do us good—to protect us from the devil's attack so we in turn can minister to others or bring protection when needed through His power flowing from us.

We will now take a look at another reason why we worship God. There would be so many more reasons that any reader could think of but my last reason in this book is:

Worship releases living waters from within us

It is in all of mankind to worship something. God has created within us an inner drive to worship Him. Have you ever wondered why people sing in the bath or shower? Other than the water drowns out their voice. I have friends who said God filled them with His Spirit while in the shower. I have spent many hours of pleasure over the years worshipping God beside a natural running stream in the mountains near my property. Many times when I had visited there alone I sang.

Another time when I was watering my garden, I found myself singing as soon as I turned on the hose. I could not wait to go inside and accompany myself with the piano. It was then, that I wondered why the sound of running water automatically stirs up a song within my heart. The revelation I had on this was: The sound of running water activates the natural lifespring within us. It can be likened to the unlocking of the source of a river.

In teaching singing, it was my job to help my students release their emotions from their belly, to bring deeper feelings and character to what they were singing. Singers can never keep a song within themselves. It is always to be given away in some form or other and cannot be taken back once it is let out. You cannot snatch a song from the air or demand it back once it is sung.

To sing is a gift that is given to everyone and many non Christians can release such natural beauty with their voices that brings tears to our eyes. But every Christian can go deeper in pouring out from their heart, giving their whole being in worship to God, regardless of the tone of their voice. This brings a tremendous release to us.

Jesus says to us in John 7:38: *'Whoever believes in [Me], as the Scripture said, streams of living water will flow from within him.'*

To put the above verse more strongly is that out of the belly or bowels of the true believer—one who trusts the Lord and clings to Him, there will be a continual flow of living water. The living water speaks of the pouring out of the Holy Spirit. First and foremost, Holy Spirit helps us to worship in spirit and truth as Father God requires. The following scriptures speaks of this river:

Psalm 46:4: *'There is a river whose streams make glad the city of God, the holy place where the Most High lives.'*

Revelation 22:1: *'Then the angel showed me the river of the water of life, as clear as crystal, flowing from the throne of God and of the Lamb.'*

Ezekiel 47:1: *'The man brought me back to the entrance of the temple, and I saw water, coming out from under the threshold of the temple...'*

The writer of 1 Corinthians 3:16 says: *'Don't you know that you yourselves are God's temple and that God's Spirit lives in you?'*

This is powerful stuff! The RIVER of LIFE has the capacity and power to bring life to wherever it flows! (Ezekiel 47:1-10)

Jesus said that this same river will flow from those who believe in Him. Let us not hold back but flow with that river! Let worship pour from our hearts to bring refreshment to, not only ourselves, but to others and our community. This is *true* living, and life *is* for living!

Another favourite place to visit is a spillway of a very large reservoir. The thunderous roar of water from the two massive jets is incredible and the force behind that spill is awesome. The water from this dam has the capacity to service hundreds of thousands of homes. A local power station uses over 100 mega litres of water a day to drive its huge turbines. Each turbine is equal to sixteen 747 jet engines so we can have power and heat. Yet as magnificent as this sounds, it does not have enough power to raise the dead, heal the sick or bring salvation.

Think of the incredible, supernatural power produced by the river of God which the whole earth and universe can tap into. We as Christians, have been entrusted to this awesome power to bring light, healing and salvation to a dying world. I love the little song—"There's a river of life flowing out from me." It suggests that this river makes the lame walk, the blind see and opens prison doors to set the captives free: so simple yet so powerful and true.

When you think of it, most of us are not using a speck of what God expects us to. I do not know about you, but I want the big river that flows from the heart of God flowing from me. We need that release so we can minister to a hurting world.

In 1988 I was travelling with a team doing evangelism through drama in schools, prisons, hospitals, churches and street work. We travelled through the east coast of Australia from Melbourne in the south to Mareeba, north of Cairns. Then overseas to the Philippines and India. One day during my early morning prayer time I had a vision of three vessels sitting on a shelf. I felt God was asking me what they were doing. Nothing, they were just sitting there. The Holy Spirit likened them to our earthen vessels—ourselves. Each of the vessels on the shelf were filled: one with grain, another with oil and the third with wine—representing the word of God, healing and cleansing. Our job with our earthen vessel is to be continually filled with God's presence and He will use us at His will. The message was clear to wait on the Lord and be ready for Him to use us. The reality of the vision came later during the day.

That day we were performing a play on the street with a gospel message. I had the flu but, as I was in the drama and had no one to replace me, I struggled through my part. We had finished our performance on the streets of Melbourne and were waiting for the mini-bus to pick us up. I was feeling quite ill by then and hoped our driver would hurry up with the bus.

I was still in my costume and blue, face makeup, which would be odd to those who had not seen the play. However that did not deter a lady from approaching me. She needed to make a phone call from the phone booth I was near but needed help to use it. She had a heavy accent so I asked her where she was from. She replied Greece and began to sob which led into an asthma attack. I wrapped my arms around her to stop her from slipping to the ground and tried to attract attention for help. No one else could see what was happening. Suddenly the lady straightened up and looked at me in surprise and said. "You love God?" I was equally surprised by her unusual response, then she added. "Love of God flowed through you and healed my asthma!"

What wonderful things Jesus prepares for us when we are obedient to Him. He reminded me of the vision I saw of the vessels that morning. Through His enabling love I poured out the oil for healing on this dear lady without knowing it. She had not seen the drama nor did she know I loved Jesus. God revealed Himself to her. We are carriers of His love and power no matter what we feel like. What an amazing responsibility we have to spread His love and healing.

Natural rivers usually begin from spring sources in the high country or mountains. So like the river of life flowing from within us springs from the mountain top experiences we have with Jesus. Many times our prayer team would travel around the Hunter Valley to pray for rain, and for the rivers and streams to run during drought times. Sometimes we had gotten too carried away forgetting that excess rain brings floods, and with that could bring destruction and devastation to some farmers. At times we would use what we could see in the natural and pray into the spiritual for the release to come. One example of this was after a flood. A pile of rubble had built up in one of the brooks blocking the flow of water. We likened this to people of the valley whose hearts were blocked with the rubble of life preventing the Holy Spirit flowing freely in their lives. We asked God to remove the rubbish from the hearts of the people.

Meanwhile, a man with a backhoe had arrived and patiently waited until we had finished praying and singing. When realising he was there one of our team members, Stuart, wandered over to speak to him. The driver of course wanted to know what we were doing. Stuart explained how we had likened the build up of rubble in the stream to the blockages in our lives which stops God from breaking through, and how we had prayed to remove them. In turn Stuart asked the driver what he was about to do with the backhoe, and he simply answered. "Remove the rubble out of the stream."

God always has a way of giving us confirmation of the actions we do which could appear a little radical at times. The key to this is obedience to what His Spirit is directing us to do.

CHAPTER 7

Earth – First heaven

For a happy, healthy, existence the whole earth needs to respond to the blessings and goodness of God. As we have read in so many scriptures that everything that exists has the capacity to praise the Lord. This is essential for the purpose of entering into the flow of existence with Creator God to bring order and harmony in this chaotic world. Without true worshippers in each nation to hold back the wrath of God, could you imagine the devastation throughout the world!

God is all powerful and He has the capacity within Him to destroy and punish rebellion and wickedness on the spot. What holds Him back? Until the proper time He restrains himself. He is merciful and remembers that we are but dust, (Psalm 103:14). A good father may get angry when his child behaves badly but he restrains himself from dishing out punishment that would harm or kill the child. Why? It is love for the child that controls him. Love is a powerful force, much stronger than anger. Love can also become a weapon. In chapter one of this book I likened the repetitious declaration of the tribe of Judah to God's love of a battering ram.

In old movies during times of battle, battering rams were used to smash through barriers of huge solid doors of fortresses or castles. Many men would take hold of a massive log and charge with rhythmic, repeated efforts until the doors bursts open. Some translations of the Bible uses 'mercy' or 'grace' as enduring forever instead of love. These all come from the roots of God's love.

As we seek God in worship and prayer we are joining the heavenly worshippers, fanning into flame His response to the earth. It is a two-way response—we pour out our hearts to God and He answers by pouring out His grace to us and meets our needs. We then in response offer up thanks and praise to Him: then the cycle starts all over again.

A good example of this is in Joel 2:17-19. It speaks of calling a gathering to seek God in fasting, humility, weeping and crying out to Him. The reply is found in verse 18:

'Then the Lord will be jealous for [His] land, and take pity on [His] people. The Lord will reply to them: "I am sending you grain, new wine and oil, enough to satisfy you fully; never again will I make you an object of scorn to the nations.'

And there is more!

Hosea 2:21 is also interesting*: "In that day I will respond," declares the Lord—"I will respond to the skies, and they will respond to the earth; And the earth will respond to the grain, the new wine and oil, and they will respond to Jezreel."*

Look up the above verse in the Living Bible. It really makes the scripture come alive with God responding to the pleading of the sky—for clouds to pour down on the thirsty earth that has cried out for rain, then the earth will respond by producing the grain, new wine and oil. Then all will be happy and respond with loud praise and singing: *'God sows! He has given everything.'*

God responds to whatever is happening on the earth, and His response can also be according to our response. He inhabits the praises of His people.

God not only cares for His people, but the earth itself—our habitat, a place of His abundant provision.

Psalm 19 gives a wonderful picture of the splendour of God's creation of harmony and divine order:

*'The heavens declare the glory of God,
The skies proclaim the work of [His] hands.
Day after day they offer up speech;
Night after night they display knowledge.
There is no speech or
language where their voice is
not heard.
Their voice goes out into all the earth,
their words to the end of all the
world.
In the heavens [He] has pitched a tent for
the sun, which is like a bridegroom
coming forth from the pavilion,
like a champion rejoicing to run his course.
It rises to one end of the
heavens and makes its circuit
to the other; nothing is hidden
from its heat. The law of the
Lord is perfect...'*

In the beginning—God. This is no fairy tale starting with once upon a time there was a god. God is time; He *is* existence, always has been—the beginning and the end meeting up. Except there is no end.

Was there ever a beginning? This just shows us how unfathomable it is to try and describe God.

As a young person, I used to go round and round in circles trying to comprehend: What if God didn't exist and there was nothing? I soon realised it was easier to believe in something than to believe in nothing. Nothing is *nothing*. Empty space. Dead air. What is space? Because I exist—there must be something! Understand? Do not try to.

The earth began with God—definitely a beginning for the earth because the word of God tells us that in Genesis 1 and 2. Everything that God created was perfect. God said it was good. He was pleased with His handiwork just like we are pleased with our handiwork...well, sometimes. He only spoke His word and everything would come into existence. Even the soil was perfect, not defiled by death and decay or the cry of blood. It was a pure, living matter. All kinds of grasses, herbs, trees and every variety of vegetation imaginable had sprung up in this soil at God's command.

At God's command the earth produced the beasts of the field, every living thing that crawled and flew in the air: and the water produced the fish and every living thing that swam. It was so unpolluted and perfect, that God even formed Adam from the dust of the earth and placed him in this glorious garden paradise, called Eden.

Life was wonderful. Adam was in charge of this garden, naming every animal and bird but best of all, God had made him a beautiful companion to love and cherish. All was sheer bliss and they lived in pure innocence before one another and God. The whole of the heavens and creation were in perfect uniformity and balance together in relationship with the Creator. Disharmony, disorder, discord and dysfunction was far removed from this setting. It was like one, big, happy family enjoying not only the handiwork of God, but the fullness of His presence and the purity of His holiness.

God had given instructions for Adam and Eve not to eat the fruit of the tree of the knowledge of good and evil otherwise they would die. It would have been easy enough if Adam and Eve were programmed like robots, but they were far from this for God had given them a will and curiosity like any of us. Because God had made Adam and Eve in His own image, He gave them the right to have authority over their own bodies and rule over the earth and every living thing on it. They had the freedom to make choices in life, but the one they made here was very, very bad.

Unfortunately this wonderful life did not last. Satan needed an earthly body to inhabit so he used the serpent. Obviously in the innocence of the Garden of Eden a language of all creation could be understood, otherwise how could Eve be deceived by the serpent. Eve listened to the devil in the serpent's body and ate the forbidden fruit, then offered some to Adam to eat.

Oops!

Suddenly, the honeymoon came to an abrupt end! Death's hand entered their kingdom. Death to their innocence, death to their stewardship of the garden of Eden but worst of all, death to their relationship with their Creator. A chasm of sin had come between them and God. Fortunately it was not death to their conscience. They felt guilty. They had found themselves naked and feared the presence of God—a new experience they had to face. Before they had sinned they were clothed in the glory of God and innocence. Now this era of the age of innocence was closed to them.

God banished Adam and Eve from the garden of Eden. Was this a harsh thing to do? God had no choice. He is holy. That is who He is— **holy.** Nothing could come into His presence with even the smallest imperfection. Man disobeyed. He gave all his rights over to Satan, the deceiver, who now robbed him of the authority over his own body, soul and spirit. If they were to continue in the Garden of Eden they would eat the fruit of the Tree of Life which they were allowed to. The problem with this is they would live forever, but not in purity, but in their sin.

Before this terrible happening, God had only to speak the word and life would spring up from the earth but now Adam was committed to a life of toil and slavery forever, working hard to produce life from the very soil from which God had formed him. Blessings were replaced with thorns and thistles signifying that the earth was cursed because of man's sin. Mankind from this time has had to fend for himself using his own initiative in order to survive.

Because the curse of death had corrupted this perfect world, decayed matter is now used to produce the right composites of material suitable to fertilise and bring balance to the soil. Even a seed has to die to produce many seeds. A new cycle of life—death—life had begun.

Death of one thing brings life to another

I remember an interview on television some time ago, with a lady living on a property in outback Australia surrounded by a barren desert. She was asked why her garden was so luscious and flourishing, especially her trees. Her answer was simple: "All I do is dig a hole and toss in a dead sheep, plant the tree on top then back fill." She then added: "You could use any dead animal for that matter." Good advice if you could find a dead animal! In urban areas we would have to rely on road kill.

The point is that now death had entered this world, cutting man off from the security of a loving and caring God. Adam and Eve heard God walking in the garden and hid from Him. God knew where Adam was but called out to him to come out of hiding. I love the popular singer's description of this haunting scene in his song: 'Adam! Where are you!'

Down through the ages, mankind is still tying to hide from God yet the voice of the Father still cries out to mankind after many thousands of years: **"ADAM WHERE ARE YOU?"**

Devastation entered the world that God had called good. Instead of perfection and perfect harmony—famine, desolation, disease, pain, suffering, darkness and death: the earth has become what the popular term describes—the *real world*.

We are living in a time in history where we are bombarded from all angles about climate change and developing a greater awareness of environmental issues, energy and water harvesting. This is not new. Our generation was brought up to *waste not, want not*. Our family was *environmentalists* well before it became a popular trend. My father used to say that God will destroy those who destroy the earth, (Revelation 11:18).

I remember how distressed we were growing up in the 1960's when bulldozers began clearing the bush-land at the back of our property for intensive housing. As the trees fell, my sisters would quickly grab the possums, care for the injured ones, then relocate them into the bush elsewhere. Another time we found a possum had been caught in a rabbit trap. We went to the chemist, bought some chloroform, put the possum to sleep and my father cut off its mangled foot. The possum survived, hung around for take-away and brought up babies in our yard.

We loved the bush and everything in it, so we were grieved when we had lost it. Today the movement to save the planet has gone to the extreme that it has become a religion—worship of the creation: Scripture says: '*They exchanged the truth of God for a lie, and worshipped and served created things rather than the Creator—who is forever praised,*' (Romans 1:25).

People risk their own lives to save trees, forests, whales or any other environmental cause regardless of the damage they are doing to human lives through loss of work and income. They have no concern for people yet

EARTH - FIRST HEAVEN

they are seducing people into their way of thinking through citing fear. The same people who are passionate in preaching, SAVE THE EARTH! are the ones who pressed hard to pass bills to abort babies up to eight and nine months; legalising gay marriages, changing the gender of natural births; adoptions of same sex couples then of course—euthanasia.

They seem to be anti the human race or anything that is normal in God's creation! They have little interest in family life or moral values. They also want to abolish opening parliament sittings with prayer and freedom of speech (vilification laws). They complain there are too many Christians in political positions of authority. Take God out of politics you are left with the devil in office. Try handing out our well-known Christian political party's, "how to vote" flyers on polling day—many Christians give you the snub and vote for a party that supports all those issues I mentioned above. Ignorance!

Christians should check out the source and policies of a party they vote for. Jesus said to *'go out into all the world and preach the good news, heal the sick and cast out devils.'* We are to take a stand for truth, righteousness and moral values.

Why? Because our responsibility is to be concerned for human souls, and Jesus not only has the answer to life, but *is* the answer. We have a cause to stand for—bringing souls into the kingdom of God.

Yes, we must preserve what we have been so blessed with, and I praise God for genuine people who work overtime to try and reverse the mistakes of our early settlers in unwarranted clearing of the land. Someone has to do it. And the pollution levels in some of the mining towns are becoming almost too hard to live in for those with respiratory problems. These are problems that man *can* fix but climatic change begins in the heart of man and his relationship with His Creator. When God spoke to Adam after he disobeyed, He said in Genesis 3:17-19:

'Because you have listened to your wife and ate from the tree about which I commanded you, "you must not eat of it," "cursed is the ground because of you; through painful toil you will eat of it all the days of your life. It will produce thorns and thistles for you, and you will eat the plants of the field. By the sweat of your brow you will eat your food until you return to the ground, since from it you were taken; for dust you are and to dust you will return.'

It is through man's SIN the climate is changing

I praise God that it is not in His nature to give up on the objects of His love. He had another plan to reach mankind and that is in the person of His Son, Jesus Christ. As we explore the Bible, we find it is a love story between God and man—God wooing mankind and man rejecting His love and forgiveness preferring to worship other evil gods.

God formed man from the earth to rule over the earth and its affairs, so God always needs and uses *earthen bodies*—prophets and preachers to be His voice and draw His people back to Himself. Down through the ages many of these prophets had been scorned or killed.

Had God been fighting a lost cause? No, definitely not. Right from the beginning there have been many godly people who would worship and serve the true, Creator God, to keep a remnant of His people through future generations. He understands the corrupt nature of man and is ready to forgive when prayers of repentance are offered up to Him. It was required by Old Testament law to offer up animal sacrifices on behalf of the people's sin. This act only *covered* the sin and was not a permanent solution, because man does not have the power within himself to refrain from sinning. God needed a perfect sacrifice once and for all!

He put His ultimate plan to work. He needed another *earthen body*—His only begotten Son, Jesus! Jesus Christ came to earth as a baby. He did not come from the line of Adam as His seed was corrupted by sin. Jesus was planted supernaturally by God Himself in the womb of the virgin, Mary. He came into this sin-laden world in such lowly conditions that God's very own people could not recognise Him as the promised Messiah, who was to save them from their misery.

Man had already been subjected to the physical world of slavery, death and losing sight of the realm of the spirit. The Messiah's kingdom was to restore man back to his spiritual world that is eternal and living, and the Creator in whose image he is made.

Jesus' ministry was one of reconciliation, love, forgiveness, healing the sick and casting out devils. He opposed the religious leaders who brought bondage to the people. He opposed the money grabbers and the greedy but rather spoke of the wonders of heaven and the Father's love. He was sinless and yet was accused of being full of demons.

He was hated for not being *politically correct*. He suffered such horrendous torture—His body was so battered, His flesh torn, that He was unrecognisable when He was nailed to the cross. The Roman soldiers jammed a crown of thorns on His head. The thorns are symbolic of the curse that sin had brought on the earth. Jesus became King of the cursed: King of the diseased, broken, dying, downtrodden—all who were sinful without hope. All of hell's fury and evil was vented against Jesus yet it was Father God's plan that His Son should die—for us! (Galations 3:13).

Jesus Christ was the only perfect man who could die in our place. He was the only earth-man who did not bow to Satan. He had not sinned in any way. On the cross, for every generation to come, He willingly took on our sins, our pain and suffering that we may live a life of freedom. His blood poured out and washed our sins away for good.

His blood poured out onto the earth and broke the curse over the whole of creation.

Jesus Christ has taken back the authority that Adam had given to Satan! Jesus said in Matthew 28:18-20:

'All authority in heaven and on earth has been given to me. Therefore go and make disciples of all nations, baptising them in the name of the Father and of the Son and of the Holy Spirit, and teaching them to obey everything I have commanded you. And surely I am with you always, to the very end of the age.'

Jesus has been given all the authority on earth! Then how do we fit in? Let's look at Luke 10:19:

'I have given you authority to trample on snakes and scorpions and to overcome all the power of the enemy; nothing will harm you.'

Wow! This is powerful! The curse over mankind and all of creation has been broken. Man now has the opportunity to take back the authority ordained to him from the beginning!

The most awesome thing is that through the death of Jesus Christ, we now can live to worship the Living God and enter into the fullness of His presence once again!

And the earth? Romans 8:19-22 says: *'The creation waits in eager expectation for the sons of God to be revealed. For the creation was subjected to frustration, not by its own choice, but by the will of the one who subjected it, in hope that the creation itself will be liberated from its bondage to decay and brought into the glorious freedom of the children of God. We know that the whole creation has been groaning as in the pains of childbirth right up to the present time.'*

The good news is: this earth is going to be restored when Jesus returns and sets up His kingdom! I love the promise of restoration in Isaiah 55:12-13: *'You shall go out in joy and be led forth in peace; the mountains and hills will burst into song before you, and all the trees of the field will clap their hands. Instead of the thorn bush will grow the pine tree, and instead of briars* the myrtle will grow. This will be for the Lord's renown, for an everlasting sign which will not be destroyed.'

What a wonderful provision God has made for His people. It could only happen through His son, Jesus Christ. When we are released from the captivity of Satan and born-again by the Spirit of God, He births a new song in our hearts. We cannot help but sing the songs of our Redeemer. Those trapped in sin cannot have lasting joy or sing the songs of heaven.

Psalm 137:1 says: *'By the rivers of Babylon we sat down and wept when we remembered Zion. There on the poplars we hung our harps, for there our captors asked us for songs, our tormentors demanded songs of joy; they said, "Sing us one of the songs of Zion." How can we sing the songs of the Lord while in a foreign land.'*

What a difference when the tribes of Judah were released from bondage— *'When the Lord brought back the captives to Zion, we were like men who dreamed. Our mouths were filled with laughter, our tongues with songs of joy. Then it was said among the nations, "The Lord has done great things for them." The Lord has done great things for us, and we are filled with joy,'* Psalm (126:1-3).

I was brought up in a hard-line religious sect. For fifteen years my mother, sister, brother and I were controlled by brainwashing and fear. When I was the age of thirteen the elders were trying to force me away from my parents. I was terrified and hid under my bed. They were calling to me through my bedroom window that I must leave our home because it was contaminated. But praise the Lord, because five years later they excommunicated us. Free at last! This book is not to centre on these times but the goodness of God. For several years after leaving these people, I studied music and singing which brought partial healing to my soul. But nothing could compare with the joy and peace that flooded my whole being when the Holy Spirit filled me and delivered me from fear. I was overwhelmed by His love and He gave me a new song to sing in the language of heaven.

I believe the church is coming into such liberation bringing in tremendous joy. Jesus said in Luke 15:10 *'...I tell you, there is rejoicing in the presence of the angels of God over one sinner who repents.'* All heaven celebrates when a person comes into the kingdom of God.

The unwanted news is: things are going to get worse before this happens in totality! Yes, the curse over the earth is broken but we as children of God have a part to play in its redemption.

God will intervene in the affairs of earth if we will humble ourselves and cry out to Him on behalf of the land. 2 Chronicles 7:13-14 says: *'When I shut up the heavens so that there is no rain, or command locusts to devour the land or send a plague among [My] people, if [My] people, who are called by[My]name, will humble themselves and pray and seek [My] face and turn from their wicked ways, I will hear from heaven and I will forgive their sin and will heal their land.'*

CHAPTER 8

Atmosphere Around the Earth – Second heaven

When Adam and Eve disobeyed God, they gave Satan permission to torment and buffet, not only them, but all of mankind from there after.

Several years ago, a child who had a problem with all authority figures, began music lessons with me. This student refused to receive instruction and argued with any suggestion I made, insisting that the teacher at school said it was done another way. A child like this can be very abusive and controlling. A good teacher and student relationship never develops with this behaviour as the student strips the teacher of any right to become her teacher. It seemed this student had given that right to the teacher at school who was only teaching simple, basic skills on a short term level and the child would never progress any further.

Rebellion begins early in life and children can try to rob their parents of having the authority to become good parents. Rebellion is classed as the sin of witchcraft in the word of God, therefore Satan has been given the authority over their child unless they fight to take back their rights as parents.

It is like that with God. If we refuse Him, we listen to the devil and give him the authority to control us.

The way we view God and treat Him is how He reveals Himself.

2 Samuel 22:26-27 says:

'To the faithful [You] show [Yourself] faithful, to the blameless [You] Show [Yourself] blameless, to the pure [You] show [Yourself] pure, but to the crooked [You] show [Yourself] shrewd.'

Satan is out to destroy God-ordained relationships: whether it is between husbands and wives, parents and children, teachers and students, employers and employees, or any other situations. He influences the minds of the rebellious and they see these relationships from a distorted perspective—they see enemies and not friends. That is how many people view God. They create God in their own image and blame Him for not responding the way they think He should. I have heard it so many times when sharing the gospel with people and speak of God's love. A common response is, "Then where was He when I needed Him?" The point to consider is where was God in their lives before they go through trauma. Usually they have put God far away from their lifestyle. It takes a lot of grace and wisdom to answer them. John 10:10 says: *'The thief comes only to steal, kill and destroy...'*

Ephesians 6:12 says: *'For our struggle is not against flesh and blood, but against the rulers, against the authorities, against the powers of this dark world and against the spiritual forces of evil in the heavenly realms.'* These rulers of darkness are not in heaven because they were cast out with Lucifer when he rose up against God. Lucifer means, *light-bearer* and is described as the morning star—a beautiful being adorned with precious stones. He was ordained by God as the covering cherub over Eden and was a model of perfection and full of wisdom. He was puffed up with pride which led to his downfall. He exalted himself as God so he had to be stripped of his heavenly authority and thrown out of heaven, (Ezekiel 28:12-17).

Satan still has gifts that God had given him and he uses them to corrupt mankind. He still can appear as an angel of light, subtly deceiving people. He has no authority over God, the affairs in heaven, or heavenly beings but he sure knows when those on earth give him authority over their lives. Power was a gift given by God and Satan and his minions certainly know how to use it.

There is a place in the heavenly realm where these powers of darkness live. Their sole aim is to block the purposes of God and destroy mankind and drag him into the pit of hell. They are just as real as we are and they are innumerable. They are of different ranks: Satan, the highest rank; princes over nations; territorial spirits over areas and buildings, and tormenting spirits over groups or individuals. The lowest of these demons are those living among us on earth. Their aim is to cause people to sink lower into depravity; block their hearts and minds from knowing the God of love, and blinding their eyes from seeing the glory of Christ, (2 Corinthians 4:3-4).

They hate God with a passion and are like ravaging lions out to tear apart all good work—to disrupt anything God has planned. They also incite persecution against God's people, Jews and Christians alike because they are a threat to Satan's domain.

We are living in a war and cannot afford to be complacent.

2 Corinthians 10:4, (NKJV), says: '*For the weapons of our warfare are not carnal but mighty in God for pulling down strongholds, casting down arguments and every high thing that exalts itself against the knowledge of God, bringing every thought into captivity to the obedience of Christ.*'

God has given us weapons to use against our spiritual enemies but as this book is about worship, prayer and music, I will keep focused in this area.

We have read earlier on that all of heaven worships the One who sits on the throne, to bring order and harmony to all of the universe.

Psalm 24:1-2 says: *'The earth is the Lord's and everything in it, the world, and all who live in it; for [He] founded it upon the seas and established it upon the waters.'*

God created the earth and everything in it. He is the rightful owner.

Satan on the other hand is out to corrupt anything that belongs to God.

2 Corinthians 4:4 says: *'The god of this age has blinded the minds of unbelievers, so that they cannot see the light of the gospel of the glory of Christ, who is the image of God.'*

What this verse is saying is that Satan is behind the worldly systems—ungodly structures, evil patterns of thinking, motives, disease, greed, crime and all that is depraved and oppressive. He has become a ruler of this earthly kingdom because of man's fall. He is the greatest cosmic conspirator of all time. He has a plan for every nation, government, authority, religion, Christian denomination, church group, family and person. He uses his demonic followers to carry out his plans and they are tenacious as pit-bull terriers on a kill. The last thing Satan wants is people worshipping the true God.

Satan is a ruler of darkness and hates the light.

Music is a powerful tool and used in the wrong hands can be very destructive. Satan has been given creative power and uses this power to manipulate the hearts and minds of musicians, to deceive them to give him glory instead of God. We can see the effects of heavy, metal rock music with its harsh acoustic distortions, has on young people by sending them into trances. It can drive them to hate, commit evil acts including sexual perversion, suicide, murder and can cause emotional and mental problems. A heavy rock concert releases powerful, demon spirits that incites mass hysteria—a frenzy of screaming and crying audiences. There is a spiritual power or force behind it. One such rock concert can affect the whole city and the churches in that city.

Heavy rock music was also used as a form of brainwashing—played over and over, to persecute Christians in prison in communist countries. The motive is to confuse Christians into denying Christ as their Lord and Saviour.

Because Satan is a deceiver and may appear as light, it is short lived and before long when his true, evil, self is revealed he will turn against his followers very quickly.

God is LIGHT! Jesus said in John 8:12: *'I am the light of the world.'* God Himself emits light. Every source of light and energy comes from the Living God. Revelation 22:5 speaks of the New Jerusalem: there will be no need for lights, sun or candles for the Lord Himself gives light.

Scientists have found that sound waves are just another dimension of light waves. They are infinite—never stopping. The waves themselves undulate in perfect formation with hills and valleys identical in size, shape and consistency. Only divine order could bring such uniformity. Emanating from the Being of God is not only incredible glory and light, but sound and music. If God readjusted our eyes we would actually be able to see music and singing as waves of light.

Over the years, experiments have been made on plants. Plants that had classical music played to them grew towards the music. Plants that had heavy metal played to them, died. Plants that had no music at all played to them grew toward the natural light. Also, classical or harmonious music played in cow bales and chicken sheds increases the production of milk and eggs. The conclusion speaks volumes. Sometimes I wonder what would happen if some of the Christian bands were to play in these situations. An interesting point.

Some time ago the people of a community were fed up with the gangs of young people hanging around their town. It was decided to pipe peaceful music throughout the shopping centre. It worked! Problem solved. It is hard to hang around and commit acts of violence in an atmosphere of peace so the youths went elsewhere and the crime rate dropped in that particular town.

My brother in-law, who is an expert in electronics, has two speakers that flashes colour when music plays. Discordant music with a heavy, dominant beat explodes into glaring colours of red and orange. These colours are disturbing, whereas more harmonious music flashes softer shades of blue and green which are more soothing to the nervous system.

God has given us a weapon of light. Ourselves! Jesus said in Matthew 5:14-16:

'You are the light of the world. A city on a hill that cannot be hidden ... In the same way let your light shine before men, that they may see your good deeds and praise your Father in heaven.'

Matthew 6:22 says: *'The eye is the lamp of the body. If your eyes are good, your whole body will be full of light.'*

Even science has proven this to be true. Someone had invented a light meter which measures the degree of light in a Christian. It has shown that when a person is born-again and filled with the Spirit of God, every atom and cell of their body is flooded with His light. This is the genetic make-up of Jesus!

Colossians 2:9-10 says: *'For in Christ all the fullness of the Deity lives in bodily form, and you have been given fullness in Christ, who is the head over every power and authority.'*

What an inheritance! The fullness of Christ!

After surgery my sister, Lorraine, reacted to the anaesthetic and went through the death situation and had to be resuscitated. She survived to tell of the things she had experienced. For some time afterwards, when she saw people on the streets, she knew Christians from non Christians by the wonderful light that radiated from them.

The unsaved had an aura of death around them and there was so much darkness in the world, that she felt depressed. Her eyes were still looking heavenward and it was months before she could adjust into earthly vision. Imagine the damage that born-again, Spirit-filled musicians and singers could do to Satan's kingdom if submitted to the leading of God.

Christmas is a good time to reach people with the sound of music and singing. A handful of praying friends and I used to walk the streets of a few country towns around us and spread the message of the gospel in song, sharing, giving of tracts and little bundles of sweets. I played the piano accordion which was loud and groups of people would wait for us outside their homes well before we had arrived. The presence of God was so strong during these times. We had extra copies of the words of carols in booklets to give to the listeners if they wanted to sing along. One time a neighbour and her daughter stood outside their home to join us. They were used to hearing me teach singing because sound carried from my house. But on this occasion, there was a look of wonder on their faces and it puzzled us. Why did they look so amazed? It would not have been our singing. I could only put it down to—we shone with the glory of God! We moved on down the road to the next house. Sometimes we were invited into homes. Other times we had opportunities to pray for those listening. What a blessing to do God's work in simplicity and having a personal contact with the people of our community. Music opens the way into the heart of a person.

Satan is a thief and he is out to destroy our young people by luring them with the psychedelic attractions of strobe lighting, clouds of smoke, glaring coloured lights while their young bodies writhe around in a trance opening themselves up to demonic powers.

The church has so much more to offer than the world. We have the wonderful glory of God in our midst! We do not need gimmicks when God is moving by His Spirit! His glory is all we need. Keep the light of God shining in His church! Like I said in an earlier chapter, we do not need to paint the inside of our buildings black then turn off the lights during worship. We need to see the light of Jesus on each face—the glory of God. We are the body of Christ and it should inspire us to see the devotion and diverse expressions of others as they respond to the love of Jesus. We come together to be in union with Christ.

Many Christians around the world cannot freely worship the Lord together because of persecution. Others are isolated—the only one in an entire village who loves Jesus. They cannot fellowship and only can dream of meeting with others like we do. The West has it all but Satan likes to separate us in our services. It is all about Jesus and not a concert with the spotlight on the worship leaders alone. It is a distraction of the evil one to take our focus away from the One who has purchased our salvation. Jesus never encouraged us to be popular—He certainly was not. He said to deny self! Start looking beyond our music and singing and into the heavenly realm where Jesus is.

I remember when I was in India on an evangelistic team. A dear Indian pastor came from many miles away. He had walked the whole way in shoes that were too big for him. He wanted to fellowship with us and when he arrived he was so thankful to God for the opportunity. During prayer, he knelt on the floor and sobbed, pouring out his devotion to the Lord. What if he came into the body of Christ where he could not see the people because the lights were turned off. The apostles never entertained the crowd, they were serious and meant business. There was a great cost to their walk with the Lord—persecution and death.

'Do not love the world or anything in the world. If anyone loves the world, the love of the Father is not in him. For everything in the world— the cravings of sinful man, the lust of his eyes and the boasting of what he has and does— comes not from the Father but from the world. The world and its desires pass away, but the man who does the will of God, lives forever,' (1 John 2:15).

God is preparing a bride, holy and spotless for His Son. There is power and light in our music. We can have God's glorious presence that can save, heal and deliver. Christians think that using the same style of music but changing the words to the music makes it Christian. Changing the label of a bottle does not change its contents. They are drinking the world in those bottles and not separating from it. I agree that music is amoral— neither moral or immoral but it is best to look into the origin of a style before putting our heart and soul into it.

Everyone seems to enjoy the *'Hallelujah Chorus'* from Handel's oratorio, *'Messiah'*. It is powerful, spine-tingling and still very popular even after 282 years. I believe it will still be going strong to the time when Jesus comes for his Bride. Why? Because of George Frederick Handel's devotion to the Lord when composing it. He wrote it on his knees in prayer and tears before God. What a blessing all of mankind has received through this man's humility and obedience. The chorus is a finale´ to our life on earth, ushering the reign of Christ as King of kings and Lord of lords. It is a strong declaration taken from Revelation 11:15. More on that in a later chapter.

Our music needs to be purified, holy, fit to stand before God to minister and please Him first, not try to draw the crowd. Let God do the drawing as we yield to Him and the crowds will come. Then we are ready to fight the evil one. What is given by God will last throughout eternity.

In the CBD of Maitland near where I live, is a mall surrounded by many shops including restaurants. Half way along there is an open area leading to the Hunter River Levee Walk. For a few years, a group of us have been praying for the sick, sharing the gospel and giving out tracts in this area. Many times we have seen God do amazing things. For about a week I felt God was urging me to play the piano in the mall. What a peculiar request, I thought, and argued a bit in my mind. How could I take a piano into the mall? A keyboard was more reasonable but it was like God was shaking His head to that. It is always best to wait for God to speak again rather than rushing in with a substitute. Besides I was nervous with the whole idea. With a conventional piano you have your back to the people. I waited. One day I showed up to evangelise and there it was—a piano! Wow! God knew ahead and planned it for me. The local council had put it there. I knew why. Music can change the atmosphere of a city. I could not help but sit down and play as the Holy Spirit led. God opens the doors for us so I took up the opportunity. A friend who loved sharing the Lord with people never hesitated and had them dancing. Other members of the team talked to those gathered around. Joy came to that part of the town. Unfortunately the next season, Covid 19 struck and we were unable to reach people.

Like I have said before, Satan is out to block any response we have to God whether it is prayer, praise and worship. To share the gospel of the kingdom of God is a powerful weapon against the evil one and wearing masks and isolation stopped us from street work for that season. The devil will do all he can to hinder God's work through his people. A good example of this in scripture is when Daniel's prayer was blocked. A heavenly visitor came in a vision, Daniel 10:12-13:

'Then he said to me, "Do not be afraid, Daniel. Since the first day that you set your mind to gain understanding and to humble yourself before your God, your words were heard, and I have come in response to them. But the prince

of the Persian kingdom resisted me twenty one days. Then Michael, one of the chief princes, came to help me, because I was detained there with the king of Persia.'

Daniel lived a pure and dedicated life before the Lord and Satan used every strategy he could to counteract his prayers from being answered. There are battles continually between the devil's angels and God's holy angels in order for God's will to be executed without resistance. Michael, the archangel, came to assist in the spiritual warfare surrounding Daniel. Just imagine: this magnificent being, spoken of in Revelation 12:9 as Michael—the mighty, warring archangel, who will in the future, fight and subdue the dragon—fronting up to clear the airways so God can respond to *your* cry!

The activity in the second heaven or atmosphere is indescribable. It is alive, active and needs what I call air troopers—those on earth who will intercede and praise the Lord to clear the way so heaven can respond to us with the glory of God's presence. Just like when the tribe of Judah's praises scattered their enemies when they came in for the kill, (2 Chronicles 20:1-27).

I stress it again, the devil is passionate in trying to destroy the work of God on earth.

How passionate are we to destroy Satan's plan for the earth

Talk to ex-Satanists, they will tell you how zealous they were in bringing curses against the churches where they lived. An ex-Satanist, high priestess, once told me she wished the churches would be just as zealous in prayer for the salvation of their town as the members of the occult were in bringing destruction on the community.

As worshippers and intercessors, our group often had to pick up audio and video tape that had been strategically stretched and tied on fences or in long grass along the entrances into towns. Areas outside churches or venues of prayer were also a target of this activity. As well as the tape, we have at times found evidence of demonic rituals: a black balloon, a rabbit's foot and tail, and also chicken feathers. For those who are not familiar with this form of cursing, I will explain. Satanists and witches record curses on audio and video tape to cause road accidents or any other destructive activity. Most times when we have found these tapes on country roads, the gruesome discovery of a white cross or tell-tale signs of a road accident—skid marks and glass are found nearby. When we found these tapes, we gathered them up and then burned them. As we gathered, we declared the blood of Jesus over ourselves and over the area, commanding the curses to be turned into blessings. We also prayed for the salvation of the people who placed them there. We usually ended our time in exalting the name of Jesus in song.

You might be thinking at this point, 'I thought this book was about music.' Let me warn you that this area of ministry is not for the fainthearted but those who have been called to something deeper and vital. Those who are already using their weapons of war—praise and joy!

In our western way of thinking, we are a bit blaze` about the supernatural. How many times have people said to me, "but greater is He who is within you than He who is in the world." Yes, I agree, but that does not protect those who do not know Jesus. I do not do this because I fear for my own life, I do it to protect our neighbourhood and if we do not use God's power against the devil, he wins. I have had people report back to me that they had seen tape beside the road but due to the traffic conditions or other reasons, they had not stopped to remove the tape. Because of this, fatal accidents have occurred in that very place within days.

Yes, we are protected. One day my next door neighbour, totally oblivious to these things, pointed up into the electricity wires outside her house and said, "I wonder how that got up there?" My eyes followed the line of her finger and I laughed at the tape tied high on the wires. "I think it was meant for me," was my only answer. She would not have understood if I tried to explain. I did wonder myself how the witches had tied it up there without a ladder until someone mentioned they levitate. As a praying person the curse was meant for me but I believe they could not tie it directly in front of my house because of the protection of powers that are stronger than they are. One day during a prayer and worship time I had a strong urge to leave. The meeting was a regular gathering and held at a friend's place. She lived on a rural property with a long, gravel drive to the road. When I reached her gateway I saw the reason why God had sent me there. Tape was stretched along her fence. Satan's followers know where to send his people and while we were praying they were active to bring a disturbance. In the street where I lived, in one family alone, there had been a murder, a fatal car accident and two suicides, yet the family was surrounded by Christian neighbours who knew nothing of their need. In another family around the corner from my place, the mother died of cancer three weeks before the adult daughter was found dead in their house and her father was rushed to hospital unconscious. I am not sure of the circumstances. It was very sad. I had walked by their house every day to visit a friend who lived next door to them. They were secluded in an urban area with little, or no friends or relatives visiting.

We are seeing Satan's work of devastation all around us. Often we waltz off to church on a Sunday and mid-week for our spiritual buzz, thinking we are doing God a service, and yet we do not even know who is coming under terrible spiritual darkness in our street. If everything was wonderful, no problems at home, no problems in church—every one saved, delivered and healed: all working together as one big happy family, I will believe that the curses have no effect on us or our town. This is far from true and we have to face up to the fact. It is a struggle to keep this peace and harmony.

One time I was driving along and the Holy Spirit directed me to slow down. I knew the drill and sure enough, tape was strewn for about a kilometre on both sides of the road entering into the town where my sister lived. It took me an hour to gather it up and pray. Once that was done I was just about to continue on to my destination when I felt a strong urge to back track. I stopped the car at an area beside an embankment. What I found horrified me. There was the evidence I had been looking for! Deep down I had been wondering whether we were just wasting time with the tapes and that they were not all that significant. The reality of my actions came to light!

I had found in the ditch, twenty tapes tossed aside as if someone discarded them in a hurry. Many had been stripped of the tape but all of their casings still had their labels. They spoke of the coming of chaos; destruction; the guillotine; demonic empires; bewitches, pentagram prayers (wind, fire, earth and water); bestiality and many demonic gods were named: god of debauchery; goddess of prostitution and lust, and the god of war. These were the titles. Imagine the content of the tapes!

I did not play the tapes that were in tack but quickly burned them. I do not know if they were spoken or sung curses, with or without music. My guess—with 'music' as it is a powerful tool. I did not want to know, I just broke the curses as quickly as possible. I now had proof this was really happening.

1 John 3:8 says: *'He who does what is sinful is of the devil, because the devil has been sinning from the beginning. The reason the Son of God appeared was to destroy the devil's work.'*

Incidentally, I wrote to a church in the area where I had found the tapes explaining what I had done and its significance. Praise God they responded, not knowing who I was, and invited our team to join them in prayer for the upcoming tent crusade. During that time we were visited by the angels I had mentioned in chapter two.

We are still affected by the enemy's onslaught in one way or another, but if we make the effort to confront the darkness with our weapons of light, look at the blessings. Heaven joined us; first with the angelic choir, then the presence of angels sent by the Lord Himself!

> **We just need to clear the spiritual airways of all the rubbish the devil dumps in our way for the Spirit of God to move!**

Have you been to worship and prayer meetings that are usually alive yet sometimes it is so hard to break through. People begin to grow restless and others yawn. There is such a spirit of lethargy that no matter how hard everyone tries nothing happens. We start to make excuses that 'we've had a long day, it's so hot, we're not well ...' We have all been there!

When this happens to me—especially when hunger pangs gnaw at me, I always think of the discomfit that others tolerate in other countries and the sacrifices they make. In South Korea, the praying people kneel for hours on concrete benches outside, or on hard floors not letting up their fervour; their prayers growing more passionate and louder as the hours roll by. Our excuses have no ground—it takes sacrifice to get the fullness of what God has for us. How desperate are we?

When I was in the Philippines, the people would worship the Lord for hours. Singing, dancing and clapping. It was unbearably hot and humid! A brother would get excited and run around blowing a scout's whistle. Such joy and reckless abandonment in the presence of the Lord. It reminds me of the scripture in Psalm 89:15-16:

'Blessed are those who have learned to acclaim [You], who walk in the light of [Your] presence O Lord. They rejoice in [Your] name all day long; they exalt in [Your] righteousness. For [You] are their glory and strength, and by [Your] favour exalt our horn. Indeed, our shield belongs to the Lord our king to the Holy One of Israel.'

We read in Genesis 32:24-30 that Jacob would not let go of God until He blessed him.

God had promised Abraham that through his seed all the nations of the earth will be blessed. Jacob was of his seed but he had to wrestle with God all night to receive the promise of blessing. He said: *'I will not let You go unless You bless me.'* How is that for persistence!

Psalm 149

Praise the Lord!
'Sing to the Lord a new song,
[His] praise in the assembly of the
saints. Let Israel rejoice in their
Maker,
let the people of Zion be glad in their King.
Let them praise [His] name with dancing
and make music to [Him] with tambourine and harp.
For the Lord takes delight in [His]
people; [He] crowns the humble
with salvation. Let the saints
rejoice in this honour and sing for
joy on their beds.

> *May the praises of God be in their mouths and a double-edged sword in their hands, to inflict vengeance on the nations and punishment on the peoples, to bind their kings with fetters, their nobles with shackles of iron, to carry out the sentence written against them—this is the glory of [His] saints.*
>
> *Praise the Lord.'*

Two things I will point out: singing for joy on our beds; and praise used along with the sword, which is the word of God.

In the opening chapter we have a picture of the army of singers and how their continuous praises became the sound of a battering ram until they smashed through the forces of evil. When weariness overtakes us, it is time to get up and war!

I have often felt sleepy at prayer meetings—in fact as a child, prayer meetings were the best place to doze because everyone had their eyes closed and would not notice. This is not for me now. I have learned by experience this is also the enemy's way of shutting up our mouths from ministering to God. It is at this time, that I use music as a weapon against the powers of darkness. I start by striking a few heavy chords on the piano then allow the leading of the Holy Spirit. Usually it is not long before every one in the room is on their feet and joining in with dancing, singing, shouting, praising, clapping or whatever expression God is leading them into. Suddenly the breakthrough comes and the cloud of oppression explodes and everyone is refreshed and able to soar on heights of glory.

Those who play sports or are keen observers will know the thrill of the game—win or die feeling; the pumping of adrenaline; the dogged determination to be the best; the ecstasy when announced the winner! The aim of any game is to beat the opponent whatever the cost. None of this could ever happen without extreme endurance tests through the hard work and discipline of all the team. With highly trained skills, all must work together in trust and unity, desiring only what is best for the whole team— the goal of reaching the top, to win the premiership. The competition is fierce, only those with the killer instinct can win—those who have trained for hours in defence skills; drilled over and over in hack skills; those who have pressed on against all odds. It takes well-toned muscle power, incredible speed and flexibility far above the attacking team. All games have territory to defend and every person's aim is to score goals and to block their opponents from scoring goals.

How like spiritual warfare this is—except:

- Are we that determined to defeat the enemy?
- Are we disciplined enough to carry out our mission of fighting against the odds through trials and hardship without being crushed and wounded?
- Are we ready to work together in unity for what is best for the whole team or church.

There is no easy way. Spiritual muscles can only be developed through years of hard training in the word of God and applying the word of God to our lives.

We cannot afford to succumb to the enemy's distraction otherwise he wins—and we miss out on God's blessing!

CHAPTER 9

Heaven – Third Heaven

To give us a clearer picture of how necessary it is to worship God, we need to have an understanding of the three levels of the heavenly realm and how they respond to one another. We have already looked at the first and second heaven and now we will touch on the third heaven. I say touch on because it will take all eternity to discover the absolute magnificence of it all.

Heaven is the place where God dwells. In scripture heaven is described as a wonderful place: no darkness, fear, pain, sickness, death or sorrow—just eternal bliss with everlasting joy. It is a place of golden streets, gates of pearls, river of life, crystal sea and where all things will be made known. In other words, all those questions that we have built up over the years will be answered. But best of all, we will meet our Lord and Saviour face to face!

I had an elderly relative ask me why I talked about Jesus all the time. I asked her whether she wanted to go to hell or heaven when she died. She said, "heaven of course." I replied, "You won't like it there."

She was a bit taken aback with that answer and asked, "why not?" My response was that the whole theme of heaven was to worship Jesus Christ, the Lamb of God who takes away the sin of the world. That's what heaven is about—Jesus! Only those who are passionate about Him will be there. She responded simply by saying, "I didn't think of that."

Heaven is full of music. Many followers of Jesus have had the opportunity to visit heaven through dreams and visions. Others come back to life after being clinically dead. All have remarked on the beautiful music. It seemed to be everywhere saturating their whole being with the warmth and love of God. Music flows continuously without a sense of time or beat as heaven is eternity. There is no need for time or beat—a thousand years is as a day with the Lord.

The apostle Paul speaks of such a place in 2 Corinthians 12:2-4: (paraphrased) *'I know a man in Christ who fourteens years ago was caught up to the third heaven. v.4:...was caught up to paradise. He heard inexpressible things that man is not permitted to tell.'* (NKJV)

Although Paul could not relate what he had seen, he did say he was taken into the heavenly realm, but not taken from the earth. Heaven is not a place that is so far way in the sky that God looks down upon us. The kingdom of heaven is just another dimension that our spiritual eyes cannot see into but we can absorb with our spirit. We are surrounded by heaven. That is why when we worship God, we are literally seated into heavenly places with Christ. Heaven is a spiritual kingdom.

Matthew 17:1-6 relates the time when Jesus took Peter, James and John up a high mountain. In verse 2, Jesus became transfigured before them. '... *His face shone like the sun and His clothes became as white as the light. Just then there appeared before them Moses and Elijah, talking with Jesus...While He was still speaking, a bright cloud covered them, and a voice from the cloud* said, *"This is My Son whom I love; with Him I am well pleased. Listen to Him!"* ' (NKJV)

Before this event, Jesus told His disciples that one day they will see Him coming with His angels in His Father's glory. At this time He will reward everyone for the work they have done.

The disciples had a preview of that shekinah glory when Jesus was transformed. The cloud of glory is the portal by which we will enter heaven when we die, or at the resurrection of the saints. Again the glory cloud came and covered them but did not whisk them away from the earth. Many people who go through a death experience relate how they go through a dark tunnel and see a bright light which draws them like a magnetic force. A well known verse from Psalm 23:4 says: *'Although I walk through the valley of the shadow of death I fear no evil for your rod and staff comfort me.'* That verse gives insight into the transition between life and death. When my sister was on the border of life and death she was going through a dark valley heading towards the celestial city lit up with brilliant light. She felt the strong hands of angelic escorts on both of her arms. One angel on each side of her. It was not her time to go to be with the Lord at that stage and the angels turned her around to go back into her body.

Before my mother died, we kept the atmosphere in our home as joyful as possible and continually sang hymns and choruses that she knew. She was slipping away fast and could not speak intelligibly and only whimpered. One night Lorraine and I were sitting by her bed singing softly to soothe her as she could not sleep. Suddenly her face lit up and she reached out her hands toward the door as if welcoming a visitor. Then she spoke His wonderful name, *"JESUS!"* Following the immediate delight her face then changed to a troubled expression. She asked Him. *"WHY?"* An amazing conversation was underway between the Lord and Mum and all the shadows left Mum's face and she looked beautiful. She then smiled and waved good bye to Jesus as He went out through the bedroom door. Mum laid back against her pillow with such a blissful, contented look. Little wonder, the Lord and Saviour had just entered her bedroom and explained why He was taking her home to be with Him in heaven forever. Lorraine and I just sat transfixed throughout the whole episode.

It was like we were basking in fizzy drink as our bodies tingled all over. We did not see Jesus or hear what He had to say. It was for Mum's comfort only and she could not tell us afterwards. When she was speaking to Jesus it was in her heavenly language and she was unable to speak in English for the short duration of her life until she passed away.

We needed extra care for her but rather than place her in hospital, Bev employed registered nurses to care for her to the end. Amazingly they were both Christians. The night God had taken Mum home the nurse ordered me to bed as I had not slept for days. Mum had slipped into a coma and the doctor had come to prescribe morphine. At eleven o'clock the nurse woke me up to tell me my mother had gone to Jesus. My biggest comfort was to know that just prior to my dear mother's final breath, the nurse felt the presence of two holy beings come into the room and stand at the end of her bed. The nurse sank to her knees and worshipped God.

God is real! Heaven is a real place and not a place on a different shore somewhere over the rainbow but here with us, around us and within us. Psalm 23:6 goes on to say: *'Surely goodness and love will follow me all the days of my life and I shall dwell in the house of the Lord forever.'*

There is a fine veil over our eyes that blocks our spiritual vision but at times that veil is removed and we can see and hear into heavenly realms. Before Adam sinned, heaven and earth were in harmony. That is why Adam walked in the garden with God. He was perfect, clothed with the glory of God. After sinning Adam found himself naked—the glory of God had departed. A spiritual veil separated the earthly dimension from the heavenly dimension. He had to be clothed with materials from the earth. Throughout scripture the presence of God was represented through the cloud of glory. Moses was invited to enter that cloud of glory and meet with God face to face for forty days and forty nights! (Exodus 24:15-18). During that time he was empowered by God to lead with authority on his return. Immediately he dealt with sin within the camp of Israel as we will read in the next chapter of this book.

In chapters four and five of the book of Revelation, the whole dramatic picture of the throne room of God in heaven explodes before us, and believe me, it is not a very quiet or passive place. There is continuous sound and light emanating from the throne: bolts of lightning, peals of thunder, sounds of rushing water, constant worship of heavenly and angelic beings and every creature in heaven and on earth, sea and under the sea, crying: *'Holy, holy, holy is the Lord God Almighty, who is, who was, and is to come!'* Heaven and earth join together in a sound of jubilant exaltation of the King of kings!

The first chapter of Ezekiel describes four living creatures with four different faces attached to wheels within wheels and fire and lightning flashing back and forth within them.

Heaven is the universal headquarters or control centre—receiving and giving orders: God constantly monitoring earth and the whole existence of the universe. His voice is thunderous like the sound of rushing waters as He gives out thousands of orders simultaneously. It is a very busy place: always in motion—angels, elders, beasts and living creatures active in the presence of God, worshipping with their whole being, crying, *'Holy, holy, holy Lord God almighty, who was and who is to come.'* The whole atmosphere is charged with energy, light and power—the majesty, awesomeness and holiness of Creator God. Yet there is pure, divine order and structure which speaks of governmental authority, power and glory, (Revelation 5).

Daniel 7:9-10 describes: 'v.9b… *His throne was flaming with fire, and its wheels were all ablaze. A river of fire was flowing, coming out from before [Him]. Thousands upon thousands attended [Him], ten thousands times ten thousands stood before [Him].*'

The whole universe is held together by what happens from the throne of God. Worship around the throne room is a continuous, never-ending flow. Just as we fuel a fire with timber to keep it going to give off heat, worship can be likened to fuelling the fire of God's presence. It fans the light, warmth and power radiating from the heart of God.

In this day and age we are able to use natural elements to generate power—water, sun and wind. The more exposure to these resources, the more power is stored.

Some time ago, I saw a man on television using his own muscle power to generate enough electricity for some of his household appliances. He sat on a bicycle-like device and peddled hard. The more he peddled, the more power he generated and the brighter the lights in his house became. I remember as a child, I used to peddle my grandmother's old peddle organ. At first I could only produce a hiss and a wheeze at the best. After realising the harder I pushed down on the peddles, the more sound I could produce, so I peddled like crazy.

The principle to be learned here is that we will only get out of something what we put in. The more we worship God, the more we will reap the benefits. Continuous worship brings a response of order and harmony to the whole universe. Can you imagine if worship in heaven would suddenly stop. What would happen? There would be total chaos on earth.

A time is coming when this is exactly what is going to happen. There will be silence in heaven for about half an hour. The silence precedes the horror coming on the earth in judgement of rebellion and sin against God.

For thousands of years the prayers of the Christians have been collected in bowls as incense for this specific time.

Let us read in Revelation 8:1-5: *'When he opened the seventh seal, there was silence in heaven for about half an hour. And I saw the seven angels who stand before God, and to them were given seven trumpets. Another angel, who had a golden censer, came and stood at the altar. He was given much incense to offer, with the prayers of all the saints, on the golden altar before the throne. The smoke of the incense, together with the prayers of the saints, went up before God from the angel's hand. Then the angel took the censer, filled it with fire from the altar, and hurled it on the earth; and there came peals of thunder, rumblings, flashes of lightning and an earthquake.'*

The rest of the chapter describes in graphic detail the stages of God's wrath.

Worship stopped in heaven so God could pour out His judgements. Worshipping God prevents premature destruction on the earth until the appointed time. It took only half an hour in the heavenly time frame to prepare. It is like all of heaven waited with abated breaths in awe of what was going to happen next.

What we do in seeking God today is remembered in heaven and stored as fuel for God's coming wrath against sin. This is leading up to the final fight we have against Satan and his demons. We know the end through the word of God and if we are faithful to Him, we will be winners!

There is a close link between heaven and earth through intercession and worship and how they respond to each other. As Jesus said that what is bound and loosed on earth is bound and loosed in heaven. We have the responsibility of working with God to carry out His will on the earth. It is so amazing when God opens our eyes to see into the heavenly realm between heaven and earth to observe what He is doing.

In 2 Kings 6 we read that the king of Aram was at war with Israel and Elisha warned the king of Israel not to pass through a certain place because the enemy armies were camped there. That made the king of Aram mad when word came to him that Elisha warned the king of Israel. He sent out horses and chariots as a strong force to surround the city where Elisha was staying ready to capture him. Reading from verse 15- 16: *'When the servant of the man of God got up and went out early the next morning, an army with horses and chariots had surrounded the city. "O no my lord, what shall we do?" The servant asked. "Don't be afraid," the prophet answered. "Those that are with us are more than those with them." And Elisha prayed, "O Lord, open his eyes so he may see." Then the Lord opened the servant's eyes, and he looked and saw the hills full of horses and chariots of fire all around Elisha. As the enemy came down toward him Elisha prayed to the Lord, "Strike these people with blindness." So God struck them with blindness, as Elisha had asked.'*

Our walk is a walk of faith in trusting God and He does not always reveal to us what is going on behind the scenes in the heavenly realm. However, it is wonderful to know we are living in the midst of an amazing company of heavenly beings on guard over us, ready to work with us as God commands.

CHAPTER 10

Music and Worship in the Beginning

We know by the word of God, there was never a beginning of music that it has always been before the creation of man. We have read in the previous chapter that people who have visited heaven came back with reports of the continual flow of music without beat or beginning and end.

However, we live on the earth where time is the essence. We live in an urgent world. Our songs portray the era we live in and what is happening in the world around us. In other words the blood, sweat and tears of life. Every culture has their unique style that brings tribal communities together in celebration. We tell our stories in music, song and dance— times of happiness, treasured moments of love but best of all the goodness of God. We declare His love, peace, joy and salvation in the message of the cross. We announce in song the triumph of His resurrection and eternal glory. Down through the ages styles of singing and music have changed, but the message is the same—declaring who God is and His wonderful works. We are drawn into intimacy of worship to Him.

This generation has not been left out in Christian music and have produced many powerful songs that will go on forever. We sing about the Lord, telling the world of His great works and also we sing to Him in loving devotion. Many older people miss the songs we used to sing in church. Yes, the hymns and choruses of the past still can minister to us. But we must not overlook the talent and skills of the younger generation who are producing, through the Holy Spirit, wonderful songs to meet this day and age. God is gifting these young ones with a passion for music and it is our responsibility, as older people, to encourage them and to pray that they will walk in the ways of God as yielded instruments of His glory.

In the beginning of mankind, music, singing and dancing have been expressed. Throughout scripture it has always been the same. Wherever God has His hand there will be music. Music is mentioned in 1,150 verses in the bible; singing over 400 times, and 50 direct commands to sing. There are 185 songs written in the Bible as we see in the wonderful psalms of David, Solomon, Moses, Asaph, Ethan and Heman. This is incredible to have a record of these songs translated into over seven hundred different languages and will be ongoing throughout this age. Singing was a great part of the Hebrew culture to tell of the amazing acts of the Lord.

In Genesis 4:21, a man named Jubal was the first musician recorded in the Old Testament. All that was said of him, he was the father of all who played the harp and flute. There was no mention of him worshipping the Lord with music.

Moses wrote three songs that the scriptures tells of. The first is recorded in Exodus 15 as the song of Moses and Miriam after the miracle of God parting the red sea for the Israelites to cross when pursued by the Egyptian army. A little wonder they sang after their deliverance. What an amazing event they were apart of! Psalm 90 is also attributed to Moses.

In Revelation 15:3-4, seven angels were given harps and they sang the song of Moses and the song of the Lamb. The song declares the righteousness of the Lamb of God and the future gathering of the nations coming to worship Him in His holiness and glory.

Unfortunately, all was not always good with God's chosen people. There is also evidence in Scripture that the Israelites sang and danced during times of pagan revelling. In Exodus 32:18, Moses was on the mountain top in the presence of the Lord receiving the stones on which the ten commandments were written. He heard the sound of singing and when he came down from the mountain he saw the Israelites dancing around a golden calf they had made in order to worship it. In fury he destroyed the idol and called those who will serve God to come out from the crowd and stand by his side. The tribe of Levi rallied to him. Moses gave them swords and ordered them to kill the rest of the people—about three thousand all told. God does not allow idolatry and requires total commitment and surrender to Him. They had broken the first commandment as in Deuteronomy 6:5:

*'Love the Lord your God with all your heart and with all your soul and with all your strength.' A*nd in verse 13-14: *'Fear the Lord your God, serve [Him] only and take your oaths in [His] name. Do not follow other gods, the gods of the people around you.'*

The Levites were prepared to give up all including family, and God blessed the Levites that day and they were set apart to serve Him.

When we journey through the Old testament we come across a young shepherd boy who played the harp and sang. He knew and loved God, worshipping him with all his heart. Because of his skill of music he was taken to King Saul and while he played the harp the evil spirit that troubled Saul would depart. This opened the door for David to enter Saul's kingdom.

David was a man after God's own heart, and God had chosen him to become king of Israel in the future.

Before that could happen he had to go through many rejections, trials, battles, failures, triumphs, persecutions and sorrows. But through all of that he still kept his joy in the Lord, as we read in the psalms he had written.

Even as king, David was very demonstrative in worship before the Lord to the point his wife, Michal despised him. 2 Samuel 6:14-15 says: *'David, wearing a linen ephod, danced before the Lord with all his might, while he and the entire house of Israel brought up the ark of the Lord with shouts and the sound of trumpets.'*

Whatever David did, he put his whole heart, soul and body into it. The presence of the Lord meant everything to David and Israel. The ark of the covenant was the representation of God's residing glory. As the two cherubim overshadowed the mercy seat, God's glory rested between them. Without the glory of God's presence Israel would be lost—they had nothing. Everywhere they went they carried the ark with them. This was only a shadow of things to come. The presence of God under the new covenant resides in the kingdom of our Lord Jesus Christ made up of those whose lives are washed in His blood.

God was particular in how He was to be worshipped and how the ark of His presence was to be handled as we see in 2 Samuel 6:3-7. The ark had been in the hands of the Philistines for seven months. David's first attempt to bring the ark back to the house of Israel failed. although the whole of Israel were celebrating zealously before the Lord with songs and musical instruments. They did it all wrong—not according to God's instructions. The Ark should have been carried by two poles resting on the shoulders of Levitical priests and not placed on a cart. If anyone touched the ark they would die as the result of touching the majesty and presence of God.

MUSIC AND WORSHIP IN THE BEGINNING

This should be a lesson to all of us, as Christians, that no matter how zealous we are in serving the Lord, if we do not honour His presence with all our heart, and obey His word, our sacrifices of worship and praise are to no avail. We should never take God's presence or blessings lightly in our lives. We need to seek God in what pleases Him in our gatherings.

Psalm 22:3 says in the New King James version: *'But You are holy, Who inhabits the praises of Israel.'*

Psalm 132:13-16 says: *'For the Lord has chosen Zion, [He] has desired it for [His] dwelling: "This is my resting place for ever and ever; here I will sit enthroned, for I have desired it—I will bless her with abundant provisions; her poor will I satisfy with food. I will clothe her priests with salvation, and her saints will ever sing for joy."'*

This is a prophetic portion of scripture regarding the future kingdom of Christ. Those who are redeemed are all priests and saints before God. Praise God we have a future in the house of the Lord where there is tremendous joy and singing! Why? Because it is God's dwelling place among His people!

Our inspiration for music and singing comes from the ancient song writers of the Old Testament for thousands of years. The language of the psalms takes us through many joyous times as well as times of hardships, persecution and sorrow. But above all, every need of our own lives has also been the experience of someone else in the Book of Psalms and how God has brought them through. They are written to teach, exhort and to lift us up into higher praises and deeper worship of the Lord.

Sometimes while teaching a timid person to sing or pray, I have taken them to a quiet, high place or a lookout over a community and ask them to read the psalms with a loud voice. The height builds confidence and soon all fear goes. For many years the words to our songs and choruses were written straight from scripture. What is sung is easily remembered, and even now those scriptures come to mind when needed.

When and where were the psalms sung in the Old Testament? In order to have a full understanding of God's plan for fellowship with His people and dwelling among them we need to go right back to where worship is first mentioned in scripture. Bearing in mind there are many ways to worship God that are pleasing to Him. It is all about what brings God's presence.

Abraham

God chose specific places to meet with His servants. Abraham was a righteous man whom God had called apart from the heathen nations to bless. An early record of Abraham's worship to the Lord was when he pitched his tents near the great trees of Mamre at Hebron.

In Genesis 13:18: *'Abraham moved his tents and went to live near the great trees of Mamre at Hebron, where he built an altar to the Lord.'* While Abraham was sitting under the great oak trees of Mamre angels from God met with him. (Genesis 18:1) God met him where he was.

Sometimes our love for the Lord needs to be tested. On Mount Moriah, Abraham showed his love and obedience to God by preparing to offer up his only son, Isaac, as a sacrifice unto God. (Genesis 22:1-19) When Abraham picked up the knife to kill his son the angel of God stopped him. God provided a lamb that was caught in a thicket to sacrifice on the altar Abraham had made to cover his sin.

That lamb was a foreshadow of what was yet to come. That mountain was, thousands of years later, the place where the Lamb of God, the last sacrifice, was slaughtered to take away the sin of the world. God blessed Abraham for his willingness to give up all to show his devotion to Him. Abraham obeyed God and this was the way he offered up worship to Him. To obey God is true worship.

'I will surely bless you and make your descendants as numerous as the stars in the sky and as the sand on the seashore. Your descendants will take possession

of the cities of their enemies, and through your offspring all nations on earth will be blessed. Because you have obeyed [Me],' (Genesis 22:17-18).

We read in James 2:23, "... *Abraham believed God, and it was credited to him as righteousness, and he was called God's friend.*"

It takes sacrifice to build a dwelling place for God.

Jacob

The tribe and nation of Israel was birthed through Abraham's line. Jacob was the grandson of Abraham. God had promised Abraham that his seed would be as numerous as the stars in the sky. This promise was to be passed through Jacob's line. After receiving his father, Isaac's, blessing instead of his brother Esau—the first-born twin, Jacob left his father's house and set out for Haran. On the way he laid down to sleep with his head resting on a stone. He had a dream. He saw a stairway rising from the earth and the top reaching into heaven. Angels were ascending and descending on it. The Lord stood above and spoke to Jacob to reaffirm the promises given to his grandfather, Abraham, and his father, Isaac. The account in Genesis 28:16 says: '*When Jacob awoke from his sleep, he thought, "Surely the Lord is in this place, and I was not aware of it." He was afraid and said, "How awesome is this place! This is none other than the house of the Lord!"*'

After that he made a vow to the Lord to make the Lord his God. He then set up the stone which was placed under his head earlier while he slept and said: '*... and this stone that I have set up as a pillar will be God's house ...*' There is a pattern in all of this for the building of the house of the Lord—a place of worship. The stone from under Jacob's head had become, prophetically, the Corner Stone in the Church of Jesus Christ with Christ as the head.

Later on we read that Jacob went to work for his Uncle Laban and fell in love with his uncle's daughter, Rachel. Laban deceived Jacob by giving him his older daughter, Leah, on his wedding night. Jacob then had to work an extra seven years in order to marry Rachel, the one he really loved. After working for his father-in-law for twenty years and being cheated many times he wanted out. God spoke to Jacob and said to go back to his homeland and the Lord would be with him. In chapter 31:10, Jacob had another dream to confirm that God was on his side and had given him wisdom on how to extend his flock of goats and sheep.

Then God said in Genesis 31:13: *'I am the God of Bethel, where you anointed a pillar and where you made a vow to [Me]. Now leave this land at once and go back to your native land.'* So Jacob, his wives, children and live stock secretly left without a festive sendoff of dancing and singing. They had to make a life for themselves in order to live under God's blessing.

Laban and his men pursued them and caught up. After each party was able to voice their grievances they came to an agreement and made a covenant, heaping up stones as their witness and God as their judge. Jacob offered up a sacrifice to God and the whole family had a meal together before going their own separate ways. They worshipped God through their sacrifices.

Jacob was heading back to his homeland where his brother Esau lived. Their last interaction had not been good. Esau was angry after their father blessed Jacob instead of himself. Jacob was afraid to meet up with him in case Esau still harboured anger against him.

In Genesis 32:1,2, angels of God met Jacob on the way and when he saw them he said: *'This is the camp of God.'* Jacob named the place, Mahanaim—meaning two camps. It is interesting to note how names originated for places when the patriarchs met with God. Later we read in verse 22 how Jacob had to wrestle with God all night to receive the blessings

God had promised him. It was a memorial night, God changed his name to Israel, because he had struggled with God and with men and had overcome. Jacob was left with a limp but he had something greater. He had met with God face to face. It was so significant that Jacob named the place of the meeting, Peniel—face of God.

In chapter 35, God told Jacob to go back to the place, Bethel again— the place where he had the dream of angels climbing the stairway. The Lord spoke to him from heaven and told him to build an altar and to settle there. Bethel became a township and Jacob used this place from time to time to rest and to hear from God. Many years later, the ark of the covenant (God's presence) was lodged at Bethel.

It is wonderful to know that God works on our behalf if we seek Him. Jacob came under the blessings of Abraham and what God had promised him will surely come about. God spoke to Jacob face to face. He also spoke through angels in dreams.

The spiritual world around us is so real and the scripture says in Hebrews 1:14: *'Are not all angels ministering spirits sent to serve those who will inherit salvation?'*

God is a God of restoration and reconciliation and the meeting between Jacob and Esau had been more than anyone could have hoped for, (Genesis 33:4).

Being blessed of God often takes wrestling with Him face to face. Seeking Him in every way in all that we do. He desires more of us in all of our affairs. We are places of worship where the Spirit of God dwells. Speaking of Jacob in Isaiah 41:8 it says:

"But you O Israel, my servant, Jacob, whom I have chosen, you descendants of Abraham, my friend."

It takes wrestling with God to build a house of God

Moses

God first met with Moses in the desert through a burning bush. God instructed him to plead with Pharaoh to set the Israelites, who were slaves in Egypt, free of captivity. Pharaoh's heart was hardened and would not let them go. After God sent many plagues upon the Egyptians, and finally, the killing of their firstborn sons, the Israelites were free to leave the bondage of Pharaoh and follow Moses and his brother Aaron. God promised Moses in Exodus 23:20: *'See, I am sending an angel ahead of you to guard you along the way and to bring you to the place I have prepared. Pay attention to him and listen to what he says. Do not rebel against him; he will not forgive your rebellion, since [My] Name is in him.'*

If God gives you a task to do or sends you on a specific assignment that may be a little daunting, He will always make provision, or give you the back-up of heaven. It was a mammoth task for Moses to lead tens of thousands of Israelites through the desert, the goal being the land of Canaan—the land promised to Abraham. If anyone's patience would have been tried it would have been Moses'. The people were angry with him, grumbled, murmured, longed for the food of Egypt, and seemed to prefer the slavery of their former life to their freedom. They had no vision for the future beyond wandering around in the desert. That is exactly what happened for forty years. God inhabits the *praises* of His people. Where there is no *praise* and *thanksgiving* to create an atmosphere of sweet aromas offered up to Him, He will not stay.

During this time, God gave very specific instructions to Moses to set up the Tabernacle or tent of meeting so He could reside among His people. Psalm 127:1 says: *'Unless the Lord builds the house, its builders labour in vain. Unless the Lord watches over the city, the watchmen stand guard in vain.'*

MUSIC AND WORSHIP IN THE BEGINNING

The **Tabernacle** or Tent of Meeting was the first recorded physical structure, where the presence of the Lord resided and is detailed in Exodus 26. There was a divine pattern in the making of the Tabernacle and God instructed Moses in every fine detail. Everything had a purpose and a meaning even to the colours and type of materials used—structure, frames, curtains, hooks, clasps and rings. In the outer court stood the brazen altar for animal sacrifices; the bronze laver or basin for washing the priests hands. Inside the covering of skins, the Holy Place housed the lamp stand, the altar of incense and the table of shewbread. This section was curtained off separating the Holy of Holies. Inside this most holy place rested the ark of the covenant—a large box overlaid with gold.

It contained the stone tablets on which the ten commandants were written; the jar of manna—reminder of God's provision, and Aaron's rod, confirming God's choice that Aaron had been anointed as the high priest. The mercy seat situated on top of the ark was overshadowed with the wings of cherubim. The visible glory cloud of the Lord's presence would reside between these wings in such holiness that no one but the high priest could enter and survive. Even then it could only be once a year the high priest would enter the Holy of Holies and sprinkle the blood of the sacrifice on the mercy seat.

The sizes of everything used from frames to curtains, furnishings, utensils and how it was constructed was important. God gave Moses the details and he obeyed.

The tabernacle was erected outside the camp of the twelve tribes of Israel who lived in tents around it. God's presence was a pillar of cloud by day at the entrance of the tent. Everyone could see the cloud and when Moses entered the cloud to meet with God, the people of Israel would worship where they stood at the entrances of their own tents. At night the cloud would change to a pillar of fire. The Israelites packed up and moved when the pillar of cloud and fire moved on with the angel of God going on ahead to prepare the way.

The first house of God was only temporary, portable and always on the move. It was constructed at the Lord's command. It housed the ark of God's Presence. A place where the people gathered to worship and the priests offered up sacrifices to atone for Israel's sins. It was a type of what was to come. Things of the old made as patterns of things in the heavens, but not an exact replica of them. The tabernacle was God's way of displaying Himself, and His way for man to approach Him.

The following scriptures describes Moses. Exodus 33:11 says: *'The Lord would speak to Moses face to face, as a man speaks with his friend.'*

In Numbers 12:3, we are told. *'Now Moses was a very humble man, more humble than anyone else on the face of the earth.'*

Many times Moses stood in the gap as an intercessor of behalf of God's people. His relationship with God was secure as we can see in his interaction with him in Exodus 33:12. He did not mince his words with God. I love God's answer to him in verse 17: *"I will do the very thing you asked because I am pleased with you and I know you by name."*

It is good to remember when going through difficult times that God is pleased with us and He knows our name. He is always there not only watching over us, but with us. As in the Old Testament where God uses angels to speak to His people and lead them, they are also here for us, watching and waiting for God's command to intervene at His voice. Many times they appear to us with a message, to help us or we hear them singing but as believers in Christ, God has reserved the best for us as we read in Hebrews 1:1-4:

'In the past God spoke to our forefathers through the prophets at many times and in various ways, but in these last days [He] has spoken to us by [His] Son whom [He] appointed heir of all things, and through whom [He] made the

universe. *The radiance of God's glory and the exact representation of [His] being, sustaining all things by [His] powerful word. After [He] had provided purification for sins, [He] sat down at the right hand of the Majesty in heaven. So [He]became as much superior to angels as the name [He] has inherited is superior to theirs.'*

Moses asked God to show His glory but he could not see the face of God and live. What a privilege for us that we can look upon Jesus, the Author and Finisher of our faith. We have Jesus and the Holy Spirit as our mediators between heaven and earth. We do not need priests to offer up sacrifices on behalf of our sins. Jesus has paid for our redemption in full. Jesus is our Prophet, Priest and King.

It takes a wander in the wilderness to build the house of the Lord

David

We had a brief look of the type of worship offered up to God through Abraham, Jacob and Moses. They obviously were not into singing and music ministry, although they had laid down the foundations for a house of worship. Their obedience to God was their worship and this is what blesses God's heart. They were faithful in offering up sacrifices as God had instructed them. We can learn from each of them how they honoured God, obeyed Him, and at times showed weaknesses but did not turn their backs on God.

We will now look at the life of David who is spoken of in Acts 13:22: '... *I have found David, the son of Jesse a man after [My] own heart.'*

Although David was a worshipper of God and named as the singer of Israel in 2 Samuel 23:1, he was a man of war. Why did God use him to destroy his enemies? He had insight into the heavenly realm. He had spent all his life from childhood singing and playing his harp, offering up praises to God. This created the atmosphere for God to surround him with His presence. Because of that he knew God and what delighted His heart. He also knew God's strength and power. He saw the enemies of Israel as weaklings compared to God. He did not compare his own strength and power to that of his enemies but compared his enemies' strength and power to God's. He knew how to work with God. Most of us compare our problems and inhibitions to our inabilities to cope with them but not so with David. Just imagine how humiliating it was for King Saul to send a boy out to face a nine-foot giant who was taunting his army. Goliath would have been expecting Israel's fiercest man to confront him, instead this cocky youth appears with a sling shot. How deflating! At Christmas it is a custom for the shopping centres and even in front yards of houses, to display blown-up, gigantic Santa Clauses. I feel like sticking a pin in each of them and see them gradually fade away to a flat bag of plastic.

Maybe David saw Goliath like them—a big bag of wind who had the audacity to defy the armies of the Living God. Little children, especially boys, pretend they are superman, bat man, spider man or any other fictitious hero. David was not like that growing up, he only had God. He did not need to pretend for he had the makings through God, of a real giant killer! (1 Samuel 17:51).

We will now see how worship changes its focus, from not only offering up the sacrifices of animals to God, but also through music and singing, introduced by King David. What is the difference between the tabernacle of Moses, David's tabernacle and then the temple of the Lord built by Solomon. We will start in the beginning at the:

Threshing Floor

Although David closely followed the Lord's commands, like all of us, he was not perfect. He made mistakes as we see in 1 Chronicles 21:1: *'Satan* rose up against Israel and incited David to take a census of Israel.'* David listened and took up a census. Even Joab, David's murderous right hand man, had more sense that day and panicked. David had no right to count that which was not his. The people belonged to God and if He had ordered David to count His fighting men, each person would pay a ransom fee for his life, (2 Samuel 24:10).

Blinded by his victory and his gains, David let pride rule and began counting. As his eyes roved over the hunks of manhood before him his head swelled with pride. Well why not? These men were fierce. One killed eight hundred men with just one thrust of the spear; Eleazer's hand froze to the sword until the enemies were defeated; Shammah killed hundreds of Philistines all by himself—but not quite! The Scriptures tell us that *'God brought about the mighty victory!'* (2 Samuel 23:12).

God must get all the glory. David's act of pride and failure to collect redemption money from all those counted aroused God's judgement. Seventy thousand Israelites died with a plague, all because David listened to the devil. David soon realised he had blown it. He appealed to God's mercy as he had done so many times before. It is only by knowing God and His mercy, that we have the boldness to approach His throne of grace.

David met with the angel of the Lord at the threshing floor of Araunah. He and his elders donned sackcloth and fell face down before the Lord in repentance. David cried to the Lord saying that it was he who sinned, not the people, and asked God to spare the people and let His hand fall on him and his family, (1 Chronicles 21:17).

David's seer, Gad, told him to build an altar to the Lord there on Araunah's threshing floor and offer up a burnt offering as an act of consecration and drawing back to the Lord.

Repentance—Mercy! A perfect foundation to build a temple for the Lord. The threshing floor! Solomon's temple was built on that site, (1 Chronicles 22). What better place? Beaten and rolled until smooth.

There is a cost in building the house of the Lord. David paid for his sin. The needless slaughter of his flock was a high price to pay, but God is so merciful, he spared David's life and gave him another chance. The threshing floor was offered to David as a gift but he insisted on paying full price when he bought the threshing floor from Araunah, saying: '... *No, I insist on paying the full price. I will not take for the Lord what is yours, or sacrifice a burnt offering that costs me nothing,*' (1 Chronicles 21:24).

Isaac was offered up to be sacrificed on Mount Moriah. Solomon's temple was built on Mount Moriah. Jesus died outside the city gates of Jerusalem and many scholars believe it to be Mount Moriah.

It takes repentance, God's mercy and forgiveness to build a House of Prayer

We know that the tabernacles of Moses and David were portable. The ark of the covenant was placed in the Holy of Holies and was divided off by a thick curtain. Everything used in the function of the tabernacle was leading up to a time when God made a new covenant with His people. A time, that we as lovers of God, can enter His presence by the blood of Jesus. Each significant article of the tabernacle relates to God wanting to dwell with His people through their worship. As in ancient Hebrew law this could only happen through the blood sacrifices. Under new covenant relationship, Jesus was the Lamb sacrificed on our behalf. His blood cleanses us from sin. As God saw the blood sprinkled on the mercy seat by the high priest to cover Israel's sin, God sees the blood covering of Jesus over our lives once and for all. Our sins are totally washed away. He was not only the sacrifice but became the High Priest interceding on our behalf. As

MUSIC AND WORSHIP IN THE BEGINNING

we are made holy by His blood, the curtain or veil separating us from God has been torn away. Hallelujah! We are free to worship Him with our own expressions of love.

King David brought Israel into that freedom as we had seen earlier with his dancing before the Lord. After he made a mistake in transporting the ark into Jerusalem, scripture begins the process of naming each family and every member of that family and their function in the tabernacle of God. 1 Chronicles 6:31 details the musicians who were to minister before the tabernacle and again in 1 Chronicles 15:16, *'David told the leaders of the Levites to appoint their brothers as singers to sing joyful songs, accompanied by musical instruments: lyres, harps and cymbals.'* We read following this passage that Heman, Asaph and Ethan were appointed in leadership, and to the end of chapter 15, others were appointed in music and *'Kenaniah the head Levite was in charge of the singing; that was his responsibility because he was skilful at it.'*

All these Levites were appointed, skilled in instrumental music and singing. It must have been an incredible sight and sound. There were music, singing and dancing while the ark of the covenant was carried into the City of David. Psalm 149 says:

'Praise the Lord! Sing to the Lord a new song, [His] praise in the assembly of the saints. Let Israel rejoice in their maker; let the people of Zion by glad in their King. Let them praise [His] name with dancing and make music to [Him] with tambourine and harp, for the Lord takes delight in [His] people; He crowns the humble with salvation. Let the saints rejoice in[His] honour and sing for joy on their beds.'

It is so inspiring to read how Israel enjoyed the presence of God! Have we lost some of that exuberance in the Lord? Would our worship cramp Israel's style? We need to remind ourselves that we are the temple of the Holy Spirit. God's presence dwells within us. Where He goes, we go: where we go, He goes. Only the prophets, God's chosen leaders, high priests and godly kings were anointed with the Holy Spirit under the old covenant. The Holy Spirit would come upon them for a certain task. The people of Israel were not filled with the Holy Spirit until after Christ died and rose again. Those who believed Yeshua (Jesus in Hebrew) died for their sins received the Holy Spirit.

But in the Old Testament, they looked to the ark of the covenant to know God's manifest presence was with them. Even then it was covered over while it was being carried.

Before this event of bringing God's presence back into the City of David, there is no mention of music or singing incorporated into the worship of God until David appointed people. It must have been happening however, because of so many musicians called upon and available during this time. They were all trained and skilled in worship.

After the ark of God arrived in the City of David and set in the tent pitched for it, the people presented burnt offerings and fellowship offerings to God. David then blessed the congregation in the name of the Lord, then he gave each person gathered a loaf of bread, a cake of dates and a cake of raisins.

David committed a psalm of thanksgiving to the Lord. Asaph sounded the cymbals and his associates played the lyres, harps and blew trumpets regularly before the ark of God. David's amazing psalm of thanks is found in 1 Chronicles 16:8-36. It became a daily praise session using musical instruments and singing according to each day's requirement. A perfect setting for greater things to come.

Reading about the joyful procession of the ark of God carried back into Jerusalem brought to mind a vision I had several years ago. I saw a river flowing from the distance towards me. As it came closer I realised it was made up of the army of God. Jesus was leading this army and holding up a sword. This army was not prepared to do battle but was singing with gusto in many different languages including heavenly languages. People were lining the streets and as they did they were touched by the power of God, then joined in singing and flowed with the army. I had assurance at the time that God was going to release His people onto the streets. What an impact we would have on the cities if the church, as a whole, opened their doors and flowed into the streets. Many of us have been involved in doing that over the years.

One time I was at an International Rally in Sydney, Australia. We were based in Hyde Park and from there we grouped into our different culture groups with banners, balloons, floats and anything that we could wave or blow and flowed down the main street singing, dancing, blowing shofars, prophesying and declaring scriptures over the city. It was an opportunity for others to share the gospel and give out literature. There were hundreds of us maybe a thousand. Even the traffic lights were turned off while we passed through.

People lined the street taking photos, clapping and cheering. What a thrill it was and a testimony to the outside world that God is on the throne and His church is alive and active. This had been happening year after year at Easter and they were not reserved in their worship.

CHAPTER 11

The Temple of the Lord

It is hard to imagine the magnitude of this magnificent building on Zion's hill with its elaborate sanctuaries, side rooms and treasury, surrounded by its massive stone floor of the outer court. Here stood a huge brazen altar for thousands of daily animal sacrifices; a molten laver for cleansing of the hands of the priests, and ten other bronze basins for holding water. From the area of the altar, stone steps led up to where two huge bronze pillars with decorative capitals, supported the roof of the porch and entrance into the Holy Place. Inside were ten, solid, golden lamp stands, the table of the bread of the Presence and the altar of incense. The walls were of panelled cedar wood with carvings of cherubim, palm trees and open flowers. Separating the main sanctuary from the Holy of Holies hung a huge, brocade curtain. It was made of blue, scarlet and purple threads with cherubim motifs woven directly into the fabric from the loom. On the other side of this curtain, the Holy of Holies was entered into by the high priest once a year. Two huge, fifteen-feet cherubim stood guarding the ark of the covenant.

The walls and floors of the temple were overlaid with gold as Solomon had done with all the furnishings, articles and massive cherubim.

It has always been in God's plan for all nations to worship Him together—Jews and Gentiles. King Hiram of Tyre offered to help Solomon build the temple of the Lord by sending down pine logs and cedars from Lebanon using his own timber cutters. Thousands of workers were employed in the preparations of the temple's construction—80,000 stone cutters; 70,000 carriers; 30,000 timber cutters plus the workers of King Hiram in Lebanon. Solomon employed 3,300 foremen who directed the project. Each person received wages for their work. Huram, a highly skilled worker in bronze, did all the bronze work including the decorative work on the pillars and capitals. Only the best in their field of expertise were used. What a mammoth project! The bricks were made away from the building site and no sound of chisel, hammer or any other iron tool were heard while building the temple, (1 Kings 5:6;7).

The building of this temple could not have happened without the enthusiastic generosity of the people of Israel as we read in 1 Chronicles 29:1-29. It began with the leaders giving everything that was needed—gold, silver, bronze, iron, and precious stones went into the treasury. The rest of the nation willingly followed their example in giving.

As musicians, when we think of Solomon's Temple, we think of the shekinah glory of God filling the temple at its dedication—the music and singing; loud sounds of never-ending praise and thanksgiving to the Lord, (2 Chronicles 7:1-3). There would not have been amplification yet the sound would have been tremendous with 4,000 musicians and singers: beside the congregation of thousands, offering up their praises. What a job for the music and choir directors. Everyone with different level of skills, temperaments and ideas working together. Only with the wisdom and anointing of God could this possibly happen. It was such a vital ministry in the temple that each musician and singer were recorded by name in scripture.

Chapters 15; 16 and 25 of 1 Chronicles, details their qualifications and job descriptions. They were appointed—designated an office, ordained and equipped for this area. It was an honoured ministry to the Lord and not just a display of talent. Their gifts of music made the way to be recognised and chosen. They were well practised and they had the ability to understand and perform in the ministry to the Lord.

'Kenaniah, the head Levite was in charge of the singing; that was his responsibility because he was skilful at it,' (Chapter 15:22). "Kenaniah" means: preparation made by God; favour of God. How appropriate was his name! He was already prepared by God to teach and direct the choir and musicians. The singers were instructed to sing the songs of the Lord. They were taught to praise God in song. To have 288 singers in your choir would take quite a bit of instruction in order to release that which God had placed in their hearts. There were different ranks in Solomon's temple: some musicians and singers were leaders and directors while others had different degrees of skill. All were valuable in the service of the Lord.

Like what it is in the church today, the music ministry is a distinctive calling and appointing by God. 1 Chronicles 9:33 says: *'Those who were musicians, heads of Levite families, stayed in the rooms of the temple and were exempt from other duties because they were responsible for the work day and night.'*

Here we have musicians and singers working around the clock—24/7. The house of the Lord should never be neglected and those in the music ministry were shift workers. Worship brings the presence of the Lord as David already knew by his own experience. He said in Psalm 134:1: *'Praise*

THE TEMPLE OF THE LORD

the Lord, all you servants of the Lord who minister by night in the house of the Lord. Lift up your hands in the sanctuary and praise the Lord. May the Lord, the Maker of heaven and earth bless you from Zion.'

Not only did the music team praise and worship the Lord they sang the prophetic song and prophesied with their instruments. 1 Chronicles 25:1 says: *'David, together with the commanders of the army, set apart some of the sons of Asaph, Heman and Jeduthun for the ministry of prophesying, accompanied by harps and lyres and cymbals. Here is a list of men who performed this service.'* The next verses list names of those who functioned in this area under the supervision of Asaph who prophesied under the king's supervision. Next came sons under the supervision of their father Jeduthun, who prophesied, using the harp in thanking and praising the Lord. This list goes on until all the company of musicians and singers are named. Incredible! They were well trained, disciplined and loyal. There would have been no room for negligence. They came under the authority of their fathers who in turn came under the authority of the king David. An amazing organisation!

What blessings the presence of the Lord had brought to Israel during this time. David said in Psalm 122:1: *'I rejoiced with those who said to me, let us go to the house of the Lord. Our feet are standing in your gates, O Jerusalem.'* I do not blame him for wanting to be where there was worship and intimate fellowship with God and His people. I could imagine how overwhelming the glory would have been. The atmosphere around Jerusalem would have been alive with angels joining in with the glorious worship. The most popular scripture that the church uses today regarding the dedication of the temple of Solomon is taken from:

2 Chronicles 5:13-14 *'The trumpeters and singers joined in unison, as with one voice, to give praise and thanks to the Lord. Accompanied by trumpets, cymbals and other instruments, they raised their voices in praise to the Lord and sang: "He is good; [His] love endures for ever." Then the temple was filled with*

a cloud, and the priests could not perform their service because the glory of the Lord filled the temple of God.'

Then again we read in Chapter 7:1-3: *'When Solomon finished praying, fire came down from heaven and consumed the burnt offerings and the sacrifices, and the glory of the Lord filled the temple. The priests could not enter the temple of the Lord because the glory of the Lord filled the temple. When all the Israelites saw the fire coming down and the glory of the Lord above the temple, they knelt on the pavement with their faces to the ground, and they worshipped and gave thanks to the Lord saying, "He is good; His love endures forever."'*

"That's what we want in our Church Lord!" we cry out. Can we count the cost of such dedication and focus? The lives of the Levites revolved around the house of the Lord and His presence. They did not own houses and land for themselves like the rest of Israel. They lived on the tithes and offerings of the people. We have so many distractions and opportunities out there in this big, wide world through modern technology and other methods that enables us to be very self involved.

We also see how important prophesy played a major role in the worship within Solomon's temple during this time. Music creates an atmosphere for God to speak. Prophesy can be sung or spoken. Prophesying with instruments can open up a new realm of insight into the heavenly atmosphere. We see this happening in the following scripture:

In 2 Kings 3:13-19, the prophet, Elisha, was called upon to give Jehoshaphat, king of Judah and the kings of Israel and Edom a message from God—whether or not to do battle against the king of Moab. Elisha said he would inquire of the Lord for them because he had respect for Jehoshaphat. Before he prophesied he gave the order, *'but now bring me a harpist,'* (verse 15).

Then we read on, that while the harpist was playing, Elisha delivered a message from the Lord to these three kings. There were so many prophets before the time of Elisha who prophesied without musical accompaniment, as Elisha had done, before and after this occasion.

I wonder if the musical setting brought peace and harmony to the three kings so they could be of one mind to receive the message from God. There was obviously unrest in the spiritual atmosphere that Elisha was aware of.

In the church today, prophecy brings not only a release and edification to the musicians, but to all the congregation. I have functioned in this ministry time and time again—mainly at prayer meetings where the people are more open to the Holy Spirit. There is such freedom when I have let God take control of my fingers on the piano and just focused on Him. Music displays what is happening in the unseen realm around us. It is like a flowing river and worshippers gathered are set free to enter into the flow and begin to sing spontaneous melodies, with or without words. This brings a close intimacy with the Lord and an expectant openness to see what God is doing or saying. We first minister to the Lord and then He ministers to us.

How does God minister to His people? He embraces us with His loving presence. How do we hear what He is saying? There are many ways—through an impression in our spirit; visual pictures or visions; a scripture could spring to mind or just by opening our mouths in faith and God fills it with His words. It takes plenty of practice and waiting on God. But what a blessing it is to flow with the heart of God. I have had people describing what they would see with their spiritual eyes while I am playing and singing with the flow of the Holy Spirit. Interpretations follow and it brings the body of Christ together to use their God-given gifts. Heaven and earth mingles together as one.

True worship began with the nation of Israel. It is little wonder that for centuries the devil has been tearing around like a *'roaring lion,'* trying to destroy that nation, especially Jerusalem and the temple Mount, bringing in false religions and their gods.

God had re-affirmed His promise to David and then to Solomon after the temple was dedicated to the Lord, as written in 2 Chronicles 7:11-22:

'As for you, if you walk before me as David your father did, and do all I command, and observe my decrees and laws, I will establish your royal throne over Israel forever, as I covenanted with your father David when I said, "You will never fail to have a man on the throne of Israel."'

It is good to centre on the good portions of scripture but life has the habit of not going according to plan, sometimes through our own doing. The next part of the chapter brings out that if Solomon does *not* keep following in the ways of the Lord as his father, David, had done but follow other gods, Israel will be uprooted from the land, the temple rejected and they will be a ridicule among all peoples.

Unfortunately, Solomon did not keep the laws and decrees of the Lord which led to the division of Israel and Judah. Once this happened the door was left wide open for the defilement and plundering of the first temple. What began in unity of heart and purpose changed. The temple was a magnificent building and became the pride and glory of Israel. It went through many cycles of defilement and restoration according to which king ruled. It was finally destroyed 374 years later by King Nebuchadnezzer, of Babylon, who took the southern kingdom of Judah into captivity.

How sad an end to that magnificent temple and the glorious worship all because Solomon, although a man of great wisdom from God, did not invest into the future of Israel and keep up his side of the promise to God.

At the dedication of the temple God had said after Solomon's prayer:

'Now [My] eyes will be open and [My] ears attentive to the prayers offered in this place. I have chosen and consecrated this temple so that [My] Name may be there forever. My eyes and heart will always be there,' (2 Chronicles 7:15-16). God protects His covenant. His word is not spoken lightly. If He says

His NAME will be there forever, He means it. The very land on which the temple was built is the Lord's. Even today—thousands of years later! God is faithful! God's word is true! Seventy years after the dedication, Cyrus, king of Persia, conquered Babylon and gave orders to allow the Jews in exile to return to Jerusalem and rebuild the temple. The temple vessels taken by Nebuchadnezzer were also returned. The people of Israel returned in three different stages: firstly, led by Zerubbabel; secondly by Ezra and thirdly, Nememiah who had a vision to restore Jerusalem and its laws. Ezra also was a dedicated and passionate leader who taught the Jewish law and focused on restoring the temple.

God had chosen Zerubbabel, a descendant of David, to build the temple. Haggai the prophet had a message from God to instruct Zerubbabel and Joshua, the high priest at the time, to build the temple of the Lord. In the midst of opposition, with help from the people of Israel and generous giving as in the former temple, they were able to build. God again used a gentile, Darius the Persian King, to help restore the sacrificial system.

Once again musicians and singers come into the picture in Ezra 2:70: *'The priests, the Levites, the singers, the gatekeepers and the temple servants settled in their own towns ...'* Then they offered up sacrifices to the Lord on the area where the foundations were to be laid. At length, the big day had come! The foundations of the second temple were laid! (Ezra 3:10-13). There was great joy! The singers, after the order of David, and cymbal players together with the Israelites, lifted their voices in loud praise and thanksgiving: *'He is good, His love to Israel endures forever.'* Many of the people who had seen the former temple were disappointed and cried because it would not be as magnificent. The rest shouted loudly with joy and the sound was heard a long way off.

Finally after so much opposition, they finished building the temple according to the command of the God of Israel and again there was a wonderful celebration at the dedication.

With all that there was one thing missing—the ark of the covenant! How devastating for Israel that it had never been found and returned into the Holy of Holies. Instead, the foundation stone of where the ark had stood was the place where the high priest sprinkled the blood to atone for Israel's sins.

Nehemiah also was commissioned by God to build the walls of Jerusalem. There were more persecution and opposition by the people around them but amazingly through his godly wisdom and enabling, the wall was rebuilt in fifty two days. Another celebration of thanksgiving to God had taken place. Two choirs stationed on the wall led processions in opposite directions until reaching the temple where they had taken their positions inside. With the sound of harps, cymbals, lyres, and all of Israel rejoicing, the sound was heard a long way off, (Nehemiah 12).

In Psalm 42:4, one of the sons of Korah reminiscences of the joyous times they had in the temple of the Lord: *'These things I remember as I pour out my soul; how I used to go with the multitude, leading the procession to the house of God with shouts of joy and thanksgiving among the festive throng.'*

Later we read in Nehemiah 13:4-10 that Nehemiah had discovered at the time that Eliashab, the priest, had given one of the storerooms of the temple to Tobias to store his own belongings. These storage rooms were to be used to store tithes and offerings for the workers in the temple, including singers and musicians, to live on. Because of this, they were forced to go back to their houses and land and the temple of the Lord was neglected. Not only was this bad, but the fact that Tobias was one of the mockers of Israel. Little wonder Nehemiah was furious and threw out Tobias' household goods then purified the room. After that they brought back the tithes and offerings, grain and oil so the Levites were able to come back to their positions in the temple night and day. Worship was restored and the presence of God.

Once again, through idolatry of the Jews, Jerusalem was conquered, the temple desecrated, Jewish practices were stopped and the Olympian god, Zeus was worshipped in the temple. After a series of events, Judas Maccabeus restores Jewish ritual by cleansing and rededicating the temple. About a hundred years later, the Jews lost their independence through the intervention of Rome and was conquered by the roman emperor, Pompey, who entered the Holy of Holies and defiled it. This was the end of the Davidic pattern of the beautiful worship in the temple. The glory of God had departed Jerusalem! Israel was scattered once again. The prophets had warned of its devastation. Jeremiah, chapter 7 and Micah, chapter 3 speaks of the destruction of Jerusalem and the temple.

There is good news! Would God break His covenant with the house of David? Not at all! Amos appeared to be a prophet of doom and gloom, but at the end of all that, he came with the most astounding message of hope that would not only affect Israel but every nation of the world for ever!

His message of hope is found in Amos 9:11-12:

'*"In that day I will restore David's fallen tent. I'll repair its broken places, restore its ruins, and build it as it used to be, so that they may possess the remnant of Edom and all the nations that bear my name," declares the Lord, who will do these things.*'

In our day and age, the preparations for a third temple are under way. This is not the temple mentioned in the book of Ezekiel when the Messiah Yeshua will rule and reign from. This temple is where the Antichrist will rule from and defile it, (2 Thessalonians 2:3-4).

God had a much greater plan for His chosen people, Israel, that includes all people of the earth. It was much bigger than any temple made with human hands. Abraham saw it, (Hebrews 11:10). Ezekiel saw it and Haggai saw the temple more glorious than the former temple.

Ezekiel 43:7 'He said: Son of man, this is the *place of my throne, and the place for the soles of my feet. This is where I will live among the Israelites forever.'*

Herod's Temple

In the meantime, while Israel was under the occupation of Rome, Herod became ruler of the Jews. In order to be able to do this he conformed to Jewish traditions and practices by converting to Judaism to please the priests. Before the time of Christ, he set about to renovate the second temple built by Zerubbabel. It was in a state of disrepair. He was particular to follow the biblical pattern laid out previously and the legal requirements. However, being under Roman authority, he had to please other parties and compete with other magnificent Roman architecture structures at the time. He was divided in his beliefs and motives and introduced bits and pieces of Roman and Greek styles. Unfortunately he favoured Rome during conflicting laws with the Jews and placed a golden eagle over the eastern gateway of the temple. As a bird of prey this symbolised Rome and was not done to please God.

There is no mention of worship with music, or the manifestation of glory of God in the New Testament regarding Herod's Temple. Was this the glorious temple the prophets spoke of?

Not at all! In 70 CE, Herod's temple was also destroyed The Jews seemed to be proud of it as we see in Luke 21:5-6:

'Some of [His] disciples were remarking how the temple was adorned with beautiful stones and with gifts dedicated to God. But Jesus said, "As for what you see here, the time will come when not one stone will be left on another, every one of them will be thrown down."'

Jesus of course was looking ahead and knew what would happen in the future. To Him the temple was only a foreshadow of the temple in the future—His glorious body. Nevertheless, Mary and Joseph had taken Jesus as a baby to be dedicated to God at the temple, as it was required by Jewish law.

They were first met by Simeon, a righteous and devout man who had been waiting for the consolation of Israel. He recognised Jesus as the Messiah.

Anna, a prophetess, had been praying and fasting in the temple for eighty four years. She also spoke about the baby, Jesus, to all who were looking forward to the redemption of Israel, (Luke 2:22-39). God had His true servants who worshipped Him, and they were waiting for the coming of the Messiah to greet Jesus in the temple that day. They were close to God and His Holy Spirit came upon them. Amazed by what was spoken over their child, Mary and Joseph went on to complete everything that was required by the law of Moses. There was no mention of the priest recognising Jesus as the Messiah. Only those who were open to the Spirit of God could see through His eyes.

At the age of twelve Jesus was found by His parents, sitting in the temple with the Jewish teachers and asking questions. He was surprised His parents had been looking for Him as He automatically thought they would know He would be – *'in His Father's house,'* (Luke 2:49).

This is the same temple in which Jesus made a whip of chords and drove out those exploiting the pilgrims coming to pay their dues. In righteous fury He overturned their money tables and benches with cages. Imagine the sound of the men shouting, sheep and cattle blaring, doves and pigeons flapping, piles of money clashing, furniture crashing and Jesus roaring: 'Get out of here! How dare you turn my Father's house into a market!' (John 2:15).

Matthew 21:12-13 also records the incident of cleansing the temple of the merchants by saying: *"It is written [My] house will be called a house of prayer for all nations buy you are making it a den of robbers."* Zeal for His Father's house had consumed Him. He was not passionate about the magnificence and wealth of the building. He was passionate about the fact that the people were being exploited and robbed of the wonderful worship that was clearly set out in Solomon's temple. They had settled for substitutes and counterfeits defiling the temple, which should have been all about the manifest presence of God.

Instead of being filled with the glory of God, it housed a market for buying and selling. Their thinking had grown materialistic and they worshipped the building and not the Living God.

This was prophetic of what was to come. Jesus Christ was the Living Presence of God on earth. He had become the Temple. On the cross, He suffered all of Satan's defilement and wrath and as the glory had departed from the temple, He also experienced the horror and blackness of the desertion of God His Father. His final cleansing came with the pouring out of His blood. Immediately after His death, the massive curtain in the temple that separated man from God was ripped from top to bottom.

Before His death Jesus began a peoples' ministry. He ministered to the needs of people. He sought out the broken and lost sheep of Israel—to restore the Tabernacle of David as we read earlier in Amos 9:11-12.

That is why He quoted from Isaiah 61:1 while in the synagogue in Galilee: *'The Spirit of the Sovereign Lord is upon [Me] because the Lord has anointed [Me] to preach good news to the poor. He has sent [Me] to bind up the brokenhearted to proclaim freedom to the captives and release from darkness the prisoners ...'*

His dwelling place was not with the building but with the people. Isaiah 57:15 says: *'I live in a high and holy place but also with him who is contrite and lowly in spirit, to revive the spirit of the lowly and to revive the heart of the contrite.'* He came to heal, restore and repair the broken lives of people.

Preceding this incident of the merchants, Jesus rode into Jerusalem on a donkey. A sure sign He came to serve, not to conquer. The crowds made a way for Him and threw their cloaks, shawls and palm branches across the path for Him to ride through in honour. Others waved palm branches and cried out. *'Hosanna to the Son of David! Blessed is He who comes in the name of the Lord!'* The scriptures recorded that after the cleansing of Herod's temple, the blind and the cripple came to the temple courts and Jesus healed them, (Matthew 21:9).

They recognised Him as coming from the line of David and coming from high distinction. They again cried out, *'Hosanna to the Son of David! Blessed is He who comes in the name of the Lord!'* The priests and religious scholars hated what they were saying and told Jesus to rebuke His disciples. The word 'Hosanna' alternates between praise and 'save us.' This kind of praise was only offered up to God and reserved for special feasts. In another passage in Luke 19:40, He says to the Pharisees: *'... if they keep quiet, the stones will cry out.'* Although Jesus came as a servant riding on a donkey, His feet would have been on the colt which again spoke of Kingship. The people saw Him as God and Saviour! They cried out to Him to deliver them from the Roman rule at the time.

We can learn a lesson from the desecration of the temple and ask ourselves what truly pleases God. We can centre on so many different activities which we call 'ministries', yet neglecting why we come together—that is to pray and worship. The devil is out to rob us of even that in the church. Like in the modern church as a whole, there would have been many things in the temple that displeased Jesus at the time, although He did not confront the leaders. God in His wisdom deals with issues in His own time, when it gives Him the greatest glory. It is like the parable of the wheat and weeds growing together until the harvest. They will then be sorted out without bringing harm to the wheat. A time is coming when God will separate the sheep from the goats—those who will follow Him and those who will rebel.

Jesus, the precious Lamb of God, was the cornerstone of the new temple, the Church. All focus is now taken off the building and onto Christ. The temple of God is now formed with the hearts of those who love Him—not made with human hands. We are the 'stones' that are crying out praises! It all began in Jerusalem. God's eyes are still on that Holy place forever where the first temple was built, because He has made a covenant with His faithful ones, Abraham, Isaac, Jacob, Moses, David and Solomon. Jesus heard their cries of *'Hosanna,'* and offered up His own life to save all from their sins who believe and receive Him. Not quite what the people of Israel had in mind.

Satan is out to rob and destroy the temple by snatching that place for his own, but a time is soon coming when his altars of evil will be smashed to smithereens and Jesus will set up His kingdom with His bride. Each of us are temples of the Holy Spirit where God's glory resides.

We have learned that a temple is a place of worship and prayer—a place where we meet with God. Everywhere it is mentioned in the scriptures it is built on a foundation of sacrifice, struggle, wrestling— blood, sweat and tears. As we are temples of the Holy Spirit, through our struggles, groaning and crying, the sweet fragrance of the Lord is produced. Hardships causes us to seek God, creating a deeper yearning for His presence. In Isaiah 66:8b we read: *'As soon as Zion travailed, she gave birth to her children.'*

Travail speaks of labour, pain and giving birth. Israel had suffered to bring to birth Yeshua, the Messiah—the sacrificial Lamb who takes away the sin of the world.

We can thank Israel for this birthing role, priestly role, sacrificial role and their suffering role. Romans 9:5 adds to these roles: *'Theirs is the adop-*

tion as sons; theirs the divine glory, the covenants, the receiving of the law, the temple worship and the promises. Theirs are the patriarchs, and from them is traced the human ancestry of Christ, who is God over all, forever praised!'* In John 4:22, Jesus said that *'salvation is from the Jews.'* In other words, salvation is made available to everyone through the lineage of the Jews.

At the dedication of Solomon's Temple, three events happened:

- The priests purified themselves before performing their rituals and sacrifices.
- The musicians and singers played with one voice.
- The glory of the Lord flooded the temple—priests could not perform their duties because of God's presence.

How should we relate to the new covenant temple?

- Purify ourselves from anything that contaminates our body, soul and spirit.
- Be in one accord as we worship and pray together— be in unity.
- Create an atmosphere for the glory of the Lord to reside by allowing the Holy Spirit to lead.

CHAPTER 1 2

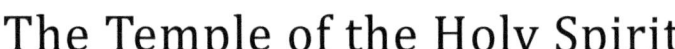

The Temple of the Holy Spirit

GOD IS RESTORING THE TABERNACLE OF DAVID

In One Day

Acts 2:1-41 says: *'When the day of Pentecost came, they were all together in one place. Suddenly a sound like the blowing of a violent wind came from heaven and filled the whole house where they were sitting. They saw what seemed to be tongues of fire that separated and came to rest on each of them. All of them were filled with the Holy Spirit and began to speak in other tongues as the Spirit enabled them ...v.17 "I will pour out [My] Spirit on all people. Your sons and daughters will prophesy, your young men will see visions, your old men will dream dreams. Even on [My] servants, both men and women, I will pour out [My] Spirit in those days and they will prophesy. I will show wonders in the heavens above and signs on the earth below, blood and fire and billows of* smoke. *The sun will be turned to darkness and the moon to blood, before the coming of the Lord and everyone who calls on the name of the Lord will be saved"...' v.41.*

Three thousand were added to their number that Day!

It happened just like the prophet said it would. Between 400-500 years before Christ was born, Joel a prophet, announced that God would pour out of His Spirit on all people, (Joel 2:28-32). Preceding this passage and speaking of restoration, verse 4 says: *'The threshing floors will be filled with grain; the vats will overflow with new wine and oil.'*

It is back to the threshing floor again where the temple was built. At the threshing floor there is a separation of the grain from the rubble. It speaks of the promised harvest of souls coming into the threshing floor and with it comes the cleansing and anointing oil. There is always abundance with God.

Within a day the Church was born! From the natural to the spiritual! A Holy nation and a royal priesthood! (1 Peter 2:9). Suddenly there was a sound that caught the attention of the people witnessing the disciples' joy. Such glory, such freedom to the point of being accused of drunkenness.

They were speaking of the wonders of God in the languages of the Jews around them from other nations. Peter rose up before the crowds and spoke with boldness. The books of the prophets became alive and he was able to preach the gospel and quote long passages of scripture by the Holy Spirit's enabling.

They were now walking with the Spirit of Jesus and not His physical presence. They were instantly changed from the natural to the spiritual; earthly to the heavenly; from the structured to the unstructured; from the intellect of Judaism, where the Torah was read and discussed in a lengthy manner. Now it became action using the power that was within them through the Holy Spirit. They could now understand that the kingdom of heaven is not one of words but of the *'demonstration of the Spirit's power,'* (1 Corinthians 2:4).

The early church was vibrant, moving in signs, wonders and miracles as Jesus had promised in John 14:12-14: '... *"I tell you the truth, anyone who has faith in me will do what I have been doing. He will do even greater things than these, because I am going to the Father.'*

That would have been hard for the disciples to fathom what He meant at the time. He was going to leave them? They would do greater works than Jesus? In modern terms, "Come on, get real."

From the old covenant of keeping the laws of God to the new covenant of the Torah written on their hearts. They had to be changed by the renewing of their minds and working with one another. This could only come about by a close drawing together daily in worship and prayer. They needed to in order to be spontaneous and radically obedient to obey the commission of being witnesses in Jerusalem, Judea, Samaria and to the ends of the earth, (Acts 1:8).

Now they could also understand Jesus' words: "*Upon this rock, I will build my Church."* Revelation of what Jesus taught them had now become reality. They began to live in 'heavenly places' with the Spirit of God. Their lives became worship through their obedience. Jesus' words to them in Matthew 28:18-20, consumed them with a passion.

'... *"All authority in heaven and on earth has been given to [Me]. Therefore go and make disciples of all nations, baptising them in the name of the Father, and of the Son and of the Holy Spirit, and teaching them to obey everything I have commanded you. And surely I am with you always, to the very end of the age."* They also took Jesus' words to heart in Matthew 9:37: '... *"The harvest is plentiful but the workers are few. Ask the Lord of the harvest, therefore, to send out workers into His harvest field."*...'

On the day of Pentecost, God poured out His Spirit on the one hundred and twenty disciples gathered. They had become the first fruits of the abundant harvest that was to follow right through all the nations of the world. They were to be a 'light to the nations.'

Through the power of the Holy Spirit they obeyed the Lord's commission with selfless abandonment. And because of that, 3,000 were added to their number THAT DAY!

In ONE DAY, the church of Jesus Christ was born! Imagine all the baptisms!

Isaiah 66:8 says: *'Before she goes into labour she gives birth; before the labour pains come upon her she delivers a son. Who has ever heard of such a thing? Who has ever seen such things? Can a country be born in a day or a nation be brought forth in a moment?'*

Yes, yes, yes! It happened as the prophet, Isaiah, had declared! God had done it! All things are possible with God!

In one day in 1948 Israel became a nation. In one day the Messianic Kingdom of Jesus Christ was born! In one day the holy nation—the church was born!

Song of the harvesters

I can imagine the sound of applause in heaven. Jesus said there is rejoicing in heaven over **one** repentant sinner not to mention **three thousand**! Joy would have exploded in heavenly realms. The beginning of the restoration of the Tabernacle of David! It was happening at last! A King has taken His rightful place on the throne of David. The earthly becoming heavenly! All things becoming new.

There was a new song in the air. The song of the harvesters! *'Those who sow in tears will reap with songs of joy. He who goes out weeping, carrying* seed to sow, will return with songs of joy, carrying sheaves with him,"* (Psalm 126:5-6).

We read in Genesis 8:22: *As long as the earth endures, seedtime and harvest, cold and heat, summer and winter, day and night will never cease.'*

These words were spoken to Noah after God destroyed the earth with water. As there is to be always a natural harvest so there is to be a spiritual harvest. There will always be times of joy and times of sadness but the promise of spring and summer always comes. In any season we go through we can still reap a harvest of souls for the kingdom of God.

Jesus said in John 4:35: '... *"Do you not say, "four months more and then the harvest? I tell you, open your eyes and look at the fields! They are ripe for harvest."...'*

Jesus is saying the harvest is plentiful. Do not miss out on the harvest. Jesus did say to make disciples not to make Christians or church goers. I have seen a sign on a local church which I think is appropriate— *"Jesus said to be fishers of men not the keepers of the fish bowl."* The kingdom of disciples are dedicated by putting Christ first in their lives and moving in the power of the Lord. Reap while there is still time! We tend to expect Jesus to do it for us and keep praying for a harvest of souls to come into the church and that *can* happen through the drawing of the Holy Spirit. But that is not the usual way to reap a natural harvest. The farmer needs to go out into the field and plough. Preparation of the soil with the right composites of minerals and fertilisers are needed before the time for planting seed has come. At the right time the seed bears a crop and when ready the harvesters go out and bring the crops into the barn. The crops cannot bring themselves into the barn.

The disciples had spent night and day in prayer for fifty days before the Holy Spirit came upon them. Then they went out. They taught what Jesus had taught them. They did what Jesus had done. They became love- slaves of Him. That is true discipleship.

Harvest is spoken of a lot in scripture. In Israel, during the Feast of First Fruits of the harvest (Shavuot), the Jews would come from all over the land to the temple of the Lord in Jerusalem. They presented the first fruits of their summer harvest, a sheaf of wheat, in celebration and thanksgiving to the Lord for the abundant harvest that was to follow and to be reaped. By offering the first fruits to the Lord is was deemed holy and the rest of the harvest to follow. Afterwards they went back home to their individual fields to gather the rest of their harvest.

Over two thousand years ago, on the Day of Shavout or Pentecost, the Holy Spirit was poured out on one hundred and twenty disciples gathered together in an upper room. They were the first fruits of new life in the Spirit of God: they had gathered on the same day before the Lord in Jerusalem where every first fruit must be presented and consecrated as holy. They were the first fruits of the harvest of souls to come to Jesus right through to the end of this age. They spoke in foreign tongues of the surrounding nations as the Holy Spirit gave them utterance. Because, as first fruits, they represented every tribe and tongue and nation of future harvests. They immediately went out in the fields to reap a harvest of souls where thousands were added to the church.

This was a sign that all who came after them would likewise be consecrated as holy to God. They will be given the same anointing, the power of the Holy Spirit, as the first disciples. We are included in that harvest! Jesus has given us the same commission as in Mark 16:15 and Matthew 28:18-20. We are to bear fruit! Jesus said in John 15:8: '…"*This is to [My] Father's glory, that you bear much fruit, showing yourselves to be [My]disciples*"…'

There are many different harvests in Israel like in every country according to the season. The barley harvest is in spring followed by the wheat harvest in summer. Then comes the fig, date, pomegranate, olive and the grape harvest in autumn.

So are the harvest seasons in our lives. There are many harvests to reap throughout our lives. Our harvests are souls—family, friends, acquaintances, those around us in the communities. Year after year the seasons of these people in our lives may come and go and still we may not have brought them into the kingdom of God.

The prophet Jeremiah paints a dismal picture in Jeremiah 8. The nation of Israel was in a state of apostasy where they had never repented of their rebellion against God—all shame and remorse for sin were gone. God said in verse 13: '... *"I will take away their harvest ... There will be no grapes on the vine. There will be no figs on the tree, and their leaves will wither. What I have given them will be taken from them"...*'

Later on in verse 20 we read: *'The harvest is past, the summer has ended, and we are not saved.'*

That is so sad. When I was in Israel with the Australian Prayer Network, I had a go of turning the huge grinding wheel used for the wheat and barley harvest. It was so heavy I was not really strong enough to turn it. The wheel, of course, has a very distinctive sound which could be heard at some distance. During times of summer harvest in ancient Israel, the sound of the grinding wheels were heard across the land showing that all was well as the women ground down the grain. It would be music to the nation's ears. But during times of famine and God's judgement on the nation, grinding wheels remained silent.

We need to hear the sound of the spiritual grinding wheels throughout our own nations. The sound of celebration of heaven and earth as people are born-again into the Kingdom of God. Let us not miss out of reaping the harvest of our time by disobeying God's word. We do not want to hear the lost crying out: *"The harvest is past, the summer has ended, and we are not saved!"* We want to hear the songs of the harvesters and the songs of joy from each repentant sinner.

I love to hear tribal people in other countries singing while they bring in the harvest. What a blessing to hear the Tongan rugby team singing praises to God before the 2023 world cup here in Sydney, Australia. They were recognised by the media and viewed on television. They were not there to evangelise but what a testimony of God's goodness to them. It was their response of love to God by putting Him first before the game. If we love the Lord, we have a song to sing! First to God and second, out to the lost with a message of hope.

In Psalm 126, the Jews, when released from captivity, laughed and sang without restraint. God had answered their cries and faith rose. This brought the attention of the people around them and they were so impressed that they said: *'The Lord has done great things for them!'* Their joy was contagious. I like the verse in Psalm 68:6: *'... He leads forth the prisoners with singing ...'*

Over the years we have seen moves of God come and go through the churches. One move brings joy and laughter as people are set free from bondage in their lives. It is a normal reaction if we are released from captivity. I remember years ago at a prayer meeting praying for a man who was seriously ill in hospital with a heart condition. We were *meant* to be praying but instead I began laughing and soon others joined me. Obviously it was a type of warfare against the devil, because during that time, the man jumped out of bed and started dancing with the nurses. He told us his story some time later.

God touches those who need Him. Jesus sought out the individuals who needed a touch from him. Not everyone, but only to those whom the Father sent Him to.

This reminds me of the time when our group was travelling around praying for the towns in the Hunter Valley where we lived. We were at a quiet, high area overlooking a town. Not far down the hill was a street with homes and sound often carries further than you realise. After praying for the town, we raised our hands to heaven and sang to the Lord—our usual practice of thanksgiving for answered prayers.

It was not long before we saw a young girl struggling to push a baby in a pram up the hill. There were other small children tagging along with her and when they reached us they stood quietly listening. They seemed to be transfixed, especially one little boy of about three years of age. After worshipping the Lord we sang a few children's songs and Jennifer, the member of our team whose ministry was with children, shared about Jesus and prayed for them. We then blessed them.

What a special moment and a privilege it was. It was so unexpected. Sometimes we are looking for the big things to be momentous times in our lives but God sent humble, little, children to hear about His love for them. We do not know the results of this occasion but I really believe seeds were planted in their little hearts and their names are written in the Lamb's Book of Life. Singing is so important in the church as worship but let us not forget what a powerful tool it is. The outside world needs to hear the message of salvation through song. It is so important to gather in the children and pass on the mantle of singing.

During the early to mid twentieth century in China, there was a community of Christians living hidden away from the totalitarian regime. Five hundred people lived on the forty three acres of land. They lived off the land and worked hard. Compared to the surrounding villages, they lived in luxury. They were joyful in everything they did including menial tasks. The leaders believed it was their job to clean the latrines and push loads of animal dung in carts. They had taken the words of Jesus: 'if you want to be great in God's kingdom you have to be the greatest servant of all,' seriously. Many leaders today need to take a lesson in this.

What was impressive with this community was everything they did was accompanied by music, singing and prayer. The children were taught at an early age to pray and sing. They did not have the toys, games or other activities like children today, so music and singing were their focus. No games were organised for them but they would go to the threshing floor and sing and dance spontaneously. That was their fun.

They were well educated and happy—work was their play. When asked what they would like to do when they grew up, most had an idea of what type of work they would like to do, but their main focus was to preach about Jesus.

There is room for music and singing in so many different situations. The world needs to hear our joy. That is a testimony to the goodness of God.

Christian flash mobs in busy places, malls, shopping centres and food courts open the hearts of the people flocking around. With delighted faces and mobile phones raised for photos, the onlookers are caught up with the emotion of the choir or orchestra. Music is the language of heaven and brings God's presence into our towns releasing a spirit of joy.

Psalm 30:11-12 says: *'You turned my wailing into dancing; [You] removed my sackcloth and clothed me with joy, that my heart may sing [Your] praises and not be silent. Lord my God, I will give [You] thanks forever!'*

What is happening to music and singing in the house of God today? God said He will restore the Tabernacle of David—repair its broken down walls. The disciples in Acts 15:16-17 quoted the scripture from Amos.

'... "After this I will return and rebuild David's fallen tent. Its ruins I will rebuild, and I will restore it, that the remnant of the people may seek the Lord, and all the Gentiles who bear My name," says the Lord who does these things."...'

What is David's Tabernacle? Is it the worship—all the music and singing? Is it the tent-like structure for temporary use? Is it a particular building, temple, synagogue or church? It is so much more than that. It comes back to the house of David—all of the twelve tribes of Israel coming back to their homeland from the nations where they have been scattered. It has been happening since their nation's rebirth in 1948.

Even so, the House of David is much bigger than that.

God has made provision for all mankind to come into His house where He will come back to Jerusalem to rule and reign as King over all kings, rulers, heads of states, presidents and prime ministers.

Psalm 22:27,28 says: *'All the ends of the earth will remember and turn to the Lord, and all the families of the nations will bow before [Him], for dominion belongs to the Lord and [He] rules over the nations.'*

Many say that God has done away with Israel—He had divorced them. Their doctrine is that the church has replaced Israel. This is a theology of replacement by the gentile church and is not true according to Jeremiah 31:31-36.

'... "The days are coming," declares the Lord, "when I will make a new covenant with the house of Israel and with the house of Judah ... I'll put [My] law in their minds and write it on their hearts. I will be their God, and they will be [My] people ... This is what the Lord says, [He] who appoints the sun to shine by day, who decrees the moon and stars by night, who stirs up the sea so that its waves roar—the Lord Almighty is [His] name. Only if these decrees vanish from [My] sight," declares the Lord, "will the descendants of Israel ever cease to be a nation before [Me]"...'

The sun and moon are still shining and Israel is still a nation and always will be. God has made a promise to Israel and to Judah and He will not break it because He is faithful to His promises to Abraham and David, His servants.

You might think, "then how do we fit in?" The answer is in Romans 11. It speaks of an olive tree, The root and trunk is YHWH and Messiah

Yeshua. In English we say Yahweh and Jesus. The branches of the olive tree refers to all the tribes of Israel. During the times of David and Solomon they were all together worshipping God. Later on in the course of history ten northern tribes separated and adulterated themselves with the nations around them. The olive tree split in two—Israel (Ephraim) to the north and Judah in the south.

God rejected the tribes of Israel because of their lack of repentance, and broke His covenant with them. The natural branches of half of the olive tree were broken off but the roots and the trunk remained. They were scattered among the gentiles, multiplied and lost their identity. Judah also sinned against God and their branches were lopped. The good news is God brought a message of hope through Jeremiah the prophet as we read above. God has made a new covenant with the house of Israel and Judah. He is a God of mercy, forgiveness and restoration.

Back to the question of—what about us? Israel or Ephraim mingled with the gentiles and became gentiles not Jews. Jews are from the tribes of Judah—Benjamin and Judah. If we are not Jews we are gentiles. God's promise is to all mankind that if we recognise Yeshua as Messiah, repent of our wickedness and be immersed through the waters of baptism to identify with Christ in death and wash off the effects of the world, we are grafted into the olive tree becoming the whole house of Israel and making us one as the body of Christ. If anyone, or branch, rebels against God they will be cut off from the tree and of course the root who is God. Grace and mercy extends to Jew and gentile if they repent and return to God they will be grafted back into the olive tree. God has partially blinded the eyes of the Jews for a season so that the gentiles can be grafted in. There is coming a time when the veil will be taken off their eyes and they will mourn for the one they had pierced realising they have killed their Messiah.

Zechariah 12:10 says: *'And I will pour out on the house of David and the inhabitants of Jerusalem a spirit of grace and supplication. They will look on [Me], the one they have pierced, and they will mourn for [Him] as one mourns for an only child.'*

God's wonderful mercy and forgiveness is going to give the whole of Israel repentance to be saved. He will cleanse their land from their iniquity.

In Romans 11:26b-27, *'Israel has experienced a hardening in part until the full number of the Gentiles has come in, and so all Israel will be saved. As it is written: "The deliverer will come from Zion; [He] will turn godlessness away from Jacob and this is [My] covenant with them when I take away their sins."'*

God has done this through Christ to bring all nations together—the house of the Lord and the tabernacle of David under the authority of the King of kings, their desired Messiah. God has promised to raise up its ancient ruins and repair its broken down walls. It is a slow process but God is doing it.

I suppose to us it makes more sense to our human thinking, to rebuild Solomon's temple with all the music and worship than a portable tent. If we look at it, just from that perspective of music and worship, it does seem a better idea especially when we read in Matthew 16:18: *'Jesus said to Simon, "And I tell you that you are Peter, and upon this rock I will build [My] Church, and the gates of Hades will not overcome it"...'*

I	He is personally committed to building His church.
WILL	He is determined to produce perfection in His church.
BUILD	A slow and drawn out process—stone upon stone into His church.

THE TEMPLE OF THE HOLY SPIRIT

MY   Jesus loves His possession, bought with the price of His blood.

CHURCH   All believers made holy in His sight. The Greek meaning is *'Ekklesia'*—called out ones.

Jesus told Peter He will build His church after Peter confessed that Jesus was the Son of God. Before the Holy Spirit filled Peter with power, Peter feared for his own life when Jesus was captured and crucified. After he was filled with the Holy Spirit he went out fearlessly and healed the sick, cast out devils, preached the gospel of Jesus Christ and baptised new believers. That is how wonderful God's love and forgiveness is. He does not see our failures but what we can do through His Spirit's enabling. Peter's name, along with the other Apostles' names are written on the twelve foundations of the New Jerusalem and the names of the twelve tribes of Israel are written on the twelve gates of the New Jerusalem as we read in Revelation 21:12-14. Our heritage is deeply rooted in Christ and the nation of Israel.

Peter and all the other disciples of Jesus had to birth the church on the day of Pentecost. They travailed in prayer and praised God in preparation for the Holy Spirit to be poured out.

It is only by the Spirit of God, that any of us can change—from timidity to boldness; from rigid traditions to freedom in Christ: from lengthy discussions of the scriptures to active obedience and the working of signs, wonders and miracles.

I encourage everyone to seek more fullness of the Holy Spirit in order to bring change to the community around us like on the day of Pentecost when a small band of faithful Jews kick-started the greatest Kingdom on earth and three thousand of their countrymen were added to the Church. The Church grew and spread to the Gentiles through God's chosen vessel,

Paul, and we today, have been truly blessed because Zion travailed and gave birth to her children.

The church, unlike Solomon's temple, is the whole, global, body of Christ. This vibrant body is always on the move by the Spirit of God. We do not have to go up to Jerusalem to worship God but a time is coming when we will. Even though there are thousands of churches and meeting places around the world we are only ONE huge house of the Lord.

As the body of Christ we have gained so much knowledge through David's tabernacle in music and worship which has been such a blessing throughout Christendom. With Pentecost came the baptism of the Holy Spirit and with it a release in the singing in the Spirit. What does this mean? It means we sing to the Lord with a love song from our spirit through the release of the Holy Spirit, using our voice in the same way we worship God with a natural song. It can be in tongues (heavenly language), or just a melody on our lips. When you are gathered with thousands of people singing with their spirits it is the most glorious sound you could ever hear on earth. It is like the angels of heaven singing. To be a part of this love song takes you into heavenly realms with Christ. It usually begins gently and softly as if wooing the voices of those gathered to enter the courts of heaven. When enough has entered into the sound then it rises to a crescendo. Like waves of a seashore rising and falling in perfect unity, until the singing fades to a gentle sound sometimes with only one voice lingering with a message in song. This prophetic song is understood in the native language of the crowd gathered. This is the sound of heaven: a unity that only the Holy Spirit can bring. No earthly choir director could ever bring in such beautiful harmonies.

Sometimes I think that we try and force the pattern of David's tabernacle into our liturgy in church forgetting that David's tabernacle brought the rituals of worship into freedom compared to Moses tabernacle. Yet God has brought the church today further into a greater freedom to worship through the Spirit of God. It is not confined to one church or place: it is spread out across all Christian denominations around the world. There is global worship around the clock, 24/7 in churches, houses of prayer, private homes, nursing homes, hospitals, schools, colleges, on the streets, in the mountains, valleys and cities. Everywhere!

The shepherd king of Israel led the way in true, heart worship in music, song, dance, lifting up hands and clapping. But the Holy Spirit has brought us into a *love song to Yeshua HaMashiach!*—Jesus the Messiah. There is so much more the Holy Spirit wants to lead us into because Jesus has lifted us up into *heavenly places* and His banner over us is love. When we meet together it should be the most glorious experience of the week to meet with all of heaven in worshipping Jesus.

**This is the worship of the Temple of the
Lord under the New Covenant.**

CHAPTER 13

The Holy Spirit

You have been reading how the Holy Spirit works within our lives but maybe you are more confused because many people accuse Christians for worshipping three Gods.

Who is Holy Spirit? We know who God the Father is and Yeshua— better known in the English language as Jesus, the Son of God. Holy Spirit is the third divine person who makes up the Trinity— Father, Son, Holy Spirit. God in three persons. It may be hard to understand, but if we think of the sun having three elements—heat, light and energy yet still only one sun in the sky. Some say we can liken Father God to the heat, Jesus the light and Holy Spirit the energy. Water is made up of three components—liquid, steam and ice but is still water. Holy Spirit is the unseen worker dwelling within a born-again believer of Jesus. He is our counsellor, comforter and teacher and guides us in all things, (John 14:26).

In the 1970's, I was hungry for more of God. Looking through my journals I came up with my first experience of being in a church that sang in the Holy Spirit as I mentioned in the last chapter. First time experiences are always so special and I would like to share it with you.

I had written: "I stood there all alone although I was surrounded by many people. I tried to tell myself that these people were crazy and must be worshipping a different God to me. I couldn't understand what they were singing but they sounded like angels. They were lifting their hands. I didn't think I could do that. Yet something inside was stirring me. I wanted to lift my hands, so why couldn't I?. Was it fear? Was it pride? Was I stubborn? Am I good enough?

Condemnation and fear had been my bad companions for many years. I had grown comfortable with them. I had never heard of a release in the Spirit of God. I had come out of religious bondage and it took all my courage just to attend the church among such seemingly spiritual people.

I was crying inside but no tears would come. I wanted to raise my hands like everyone else was doing but they were glued to my side. *Lord!* my heart cried, *I want to be like them. I want to meet with You, the way they seemed to be doing.*

Suddenly a holy Presence wrapped around me. I was aware of the singing coming into the familiar chorus, *'O come let us adore Him!'* It was an automatic reaction. My hands shot up. Tears began to stream down my face. My heart began to overflow as I sang out praises to God. My body seemed to tremble violently with the powerful presence of God. As my spirit soared higher and higher my voice grew louder and higher. My heart melted as I gazed in awe, transfixed by Jesus' beauty. I was lifted out of myself and into Him. I gave myself wholly over to Jesus."

This was my first experience with worshipping the Lord of lords with my whole being. It was some months later I was seeking the Lord for the baptism of the Holy Spirit. I had been praying, fasting and reading the book of Acts. My biggest fear in life was to be stuck in a rut. This has been the driving force that made me seek God more and rise to the next level in Him.

I did not want to be like a stagnant pool of water but a flowing river for God. I needed more of His presence. I needed His Spirit. I was quiet and shy and easily offended. I sat at the back of the church hoping no one would see me. I laugh now when I think about it. God must too. I was so hungry for a life in the Spirit as I had seen the changes in Jesus' disciples after power came and fell upon them as tongues of fire. They spoke in other tongues as the Spirit gave them utterance. Then they stood up boldly and spoke. That was it—I wanted that to happen to me! And it did! The joy came first so much so that it was hard to contain. I was younger—a lot. I could climb up on my bed and jump up and down!

After this event I had been praying for my brother, Matthew, and cousins to come to Jesus. I remember kneeling beside my bed, my body wracking with agony as I cried out to God to save them. I knew my prayers had to take action and one Sunday I scraped up enough courage and invited Matthew to come to church with me. To my absolute surprise and joy, he did. Why are we surprised when God answers prayer? These days, after many years of God's goodness, I just settle for the joy. The evening Matthew came, he brought our cousins as well. The pastor preached a timely message on salvation and the baptism of the Holy Spirit. I began to tremble as the power of God surged through me. The Pastor gave the appeal to come to the front to receive Christ, or if you would like to receive the Holy Spirit.

The music started and the congregation sang, *Let the fire fall, Let the fire fall, Let the fire from heaven fall!* What a stirring and powerful moment! I do not know how—whether I ran, flew, leapt or slid but I landed at the front of church with Matthew and cousins in tow. I sang that old Pentecostal hymn with gusto until I could no longer sing in English as my tongue seem to form words unknown to me. They came faster and faster. I heard someone say: *'Let it go, Margaret.'* Did I ever. It came out like a rushing torrent.

It came as a glorious song of heaven with such beautiful freedom that I had never experienced before. From that moment on I have never lost the gift that God has given me. It has only developed more and more as I grew in this new fellowship and walk with the Holy Spirit.

Matthew and cousins gave their lives to Jesus that night and the one who was kneeling near me was caught in the overflow and began to speak in tongues as well. She had no idea what was happening but flowed with it. From that moment onward we all have never looked back but moved on forward in God.

My mother had a similar experience when God filled her with His Spirit. She could not stop singing in the Spirit with her heavenly language all through the night. It was wonderful for her but not for me. She kept me awake all night. Baptism in the Holy Spirit means a total immersion of the Spirit of God which brings liberty. Speaking or singing in tongues is the evidence of this freedom to worship God in spirit and truth.

Matthew finished his Clerk of Work course as a bricklayer and builder. Before settling down he travelled around Australia and ended up in a small country town called, Narromine. He was only in town for a few days, but while he was there he visited a vibrant Church mid-week and was filled with the Holy Spirit. He was only about 20 years of age then. From that time he has powered on for God and has done extraordinary things.

It is amazing how God orchestrates our lives when we yield to His Spirit and plans. Over thirty years later I met a man, Peter, at a church in Maitland. One day I shared about Matthew's ministry in Indonesia. Peter afterwards commented he knew Matthew from Narromine. I was surprised and said I didn't think so as Matthew's ministry led him to Indonesia for years and other nations. Peter insisted and began to tell me how he met him. He witnessed Matthew being filled with the Holy Spirit at the church he was attending. They had worked on a job together and he was disappointed when Matthew did not show up at church on the following Sunday.

He wanted to meet up with him again but it took over thirty five years before that could happen. Life changes a lot in this length of time. God takes you on journeys you do not plan to go. Peter settled in the Maitland district and Matthew came back home, about a half an hour drive from where Peter lived. Their lives had never crossed and Peter wondered where he had ended up. And all those years later I met this man I did not know and told him about my brother. Never did Peter imagine that the young guy he met about five hours drive away would end up his brother- in-law! Not only that, I found out recently that the pastors of the church at Narromine were the same couple who had a music ministry and came to the church I had attended at the time. They held a seminar to release our music team in singing the prophetic song. Coincidence? Not at all. It was a God incident and this world is not so small or big to Him. He is a famous net-worker bringing like-minded people together.

After reading a few testimonies of what God has done in our lives, you may think you have missed your opportunity. My question would be: "Have you been filled with the Holy Spirit bringing freedom with the evidence of speaking in tongues?" If not, keep seeking God and study His word. Read the Book of Acts. It is still relevant today, even more so. Jesus does not want a bride who is lukewarm or asleep when He comes.

I have heard people say that tongues are not for today and are of the devil. Then why did Jesus say He will fill His disciples with the Holy Spirit? Why did John the baptist say that the one who will come after him will baptise you with fire. And it happened as we read earlier in Acts 2. It was prophesied by the prophet Joel hundreds of years before Christ was born.

The early church was speaking in the tongues of the different dialects of the people around Jerusalem. It can still happen that way. I know by my own experience when visiting my sister at the nursing home where she resided.

When Lorraine and I used to sing Christian songs, an elderly Filipino lady would come into the room and sing with us and her voice was beautiful. She also had dementia and I could not converse with her. As she deteriorated with the disease, I did not see her for some time. I was asking the Lord one day where she was and between Covid 19 lock downs, I was able to visit the nursing home again. Who should I see but this dear lady in the community room. Her face lit up when she saw me and began speaking in her native tongue, Tagalog. Even though I had done short missionary trips to the Philippines a couple of times, I could not speak the language. She seemed excited and by the inflections in her voice, along with her body language, made me aware she was asking questions. Without second thoughts I began to have a conversation with her in her own language. It just rolled out from me. I did not need an interpreter to understand the conversation because my spirit was in tune with the Holy Spirit. We were sharing about the glories of heaven! I went home with an overwhelming sense of the presence of God. After that experience I did not see her again.

This is one way that God can use us as we have seen by reading Acts 2. Other ways we can use tongues is in our own personal prayer times. It is given as a prayer language. Praying in tongues as the scripture says, edifies us, (1 Corinthians 14:2). In other words it makes us spiritually strong and aware of what is happening in the spiritual realm around us. The apostle Paul says he spoke in tongues more than any other person around him at the time. He could see the benefits of a heavenly language in order to communicate straight to God and pray according to God's will. Praying only with our minds can, not only tire us, but we run out of things to pray in ten minutes. Praying in tongues is a safe way in praying according to God's will. Sometimes we do not know how to pray so it is a blessing to be able to activate the river of prayer in tongues.

Speaking in tongues through the Holy Spirit glorifies the Lord Jesus. If you have doubts that speaking in tongues is of God, check out the evidence and life style of those around you who speak in tongues. Ask yourself if their lives manifest the fruit of the Spirit as in Galatians 5:22,23—love, joy, peace, patience, kindness, goodness, gentleness, faithfulness and self control.

The devil is a deceiver and a copycat, and some people have spoken in counterfeit languages. If you are still unsure, points to note are:

- The devil does not give you joy, or make you love Jesus more and want to serve Him.
- The devil does not allow you to praise and glorify Jesus from your lips.
- The devil does not set you free or heal you of trauma or disease.
- The devil does not like to testify about Jesus' redemptive plan for mankind.

Gifts of the Spirit —Read whole chapter of 1 Corinthians 14.

With the outpouring of the Holy Spirit God gave gifts to His church. They were gifts to minister and to build up His body. These gifts are still for today and they have not disappeared after the disciples died out. These gifts are stronger because the body of Christ has spread like a grass fire around the world. We are living in days of uncertainty. There are famines, earthquakes, cyclones, tornadoes, fire, floods, wars, terror attacks, persecution, sickness, disease and much more. The body of Christ needs to be lifted above all this—to be strong in faith. To be able to combat the powers of darkness rampaging on the earth, we need the gift of prophecy to edify the body of Christ. We need the gift of discernment of spirits to be able to deliver people from demonic strongholds. The body of Christ needs to be filled with the scriptures to draw upon when bringing the word of wisdom to someone who needs guidance.

The word of knowledge is so useful to discern something about a person that God wants to draw attention to: it opens the heart of a person to receive what God has for them or what He is saying. God's people do extraordinary things which requires tremendous faith and that can only come through God's supernatural intervention. Gifts of healing and working of miracles is a must in this day and age.

Our world in which we live is very sick. Our health system is in decline. Sick people can wait years just to see a specialist: then even after that, wait up to twelve months or more for surgery. There are major delays in the dispatch of ambulances because of the extreme waiting times in the emergency department of hospitals—sometimes up to six hours or more where there is a lack of staff. People are dying in the meantime. More mystery diseases and viruses are raging around. Mental illness in children is on the rise and it is hard to get help because of the high demand for child psychologists. In other countries of course, it is impossible to get medical attention at all. Praise God for the different aid workers, medical teams and organisations that go out into all the world and help humanity in their time of crises.

High cost of living is causing homelessness in our society in the west. Imagine what it is like elsewhere in other countries where famine and disease are rampant. Millions of refugees in war-torn countries, and for many reasons, have no country or home to rest. They find it hard to survive in this world, that at creation, God called—good. These are the lost sheep that are bleating out, and their cries are heard by our Father in heaven. This is the harvest field that Jesus said to lift up your eyes and see it. This is the harvest that Jesus said to pray to the Lord of the harvest to send out labourers into the fields. This is the harvest where He said the workers are few. The harvest is ready and waiting. Are we ready to reap it. We were born for such times as this—to bring healing to the nations.

God works through His church in the affairs of mankind. He went home to His throne in heaven. He sent the Holy Spirit to be poured out on all of His church—every individual. Every one of us has a responsibility; has supernatural gifts to use for His glory. I repeat what Jesus told His disciples—they will do greater works than He did. That includes you and me. We are the generation living today. We have the power available. We have been equipped with tools by receiving the gifts of the Spirit. We need them more than ever, and also to train others in those gifts we have received, to be continually making disciples to follow in the footsteps of Jesus.

CHAPTER 14

Prayer for all Nations

'It is written, "My house shall be called a house of prayer for all nations."' **Matthew 21:13**

The sound was growing louder and louder. It exploded like the gathering of rushing waters. Wave after wave pulsated through my body. My spirit soared into higher realms. I was driven with a supernatural passion I had never known before and flowed in the river of prayer with the thousands of Christians around me, crying out to God. We were of different nationalities, cultures and tongues but it made no difference. The consuming hunger for the presence of the Lord made us one—unity like this I had never experienced before. My body shook with the power of God like charges of electricity energising my spirit.

The hours swept by—one prayer meeting flowed into the next. The evening prayer meeting started at 6 pm and it was now 9 pm and still growing more and more intense. It was the fourth meeting for the day but we did not let up in our fervency.

This was the introduction to my month's stay. I had another 30 days to enjoy just living in heaven as it seemed. Now I understood the scripture in James 5:16b where it says in the Amplified Bible:

'The (heartfelt, continued prayer) of a righteous man makes tremendous power available (dynamic in its working).'

If one person can make tremendous power and be dynamic in using that power, imagine what 20,000 could do and I was only one of them. This was no special day but just a regular, week day prayer meeting. Bus loads of Koreans came every day to this house of prayer. The church connected with it had been in revival for thirty years since it started in a tin shed with only five members.

Seeking God with prayer and fasting brings the presence of God, and from humble beginnings, the church had grown to a massive congregation of over 500,000 members when I visited in 1987. Ten years later when a friend and I visited, it had grown to 700,000 people and was still growing. They had many choirs and more than one full orchestra. But as incredible as these sounded, it was the sound of the multitude praying that really captivated me. You can get to a place of total surrender to God where there is no end to the river of prayer that continually flows from inside of your whole being. Hours slip by unnoticed, for there is no awareness of time in the presence of God. He is the Lord of eternity and He has placed that within us.

This community of prayer is set among the hills on the border of North and South Korea and believe me, the hills were alive with the sound of music. While we were visiting, constant prayer and singing filled the whole complex and property. The sound of praises came from indoors and also outdoors as people wandered around the hills alone or together.

Worship releases us from earthly inhibitions and lifts us into new dimensions of the Holy Spirit where the river of life never dries up.

When we have entered into this dimension, scripture seems to flow into you, and through you, with such oneness with Jesus as the Living Word. I found during these moments of praying in tongues that scripture verses would come to mind and when I opened up the Bible randomly it would fall on the exact passages. This is the heavenly place where we are seated with Christ for eternity. The weight of God's presence fell heavily on me and I was one with the Father, Son and Holy Spirit. I heard their voice clearly saying: *'My house will be a house of prayer for all nations.'* The first time I heard those words jolted me from my sleep. The voice was so loud that I sat up startled and turned on the light. I grabbed and opened my bible because the voice came from the Word. The pages fell open to Isaiah 56. It speaks of salvation coming to all those who keep God's Sabbaths holy, live consecrated lives to Him through love and devotion. God includes all of mankind if they hold fast to His covenants which He has promised in verse 7:

'These I will bring to [My] holy mountain and give them joy in [My] house of prayer. Their burnt offerings and sacrifices will be accepted on [My] altar; for [My] house will be called a house of prayer for all nations.'

When reading this I responded by saying He had told me that several times before, even before I came to Korea. That is why I came to Korea in the first place. I had always sought the Lord as a child but there came a time when I was so low physically and emotionally, I needed a refreshing of God's Spirit. I wanted His glory so badly. I felt I was in a rut although I was seeking the Lord night and day. I was heavily involved in the music and prayer ministry at church but that did not bring joy. I felt my prayers did not reach heaven and just gathered together on the ceiling of my bedroom to taunt me. I had read every book on healing and applied the principles.

Yet I still had not been healed and had not slept for many months. I was suffering burnout and could not last much longer in that state.

Finally, a book that caught my attention was, "Korean Miracles," by Jasil Choi. As I began reading story after story of the miracles that were happening on the prayer mountain in South Korea my heart began to thump. Hope and faith rose! I knew beyond doubt I needed to go there to get healed—or so I thought.

God had other plans. He is such a good God and does hear us when we cry out to him. Sometimes not so pleasant things happen to us to break the cycle from what we are caught up with. In my situation, it was music ministry, teaching and other things that needed to be done. Sometimes we cling to what we are doing thinking no one can do without us, especially when told it would take four people to replace us. Although we sense something is not quite right in our lives we still cling to the old things we have always been doing. I sank to my lowest point before I heard God's voice through the Holy Spirit telling me to go to South Korea in April the following year. He was so direct and specific. God does not joke or clown around. I knew He was serious.

It was the Christmas season and a busy time at church with carol services coming up and training the singing groups and drama team for special events. I now was at the point of desperation. My whole body was wracked in pain with infection and sleep deprivation. Fellow believers, thinking they had my best interests at heart, kept saying, 'just have faith, and you'll be healed' — 'just confess the word'. Confessing the word was not helpful because I had been doing that for months and switched my trust in God, to having faith in my confession just to please them. Something had to break soon as I was getting to a point I wanted God to take me home to be with Him. Battling an infection in my trachea I would choke and struggled to take in my breath.

It was a very frightening experience especially while driving the car. One day while in the church offices I began choking and collapsed to the floor. Apparently I had gone blue and two pastors did all they could to revive me. *This was it*, I thought. *I was going to die*. It was at that moment I heard the Holy Spirit speak to me so clearly: *'Fight Margaret, I have not finished with you yet.'* I did fight and survived.

One Sunday morning service at church, I left the piano, stepped off the platform to stand at the altar for prayer. The Pastor called people from the congregation to come and pray for those gathered at the front if God had laid someone on their heart. A lovely lady, who was new to the church, approached me with a little trepidation and shared what God had put on her heart to say to me. It was just a few words that spoke volumes: "God wants you to go somewhere. I don't know where, but I believe it is overseas." She was spot on and I told her where God was asking me to go. She was thrilled that God had used her for the first time with a message for someone.

I booked my flight to Seoul, Korea for April in 1987, and the return flight a month later. Now I had to tell my mother whom I lived with, that God was sending me to South Korea, alone. The key word that would cause her anxiety would be—'alone'. I was not used to going anywhere alone. I was always surrounded by a team, either on one or leading one. However I was waiting for the right moment to tell her when she came inside our house from working in the garden. She was wearing a puzzled expression on her face and told me she had a vision. In her vision she saw lots of Asian faces and my face was with them! I shared what God was telling me and we rejoiced together, still with the idea I would be healed at prayer mountain.

I was at a church barbecue with the ministry team and as we were packing up to go home, I was approached by a visiting Pastor who also was the Australian superintendent of the Pentecostal church I was affiliated with.

He told me that the day before God had laid on his heart to pray for me, but every time he approached me, I would disappear. He knew nothing about me, had no idea I was ill, but when he laid hands on me, the power of God fell. He commanded healing to my body, broke off old chains that bound me, and released me into the new ministry God had planned for my life.

Wow! Praise the Lord! For the second time in my life I was free at last! I was totally healed, slept twelve hours a night for about a month to recuperate from the trauma of the past eighteen months. I flew off to South Korea well in body, soul and spirit, and released from ministry at the church to obey God's call on my life. The church had prayed for me, sent me off with their blessing and a love offering to help me on my journey.

During the event of being healed and flying out, I had done research on accommodation at the huge church in Seoul. Internet was not in vogue those days. I contacted a well-known Pastor who had been to this church in South Korea with a team several times before. She insisted that I should not go on my own. It would be hard for a foreign woman because most Koreans do not speak English. However she gave me an address to the big, Full Gospel Church in Seoul to give taxi drivers from the airport. I had already booked my flight, so I had to obey God and go whether I had accommodation or not booked beforehand.

I arrived in Seoul, Korea, at 9 o'clock at night. It was cold and I had no idea where to stay. I gave the address in my handbag to a taxi driver and he drove me to the church. I had been given photos of the whole complex and recognised the missions building where foreign visitors could stay. Fortunately, I was able to attract the attention of someone who could speak English, just to be t o l d I could not stay there because the building was under renovation. I was offered two options: one was to stay at the church for the all-night prayer meeting and catch a bus to prayer mountain the next day. What! I was travel-wearied, cold, hungry and wanted a bed. Option two was to try the hotel across the road. The hotel also gave me the brush off and said they had no room. "Lord I cried, you sent me here only to be left stranded."

The church rejected me; the nearby hotel rejected me. What was I to do. A bellboy at the hotel took pity on me and put me in a taxi and after some discourse with the driver, sent me to the other side of the city.

I arrived at another hotel which was costing me $100 for the night! A lot of money those days. I was too tired by then, and resigned to the fact that I could at least go home the next day. No, my pride would not let me go down that trail of thinking. I told the leadership at our church that God had told me to come to this country and they accepted that. So I decided in the morning that I would taxi back to the church and take the bus to the prayer mountain which was an hour away. With that I laid in bed, peace covered me like and blanket and I slept soundly. This of course was where God wanted me.

The next morning I awoke with a sense of excitement of what God was going to do. I arrived back at the church lugging my over-sized suitcase. Everything looked bright and wonderful—and huge. Someone spoke English and showed me where to catch the bus to the prayer mountain. It was a free ride on the shuttle service running to and from Prayer Mountain every hour. As soon as I sank into a seat, I sighed with relief—I'm home! Choir music was playing through the PA and it was beautiful.

I am sure every reader has had that exhilarating feeling of joy when you know beyond doubt that you are in God's will and He is directing your path as we read in Proverbs 3:5-6:

'Trust in the Lord with all your heart and lean not on your own understanding; in all your ways acknowledge Him and He will make your paths straight.' God promised me joy in the house of prayer as written in Isaiah

56:7 and I certainly had my own full dose of it among the thousands gathered. Everyone else seemed serious as they cried out to God. My turn came later when I entered one of their prayer grottoes.

God's plans are always for our eternal good, whereas our vision is limited and we want personal comfort and gratification, right now. This can cause us to go through trauma. When the sun shines on a clear mountain stream you can see the coloured rocks on the bed of the stream, but when the sun is blocked by clouds the water looks dark and murky.

Early morning where I live, a fog often comes creeping across the valley and blocks out the morning sun. It is like our spiritual vision can be clouded by our own way of doing things and not seeing God in it all and surrendering to Him.

I was never the same again after spending time on the South Korean prayer mountain. I need to write another book on the experiences I had in that short month alone and the three weeks with a friend ten years later. I learned there is nothing the world can offer that can give you peace and fulfilment as being in a place where the heavens are open and prayers and unspoken desires are granted instantly.

As I sought God for His glory, I agonised in the little underground rooms called prayer grottoes. The more the glory wrapped around me the more I saw my unholiness. The Lord began to challenge me in a similar manner when Jesus asked Peter if He loved Him. God went through each member of my family and asked if I would give them up to follow Him. Finally, when through my tears, I said yes to all, then peace and joy would come. I needed to surrender my ministry to Him—my hands for music; my voice for singing. Then He asked whether I would give up my country that I so loved. I cried and cried but I gave in and surrendered that also. At times I could not let go but I asked God to make me willing and, in

His grace and mercy, He did. It was like going through the threshing floor which is the foundation of every temple of the Lord.

I felt so much love for Jesus once I yielded my will to His. I said I'll even go to Turkey if He wants me there. Somehow in the back of my mind I thought Turkey was the worst place in the world to go. I envisioned cutthroats and pirates on every street. Twelve years later God did send me to Turkey on team with the Australian Prayer Network to declare His word from the ancients sights, and spend many hours of worshipping with thousands of Christians from other nations. It was wonderful to worship God for four hours in the same arena at Ephesus where the apostle Paul confronted the crowds for their idol worship of Diana queen of heaven.

After a time of totally surrendering to God, He began to show me the plans for a house of prayer for all nations.

I also saw God's healing power at work on Prayer Mountain. People would turn up to pray carrying their weak, adult relatives on their backs. Other elderly men and women would come bent over almost horizontal to the ground from their labour in the fields. But I would never see them leave like that. Hundreds would bring bedding to lie on the floor in the space at the front of the chapel between the platform and the beginning of the pews. Leaders would walk among them to lay on hands. Deliverance would happen during the services and others would be wailing as they repented of their sins. It was noisy as you would expect with such a crowd. If a child was sick and could not go to school a parent would bring them to prayer mountain to be healed. Before each meeting the musicians and ministering pastors would kneel on the platform and spend time with the Lord before starting the service. The presence of God and glory never waned because the people brought Him with them. As I could not understand the language, I cannot testify the types of healing I had seen, but I did know that in my own life something had changed. I was ready to go back home and share what God was doing.

We can read so many books on how to worship God and how to pray, but the biggest teacher is the Holy Spirit. Seeing Him at work through others and being with others who carry the anointing in prayer has the biggest impact on our lives. Their very presence around you is like a magnetic force that draws you into their anointing. It is like coming under their umbrella or as the scripture says—mantle. This mantle is from God and is to be always passed on.

We read the story of Elijah, the prophet, and his apprentice, Elisha, in 2 Kings 2. When God had taken Elijah up into heaven in a whirlwind, Elisha was distressed. Elijah had been his mentor and teacher, and he drew strength from the prophet. Like a puppy, he followed him wherever he went. God had taken Elijah from him and he was all alone. Elisha had already asked Elijah for a double portion of his anointing or spirit when Elijah told him the Lord was taking him away. He needed a moment to grasp the impact of that request as he mourned for his master. Without wasting anymore time he picked up Elijah's mantle from where it had fallen. Suddenly his focus changed. He looked for the *God* of Elijah instead of Elijah and said, *'Where is the God of Elijah'.*

He was soon to know, for when he slapped the waters of the Jordan River like Elijah had done previously the waters parted. He had received what he had asked for—the double portion of Elijah's anointing! The God of Elijah was also his God. Then the miracles began and the prophets and people around could see that he became like Elijah and called for his help. I carried the mantle of prayer I had received in South Korea back to Australia and with it came a strong message from Jesus, *'My house will be a house of prayer for all nations!* I myself became a house of prayer. When I arrived home, my mother came under the prayer anointing and between the two of us we became a powerful force. The church had been a praying church well before I went to South Korea and understood the depth of this style of prayer, so the river of prayer continued to flow throughout the church.

The following year, God had laid on my heart to do some training in ministry, majoring in evangelism. I was a bit disappointed. I had done so many courses and I wanted to apply the knowledge I had stored up—always learning to fish and not going out to fish. I did not want to go away from home to do Bible College. I could not afford to live away for long periods.

News got back to me that a practical, ministry-teaching school with prospects of outreach was starting the following year. Perfect! Not only that, it was to be held in the Newcastle region. Hallelujah! As I lived in Charlestown, a suburb of Newcastle, I was pleased. God had that all planned as well, and perfectly tailored the school to accommodate my wishes—so I wanted to believe. Actually God had planted His desires in my heart according to His will not mine. The school was to be held for four months, five days a week from 9 am to 12 noon. Again, perfect times. I should be able to get back home to teach private music lessons as usual in the afternoon. I filled in the application and sent it off. I still had no idea where the school was to be held. I had not so long to wait. The principal, Gary Faull, rang to ask whether I could lead worship every day of the school. Someone had recommended me. He also told me where the school was to be held. In the same church where I was involved! Why are we so amazed when God does what He always does!

It was another life-changing experience! Life School of Evangelistic Ministries was an inter-denominational school with students from the age of eighteen to late sixties. I came in half way. Students came from almost every state in Australia and one from England. Speakers also came from far and wide and taught us the word of God to equip us for everything we needed in order to minister—healing, baptism of the Holy Spirit, gifts of the Spirit and how to use them; how to share the gospel, baptise new converts and cast out demons. And above all, the importance of worship and prayer. We also were taught the importance of knowing God more deeply and especially knowing Him as our Father. Most of us who attended received deep healing from past trauma and other areas that restricted God from moving in our lives. We were released into the community to apply what we had been taught. We saw lots of healing and people coming to the Lord. We visited various churches and were able to share the word of God, testimonies, and operate in the gifts of the Spirit.

During that time we made prayer a priority and many of us, in our spare time went up to lookouts over the city to pray and worship the Lord. We were full on. There was one thing Gary Faull stressed: that our character must always be above our ministry. He certainly practised what he preached and I have always been impressed by his humility in leadership. It was such godly advice I have always remembered and passed on to others. After completing the school four months later, most of the students went back to their home towns or to wherever God had led them.

God had still impressed upon my heart—*His house was a house of prayer for all nations.* Fifteen of us joined together to form a team to travel the East Coast of Australia from Victoria to Mareeba, North Queensland. Our starting point was Melbourne for six weeks. During this time we stayed with Youth With A Mission and trained in drama to be used in evangelism. Then began our travels heading north. It was a very fruitful time in our lives where we were able to put to practice the gifts that God had given us. We ministered in churches, hospitals, nursing homes, schools, universities, correction centres and street outreaches. Not only was it a time of growing in God ourselves by working in a team, we were able to bless the body of Christ, heal the sick, cast out demons and preach the gospel. We saw many people come to Christ which always brings joy above anything else. We felt like the first apostles of Jesus in the book of Acts. Each day it was wonderful to wake up early before everyone else and pray for a few hours before breakfast. These times were so refreshing and it prepared me for the day ahead and opened the way for the rest of the team.

After travelling in Australia we spent some time in the Philippines where we saw God do amazing things. Hearts were so open to the gospel and faith was high for healing. As hundreds came out to be healed, and because we were always on the move, we did not always see the results of our ministry. Sometimes interpreters could not keep up with the flow of testimonies to tell us the news.

One testimony caught my attention when I heard sister Margaret's name mentioned. Apparently I had laid hands on a child's broken arm and he was healed completely!

Wow! Even broken bones get healed! Just like Jesus said to do—lay hands on the sick and they will recover! I soon came down to earth after one meeting where I was praying for the sick. There were so many people lying on the floor around me after they were prayed for that I did not take any notice when the lady I laid hands on for healing, fell to the floor. But her family and friends were alert. They quickly knelt on the floor around her commanding life into her. She recovered, stood to her feet and began dancing like many others around her. We had been taught to always look at the person's face when praying for them to see if there is a demonic problem to do deliverance. When someone has notable healing on the spot their face lights up with a broad smile. I must have had my eyes closed or been distracted with so many people crowding in. I was told the next day that she had turned blue around the mouth and died. Some of us are not used to raising the dead but those dear Filipinos knew what to do. She had a heart attack.

Everywhere we went, even in Australia, I was able to share about God's dramatic healing in my own life a couple of years before, and that seemed to draw the crowds out to be healed. We were involved in water baptisms as well. Just in one area alone in the Philippines, we baptised about two hundred new converts. The joy was tremendous and contagious. We had lost count of how many were filled with the Holy Spirit.

I had always been assigned to teach on prayer. At one church I was asked to do a four-hour seminar on prayer. What! I nearly collapsed. I would run out after about an hour. There was one consolation, using an interpreter would halve the time. I told Gary of my problem and he gave me his folder with notes on prayer. Somewhat relieved, I began an incredible journey on the back of a three-wheel contraption, a jeepney, then the train. I finally arrived at my destination. I sighed with relief seeing only about sixty people gathered.

They were already in full swing, singing, clapping and dancing. By this time the perspiration was oozing out of the pores of my skin after travelling in the extreme heat and humidity. How could they dance like that?

After being treated like royalty, I began to teach. Unfortunately it was slow going because the interpreter was having difficulty with my Australian accent and everyone kept laughing. I had issues with that because in teaching music I liked undivided attention. Besides, the young man interpreting became embarrassed and it was torture for him. As usual God came to the rescue at the right moment.

A man came through the door and I recognised him. Oh no, I thought. He was the superintendent of the all of the Assemblies of God churches in the Philippines—thousands in his base church. I felt so small and my legs began to tremble. I had nothing to fear. He offered to interpret and the anointing just flowed. I ran out of my notes and started on the notes given to me but it felt like a tap had turned off. There was nothing wrong with the notes of course but God wanted me to rely on Him. I closed the folder and just let the Holy Spirit take over. I prophesied to the church. The longest I had ever spoken.

A few months later on our second trip to the Philippines, we were at a meeting, and a pastor came up to me and he was excited. "Sister Margaret! Since you prophesied and prayed for our church we have grown from 60 to four hundred in the congregation!" Praise God! He gets all the glory!

I soon learned from that experience that the same Holy Spirit who raised Christ from the dead, not only lives in the big names in the church, but also me. I can do all things through Christ who strengthens me. He can do all things through everyone who is reading this book. The key is waiting on God, spending time with Him and meditating on His word.

India was the next adventure. Because women's ministries in those days were not so accepted, and half of our group were women, we were limited. But that was okay because prayer was essential and flu seeped into our camp. Some days I was able to spend the whole day weeping for India.

However, we were able to perform our musical in the most incredible places even in a garbage dump where people lived. We just set up a platform big enough for the drama and dressed in our costumes in a Hindu temple. We took advantage of the situation by lifting up the name of Jesus and declaring God' glory in the place to break the power of Satan. We then performed the musical. This was one place where Muslims and Hindus worked together in relative harmony. It was quite amusing because when the appeal came to give their lives to Christ, the leaders of the other religions tried to force their members to go to the front for prayer. Others were pulling off demonic charms around each other's necks. We had no idea what was going on or whether we had done something wrong. Mothers also were pressing through the chaos to give their babies to us to bless.

I loved going to the villages. We performed drama; shared testimonies of what God had done in our lives. Again, my testimony of God's healing raised the faith level in the crowd and many would come out to be healed and saved.

One of our team members, Joan, and I had an experience whilst out walking. Joan had been a nurse in Cambodia and Vietnam when she was younger, and had no fear of wandering off on her own during free time. We were warned to always stay with the group so I was reluctant to do go with her, but on this occasion I did. I soon regretted that when after a long time of trying to find our way back to our hotel we were well and truly lost. We offered up a one word prayer to the Lord, "Help!" He did.

Suddenly, a young boy of about ten years old appeared in front of us and beckoned to follow him. Puzzled as well as intrigued, we did.

He did not speak but beckoned. There was a group of other boys slightly older watching us and we could tell they were jibing him. He stopped and spoke to them a few words in Hindi. Their attitude quickly changed and they greeted us in English. We asked what our young escort had said to them: they told us that the boy said he had been sent to guide us. Amazing we thought—but who sent him? We had wandered well away from where we first started out but the guide took us straight back to the hotel. Joan was wise to the ways of India and reached into her purse for money to pay him. We both stood with mouths agape. He had totally vanished! No sign of him anywhere. We then realised who sent him! No wonder he knew where to take us and his whole presence was so confident.

The whole team travelled north to the Bihar State. The Bihar State is Northern India, a vast area of 80 million people and was the centre of Hinduism and Jainism. We reached our destination and was delighted at how lovely the place was. It was a rural area and we stayed at a Christian mission which comprised a church of about one hundred and fifty members, a school and an orphanage. At the time we were there, the mission was the only outreach among 15 million people and had twenty five outreaches throughout the state. This was a more relaxed experience—a time to rest. The young ones on the team took advantage of that and caught up with some sleep. Joan and I being older and more adventurous, needed to walk and explore. I was more keen to go with her this time as there was nowhere we could get lost.

A village close by with an assortment of dwellings was our obvious goal. Joan soon found a young man from the mission who was willing to accompany us as an interpreter. The locals living near the mission were not used to white faces so came out to stare at us. That was okay and we just smiled and said hello in their language as we were instructed to. However, a grandmother who lived at the end of the village went to the mission Church. She was so thrilled for us to visit and greeted us affectionately. She then brought out some food and water for us. Even though we were warned not to accept food from the locals, we did in the name of Jesus as it was her way of blessing us with hospitality.

Every day throughout the duration of our stay in this area, we would go through the village greeting the locals who now were used to us and more relaxed. One day we reached the grandmother's house but she had not come out to greet us. Surprised we went around the house to find her. She was lying on the ground on a straw and cow-dung mat and was very ill. Joan, a nurse, examined her and said we must pray as she had malaria. We did and had an instant result. The dear lady jumped up and disappeared inside the house. She came out with her grandchild in her arms. The baby was only about six weeks old and laboured for breath. Joan looked at the yellow eyes and taut yellow skin on her little face and shook her head. I got the message and we both commanded life into this little body, and malaria to go in Jesus' name. The grandmother whisked the baby away before we had a chance to see the results. She came out of the house praising the Lord with food in her hands for us. What joy! How wonderful God is!

That night, we held an outreach meeting and who should be there — the Grandmother, her healthy, baby granddaughter, the parents of the child and the rest of their relatives. It was amazing to see how happy they were.

Word had spread around of the Grandmother and baby's healing. The next day Joan and I set out for our walk and were thrilled to see a line of people waiting for us to come so they could be healed. Mothers with the little ones were needing prayer and we were only too willing to pray. There was no adequate medical help within miles and they were desperate. Unlike in the West, there was no access to baby formulas and one little mother was distressed because she had no milk to breast feed her new baby. We laid hands on her and prayed for her but had to wait to see the results.

The next day the line was even longer and the first to greet us with a huge smile was this mother. She had milk for her baby! What was more astounding about our ministry here was that the men began to break their culture and ask for prayer. A man with poor vision was healed; another with a red and badly swollen leg was healed; heart conditions and other sicknesses were healed. We could tell by their big grins. Our interpreter was able to share the gospel with them.

There was something taking root in my heart in this rural community. I realised that I preferred to meet the people person to person, to minister to them, rather than in large, crusade-type meetings. Large gatherings have their place and I love to join massive prayer meetings. But for sharing the gospel and healing the sick, I preferred to be outdoors in their own environment than in a building. God was preparing me for what He had planned for the next stage of my life.

The last day of our stay, the leadership of men from the church were going out to play cricket with those of our team. The ladies in our team joined them and their wives, in the playing field to have a picnic before the game. As soon as the men left to play cricket, the women flocked around us. They complained that they felt called to minister like they had seen us doing but were forbidden to do so. It was the culture in this State. God had already spoken to me about releasing the women into a prayer ministry but had no opportunity to do so. It was obvious that God had planned this moment so I did not hesitate. I quickly shared what God was saying and all the ladies on our team laid hands on them. Something had broken over their lives and they were filled with joy and expectation. It was not until 2012 that I realised the full impact of that prayer.

It was time for us to leave India and head back to the Philippines before going on to Australia. We were in the city and I was up on the rooftop of the house where we were staying. It was early morning and the sun was beginning to lighten the hazy sky over the roof tops of the city.

We were due to fly out that day and it was my last chance to pray over the city and declare God's glory. I asked the Lord what other plans He had for me when I arrived back home. The Holy Spirit led me to Jeremiah 9:17-18. I was aware what the passage said. As Jeremiah was called the weeping prophet, I could identify with him in that. It was verse 17 that stood out to me.

'Consider now! Call for the wailing women to come; send for the most skilful of them. Let them come quickly and wail over us till our eyes overflow with tears and water streams from our eyelids ...'

This scripture along with: *'My house shall be called a house of prayer for all nations...'* has been the foundational scriptures to start building the house of prayer at home.

Our time in India was an experience I am thankful to have had. God had shown us that He can use those who are insecure, reserved and not fully grown in Him—just ordinary people, to do exceedingly, above all we could ask or think, as we humbly yielded to Him. Faith was high in developing countries where there is poverty, lack of material means and medical help. We hear of other missionaries leading thousands to the Lord and equally as many miracles. But everybody is a somebody to God and every time one person hurts, He is there to heal.

A few months following our time in India, I had read an article in a news letter that in the Bihar state of India a women's prayer network had started and had grown from a handful of women to a mighty force of about three hundred women. I felt so blessed that God's house of prayer was active in the most darkest place of India. The ministry of prayer is for everyone. Every ministry needs the foundation of prayer, because without it, we have no power. I felt privileged to be there at the beginning.

CHAPTER 15

House of Prayer

It was the beginning of 1989 and my mother and sister, Lorraine, began classes at the Life School of Evangelistic Ministries I had attended the year before. I was asked to take the daily prayer meetings for an hour before the starting of the classes. I was only too willing because I was able to keep in touch with everyone who repeated the school. This time it was not held at Charlestown but only fifteen minutes away and I had to take Mum there anyway. Mum and Lorraine had a life-changing experience as I had.

During that time I felt God wanted me just to devote to prayer and reading the scriptures for several months. My mother felt to sell our home in Charlestown and move up to our property at Mount Royal for a while, and devote her time to prayer as well. My father had already gone to Jesus several years before and it was a big decision for her to sell our house that he had lovingly built. As we did not have a proper house up in the mountains, just a tin shed to live in, conditions were rough. However, between working the land, painting the shed, worshipping and praying, God not only ministered to us, but provided for our needs.

When our water tanks ran dry we prayed for rain and by the end of the day a storm would come and fill up our tanks. When we needed company, someone stopped by for a chat.

One day in the distance on the ridge opposite, we could see a fire burning down towards the creek. Davis Creek is a flowing mountain stream in the gully that divided the two mountain ridges, but with the north-west wind blowing strongly, it was no deterrent to a fire bent of destruction. If it jumped the creek it would race up the hill in fury fanned by the upward current of wind. We were situated half way up the north ridge and we had no way of escape. There was no one to turn to up there alone, only God. In the distance the fire was coming closer and the wind still blew fiercely. We stood in agreement with the authority of God and commanded the wind to stop and change direction. Then we commanded fire to go back where it had already burned. To our relief and joy it did and finally fizzled out. We learned that even the wind and fire obeyed us when done in the name of Jesus. Knowledge I needed to apply for future events.

There is no end to the lessons God taught us about His power through His word and His Spirit. He taught us how to use the mantle of authority He had passed on to us through Jesus. Jesus spoke to the wind and waves to be still and they died down, (Mark 4:39). We have been given authority over serpents, demons and everything that rises up against us. Even the elements we can command to stop in their destruction.

Jesus said in Luke 10:18-19:

'I saw Satan fall like lightning from heaven. I have given you authority to trample on snakes and scorpions and to overcome all the power of the enemy, nothing will harm you.'

Often it is a very tough lesson when battling steep muddy roads after rain with the car sliding sideways down the hill. One side would be thick mud and deep ruts and the other side a steep slope into the gully and forest.

God was always there showing us how to overcome the natural obstacles as we trusted Him. Also, this was my brother Matthew's training ground for missions work in the jungles of Borneo, Indonesia, the Amazon and the steep mountain roads of Nepal.

Now and again individuals would come to join us to seek God for their own spiritual journey. They would go home changed and the overflow of the Holy Spirit would touch the churches where they fellowshipped. I had learned through our experiences that God's presence was as strong with just two of us as it was for me among thousands. We had an open heaven. The scriptures flowed through us into songs and prayer. God would speak to us through visions and dreams which were confirmed through His word. God would give us wisdom to deal with frustrating issues and incidences in practical ways.

This was our own personal, private prayer mountain in the middle of the Upper Hunter Valley region. It is an isolated area and roads are rough. What we lacked in material things and comfort, God sure provided in many other ways. We always had the opportunity to share the love of Jesus and pray with people, whether it was with neighbours passing through or when going into town sixty two kilometres away. We lived freely without distractions or restrictions on time and commitments. We did have the phone to keep in touch with family but it only worked sometimes. We had taken the passage from Jeremiah 29:7 seriously:

'... Seek the peace and prosperity of the city to which I have carried you into exile. Pray to the Lord for it, because if it prospers, you also will prosper.'

We were not in a city but were surrounded by country towns quite some distance away and our position was central like the hub of a wheel. We kept interceding for these towns and God had given us a great love for them. We kept declaring His glory over the towns. We had regular communication with a pastor of a thriving church in the closest town and would fellowship twice a week if the weather was permitting.

God still stressed on my heart to build His house of prayer. We were hoping to build where we were, but God had other plans. That came to reality when one day, He spoke to my heart to go back down from the mountains, settle in the valley and share the vision of the house of prayer wherever His Holy Spirit would lead us. He shared Habukkuk 2:2-3 with me:

'Write down the vision and make it plain on tablets, That he may run who reads it. For the vision is yet for an appointed time; But at the end it will speak and it will not lie. Though it tarries, wait for it; it will surely come. It will not tarry.' (NKJV)

I was a little disappointed as I really believed Mount Shammah, the name of our prayer mountain, was the house of prayer for all nations that God was impressing on my spirit. Often we hear God speak clearly but we do not grasp the full understanding or implications of what He is saying. He sometimes gives only the first step to motivate action on our part. I more or less had formed a picture of what the house of prayer for me to build was, and it was just the sixteen hectares in the middle of the forest at Mount Royal. He had given me the name in South Korea that it was to be called Mount Shammah. I knew it was God speaking because I had never heard of the word before and did not find out until a friend, Elizabeth, who was one of the pastors from our church at Charlestown, rang me and told me the meaning.

Something caught her notice and it is found in the book of Ezekiel chapter 10. The temple of the Lord was defiled by idolatry and the glory of God had departed. It was a sad thing when God's presence disappeared from the house which was designed for people to come and worship Him. God always restores and in Chapter 48, details of a city were revealed to Ezekiel. It was to be called: "THE LORD IS THERE". In Hebrew it is YAHWEH SHAMMAH. God once again will fill His house with His glory.

Shammah, which means: *God will bring about a mighty victory,* was one of King David's fighting men. Please do not confuse the city—'Yahweh Shammah' in Ezekiel, with 'Mount Shammah House of Prayer' which the Lord has given to us. God gave me the name while I was in South Korea for my own property as I had been always seeking to go higher into His glory and Mount means—to ascend or to go up; a kingdom, state or city and the kingdom of Christ or church.

We did buy a block of land and settled in Branxton, a small community in the Hunter Valley. Our street name was Church Street. The street name became significant to us when were studying a map of Branxton in the Real Estate office during the early years of town planning. On the original plan, the land we bought, and four blocks surrounding, were reserved to build an Apostolic Church. That did not eventuate, but instead, was divided up into smaller blocks and we took the only one left which had been left vacant for some time. What a blessing and appropriate. Within just days of settling in, the church with whom we were affiliated in a town twenty two kilometres away, asked would we be able to have a Bible study group in our home. Of course we said yes as we had been isolated for many months. Well, what a glorious time we had. I led the worship. My mother, after her mountain top experience, was on fire and showed it by praising the Lord in dancing. We had lively meetings that grew to about thirty at one stage as local Christians from Baptist, Salvation Army and Anglican Churches joined us. The Anglican Church was going through revival at the time and God was baptising them with His Holy Spirit. This meeting in our home was led by the Assemblies of God church, but at the time we mixed with the other churches around us. There was such a unity of spirit and a hunger for prayer and the presence of God.

The Assemblies of God led a combined ladies meeting in the area which was also well attended. What impressed me was the attentive care and respect everyone had for each other. We were one, big, happy family living in close proximity to one another. I led the worship at the ladies' meeting and any other special Christian week day events in the Anglican Church. Those were happy days of mixing with the whole body of Christ and working together.

In 1991, I had a phone call from a fellow musician and prayer warrior, to ask would I be interested in being a prayer coordinator for every town along the New England Highway of the Upper Hunter region. It was for an Evangelical thrust called, "Breakfree 92", into the whole of the Hunter Valley. There were eight country towns assigned to me and quite some mileage between a few of them. I was only too willing and began attending meetings in Newcastle in preparation for this big event. There were not enough public relations officers so I stepped in and doubled up with my role as prayer coordinator. Everyone who had a function in the preparations of Breakfree were anointed and prayed over for the work ahead. We were sent out with a fresh anointing of the Holy Spirit and for me, a new adventure in God where I had never been before.

I was excited but a little nervous all the same. Breakfree 92 was designed to bring the whole body of Christ together for the purpose of harvesting souls for the kingdom of God. Every town was to be responsible to create ideas that would be used to outreach into their communities. As a PR, my role was to visit the leadership of every church in the eight towns assigned to me and invite them to join in with this project. I had good results as every part of the clergy across the denominations were only too willing to stir up the members of their churches to participate.

Each town held regular meetings or prayer breakfasts for me to come and share progress reports. It also was an opportunity for the leaders to pool all their ideas of outreaches to their specific town.

We also formed a network of prayer from these meetings. First of all, a prayer leader from each church was elected, then they would relate to one prayer leader of their town who organised prayer meetings. That made it easier for me to only have to communicate to eight prayer leaders instead of many. Then I was accountable to the Breakfree prayer director and the overall director and leaders of the whole event.

Everyone plunged into the project with their own flavour to make it a success. We held months of regular prayer meetings, prayer breakfasts and prayer seminars leading up to the visiting Evangelist spearheading this undertaking. The whole time Breakfree rallies were in action, prayer vigils were happening around the clock according to rosters in place. It was an amazing time seeing all denominations involved and working shoulder to shoulder in unity and fervour.

A major input leading up to Breakfree 92 which coincided with the preparations beforehand, was a visiting prayer team, Spirit Alive, spearheaded by Brian Pickering. They travelled through the Hunter Valley at the invitation of local churches in many towns all over the vast region. Coming into the valley for six, 40 hour weekends, they led worship and prayer. Christians of different denominations and prayer groups came from far and wide to join the local people in the unity of seeking God. Spirit Alive's ministry of worship and prayer was inspirational, giving insight into the areas of spiritual mapping and the prophetic. We would come together in a building, start every session of prayer with an hour of worship, before grouping into small teams and then going out to strategic places suggested by the locals living in the towns. Many times, these places had a dark background. We were there to pray into that by digging out the roots of the problems and breaking the strongholds which bound the area. Events of the past, unless broken can hinder the town from moving on spiritually. We all had different gifts in prayer and were allowed to use them.

If the place was dark, one or more persons could have a vision of what had caused this darkness and others would pray into that. It was like putting pieces of a puzzle together as each one could add to the other's prayers. Everyone would participate in different ways of declaring God's light, reading scriptures loudly or sing appropriate songs to bring God's light and glory over the town or area.

There were so many needs throughout the towns that God drew our attention to. There was not only trouble with the youth, drugs and alcohol addictions and domestic violence, but apathy to the gospel of Jesus Christ. We also travelled into the rural areas. If it was not drought drying up rivers and creeks causing financial devastation to the workers of the land, it would be floods destroying thousands of dollars worth of crops. Sometimes this would happen a few years in a row dragging them into debt with the banks. This was enough to drive desperate farmers trying to make ends meet, to suicide.

I felt at home with this type of ministry; meeting the people and listening to their heart-breaking stories At other times we heard how God had changed lives and brought so much blessing. We prayed in businesses, police stations, schools, hospitals, nursing homes and so much more. We were all from different church affiliations and different towns but we worked together in harmony. That can only happen by the Spirit of God.

We were out on the field and we used what was happening around us as God's guidance into prayer. It was like fine tuning on the radio to hear a clearer sound but tuning into the Spirit of God to hear what He was saying. For example: if we saw a stagnant pool of water it would remind us of the flowing river of living waters of God, and pray that into the town. We could be in the middle of praying for a struggling pastor or church and an eagle would fly over and someone would respond and read Isaiah 40:31: *'Those who wait upon the Lord shall renew their strength. They shall mount up with wings like eagles; they shall run and not be weary, they shall walk and not faint.'*

This ministry involvement was preparing the towns for Breakfree the following year. It opened doors and hearts to continue to pray across the body of Christ. There was an open heaven over the whole Hunter Valley during many years to follow.

Why was this happening? Unity of the body of Christ. There is only ONE CHURCH and I began to fully understand that as I continued to work among different churches.

In my own life during this time I had answers to Jesus' command of, *'My house will be a house of prayer for all nations,'* came into clearer focus. I had a habit of drawing lines on a map to connect towns where I had travelled. I had done it in India and the Philippines. I had done the same with the map of the Upper Hunter Valley where Spirit Alive had taken us. My mother was with me at the time and suggested I turn the map up the right way. I was astounded. The formation of the connected lines to each town was the basic outline of a house! If you asked a child to draw a house, that is what they would draw. A light flicked on in my brain. This was the House of Prayer I was to build! Not a man-made building on a small property in the middle of the mountains but a whole community of towns! And not only that, Mount Shammah was positioned right in the centre of this house on the map. This is where it all began for me two years before by obeying God's call to pray for the towns surrounding our prayer mountain. From our humble tin shed in the bush from where the glory radiated into the communities below.

Oh the joy of that revelation! To be able to go into those towns we had prayed for and seek out God's people to bless them—joining them in worship and prayer. Wherever our feet walked we blessed the land, the farms and waterways—houses, businesses, schools, emergency services, police, medical fields and the list goes on. God is so good. If we walk with Him He joins all the dots together and makes straight our paths like lines on the map.

For the next twelve months I was caught up with, not only trying to earn a living through teaching music in our home, but the organisation and participation of the events connected with Breakfree. In the town where we lived, we established a prayer meeting and began to meet at the rectory of the Anglican Church. Afterwards, we felt to hold it in a neutral place to make it ecumenical. One of the ladies offered her place not far from town. Nina and her husband, Warwick lived on 30 acres of land and had plenty of room. Neighbours were some distance away, so we had the freedom to go with the flow of the Holy Spirit and not disturb them when we prayed loudly.

Breakfree was over and I kept in touch with prayer leaders of the towns to encourage them to keep on praying. Spirit Alive moved on from their ministry in the Hunter Valley and travelled to other towns out west and interstate. When we were able to go, some of us from our area would join them. I have always treasured, held and applied all that they have taught us.

At the end of 1992 my mother showed signs of a having a stroke and had to ease up in yard and garden work. Her health was deteriorating and after a series of tests the diagnosis was sinister. She had an aggressive brain tumour which took her life five months later. I was devastated. I had lost my strongest praying companion.

Through my grief I still kept up my commitments in teaching and the local prayer meetings where my friends were such a support. God was faithful during this time and carried me. I depended on Him more and His word became my source of healing comfort.

One day after five years of grieving I was sitting on the ridge at Mount Shammah overlooking the valley and the blue forested hills across the creek. The gentle breeze softly caressed my face bringing a refreshing moment in the heat. The buzzing sounds of insects around me were a reminder of praying people on the mountain in South Korea. Candy, my little, furry friend, was sleeping beside me restlessly flicking the annoying insects off her ears. Suddenly, I heard God speak clearly and He said: "I have bruised you and now I will heal you." I was surprised with my own response, when I answered: "I'm so glad it was you Lord. I would have been offended if you allowed Satan to hurt me so much." From that moment onwards the grief had lifted from off my life.

No matter what we go through, God is there with us and at the right time He heals when it gives Him the greatest glory. And it did. I have learned that people suffer from all types of pain in this life and our responsibility is to bring healing and comfort as God has healed and comforted us. At times we try to rush His healing bringing discouragement to the one we pray for.

Our local prayer meeting developed into a thriving fellowship and Christians came from far and wide. A new ministry of—'Living Springs Ministry' had sprung up. The street I lived in was Church Street and connected with a street called Spring Street. One early morning I was walking and asking God for the name of the ministry He was birthing in my heart when the sign post, 'Spring Street,' caught my notice. I love it when God puts things together for us.

People came with needs of healing and deliverance: others to pray, and still others to soak in God's presence. We would begin with powerful worship and be led by the Holy Spirit into intercession. We prayed for other nations, especially Israel. We interceded for persecuted Christians world wide. Local and federal governments and governments of other countries were major topics in prayer. We prayed for revival of the body of Christ and a spirit of intercession to stir the church. We were desperate for the spirit of repentance to come upon our own nation. We declared righteousness and stability into our nation; truth, godliness and life. But most of all we asked the Lord of the harvest to send labourers into the fields to reap and bring in the harvest.

Sometimes we were loud and expressive with the joy of the Lord. There were times we would quietly wait before the Lord and allow Him to minister to us. Other times the burden of the Lord would weigh heavily upon us and we would groan or travail in the spirit until the burden lifted. Romans 8:25-26 says:

'But if we hope for what we do not yet have, we wait for it patiently. In the same way, the Spirit helps us in our weakness; We do not know what we ought to pray, but the Spirit [Himself] intercedes for us through groans that words cannot express.'

We had incredible times and God truly blessed us. Christians would send in prayer requests for people we did not know and we would have feedback later they were healed.

One day a child had fallen from a window causing severe brain damage and God healed him. We had an urgent prayer request for a man who had a triple by-pass that was not successful and he was seriously ill. We heard later that during the time we were interceding for him, he got out of bed and began to dance with the nurses. Others were healed of cancers, skin diseases and emotional issues. Many were filled with the Holy Spirit and we baptised those desiring water baptism.

Types of prayer

We had learned there are many ways to pray: When the burden was heavy we would groan and travail in the spirit. When there was a blockage or obstacle in the way of God moving by his Spirit, we would command it to go as Jesus said in Mark 11:22-25. Other times we would declare and decree the scriptures or the prophetic word. We would impart God's blessing, peace and healing by laying of hands. Also there were times when we just simply asked according to His will—trusted and thanked the Lord for the results. All types of prayer are needed and led by the Holy Spirit, we worked together in unity to build the kingdom of God.

Praying in tongues is so vital in prayer as the hours can slip by, and instead of tiring, we revitalise. Many will say, "but you will need an interpreter." If you gave a *prophecy* or a message in tongues someone else would need to interpret otherwise no one would understand the message from God. But praying in the spirit together is the universal language of heaven and although it manifests in different expressions, it strengthens everyone present. It is praying straight to God not to each other. It is a free channel to God with no blockages on our part. We can pray with our mind but so many times we are bogged down with our problems we are confused and do not know how to pray. Praying in tongues is always praying according to God's will. When we groan in the spirit or travail it is so deep it cannot be spoken in a known language even though you usually know what you are praying. Sometimes you have no idea why you are groaning and the answer may come later.

God was impressing on my heart again to build His house of prayer. Foundations were truly laid when Mum and I established the spiritual roots in prayer while living at Mount Shammah Prayer Mountain. The structure was formed by networking throughout the towns gathering the churches together to pray. This cleared the way in the spiritual realm to change the atmosphere over the Hunter Valley for the harvesting of souls during Breakfree.

Every house needs maintenance and repairs. After my mother died in September 1993, before God healed me of grief, I withdrew and began writing novels to help deal with my emotions and sorrow. I wrote five in two years. Each were action packed from cover to cover with the traumatic lives of the people of God and how the enemy is out to destroy them. One book was inspired by my own experiences with fires and flooded streams of Mount Shammah but I changed the names of characters and towns and localities. The setting of each book is different but the message of God's love, faithfulness and deliverance from devastating situations are the same.

The Christians in the book used their skills of prayer to bring about the victory. Also their gifts in music and worship brought revival to churches and repentance to towns where they would be situated.

These books may be written as fiction but the Holy Spirit gave the inspiration. I had written so many truths from God's word put into practical use. I could see that nothing is impossible with God. Nothing is coincidental with God. Everyone in churches are crying out for revival. I could see it happening in my spirit as I kept writing and I still have that assurance that God is about to do something outstanding in this generation. God will do extraordinary things through music to break open the heavens to pour out His blessings upon the towns.

During my time out to write, the Holy Spirit was teaching me the importance to look beyond the music. In other words—not to go by what I see, hear or what other people were telling me to do. They were kind and their advice was good but not for me at the time. God was opening my eyes to see the unseen realm when I prayed and worshipped Him. I wrote what

I was seeing and the end result. It was time to stop writing for a season and move on the next stage of the journey God was leading me into.

The Holy Spirit reminded me of a scripture which I first had revelation of when Spirit Alive came through the valley.

It is Zechariah 8:20-22: *'This is what the Lord Almighty says: "many peoples and the inhabitants of many cities will yet come, and the inhabitants of one city will go to another and say, 'let us go at once to entreat the Lord and seek the Lord Almighty. I myself am going. And many peoples and powerful nations will come to Jerusalem to seek the Lord Almighty and to entreat Him.'"*

I knew what God was saying to me through this scripture. I was to reconnect with those I had prayed with several years before. I was to travel from town to town gathering praying people together to take to the next town like we had done previously. This was the repair work that God wanted me to do.

God also spoke to me from Zechariah 2:4-5: *'Jerusalem will be a city without walls because of the great number of men and livestock in it. And I myself will be a wall of fire around it, declares the Lord.'*

Yes, I could relate to that scripture. I knew it was meant for Jerusalem but scripture can direct and minister to whomever it quickens. Mount Shammah House of Prayer was huge. It was cattle, sheep and horse country. Not to mention twelve major towns and Hunter Springs at the gable peak of my drawing of the house outline on the map. This is the source of the Hunter River which flows 468 kilometres through many towns of the Hunter Valley to the delta at Newcastle. Right up on the top of that peak on the map I drew a red cross, a symbol to show that Jesus died for His church and this valley, and He takes the highest place as head of the church.

After that scripture above, I coloured in a fire around the house outline. There are many small towns and communities in this vast area and I needed God to give me contacts to pray with. I began to pray and fast to have clear direction from the Lord where to start. When I was ready I packed my little Daihatsu Feroza with camping gear, dog and canary and started out on a journey as a spiritual scout. I drove through all the towns that I could speaking the name, Jehovah Shammah, into the house of prayer. We need His presence and glory in His temple: without it we have nothing. I did not end up camping as I had a place to stay en route. It was a full, two-days journey but what a blessing.

When I arrived home and had rested, I began to make contact with the praying people on file after Breakfree. Nina and I visited key ministers in different towns to share the vision so they would know we were not out to steal their sheep. We had powerful prayers and blessings said over us to send us on our way. By this time God had made it clear to only gather in the key, praying people in the towns and share with them about the house of prayer.

Most of these were the town's prayer leaders during Breakfree and were already prepared by God. They in turn gathered people in their own town to pray. Sometimes there were only two's or three's, sometimes ten but the presence of God was upon them.

Our group in Branxton was like a watering hole. People came for a refreshing in God and moved on to bless others or start their own houses of prayer. Nina had named their property Jehovah Rohi Prayer Retreat— meaning the Lord is my Shepherd. It was certainly that for over twenty years. The Lord, not only led us into green pastures and beside still, fresh water, but He would lead others to us.

One dear lady awoke one morning and heard the Lord telling her to go up to Branxton and join the prayer meeting held there. Those days we did not have mobile phones and she had the Holy Spirit lead her right up the long, gravel drive to where we were praying. We were standing outside in the fresh air when she arrived and were making declarations and decreeing the word of God over the nation at the time. She had a release that day and when we saw her again, several months later at the book shop where she worked, she told us her story. That day she joined us in prayer, she had a release in her spirit, and with the anointing was able to go out and start six other prayer meetings! She became a powerful woman of God and was raised up in leadership.

If you want to be able to pray and worship God in the Spirit hang around those who do.

As a team, we then began our journey of going from town to town gathering with the local prayer warriors of each town. God kept giving us more and more contacts which involved more lengthy journeys out of towns. Sometimes we stayed overnight at family, owned properties and another time we camped in tents beside a brook and was so blessed.

While we were there, we met with the lady who was the holder of the key to the toilets of the camping ground. After she asked why we were there, we shared with her about our journey of prayer, and that her community was next in God's agenda. She was so excited and told the local policeman's wife who said they needed prayer. The next time when we visited that place, our contact joined us for prayer and took us over to pray for her family including a new born baby. As God gave us a new contact for prayer I coloured a little fire on my map in their locality. Many times a prayer meeting would start in their home. Fires were popping up all over the Upper Hunter Valley as God was calling His people to pray.

We were also connected with other prayer groups and churches outside the Valley and this led to visiting ministries to our small town. Three Papua New Guinea pastors visited us and we held a couple of meetings with them. One day I had a phone call from a pastor in Sydney who asked could we make use of seven Filipino pastors for the day. We had been well trained by Brian Pickering's teaching of, "being totally available and radically obedient," that we were ready for whatever and whoever God would send our way. With such short notice, we held a meeting in a larger neighbouring town and was so blessed to see decisions for Christ and people receive healing. As there were too many pastors to minister in one meeting they were given the opportunity to minister in the Filipino community and nursing homes.

Another time a visiting Indian pastor joined us for prayer and from that visit we arranged another short-notice, larger meeting in the Lower Hunter Valley. We had a good-sized crowd gathered and our Indian brother's ministry in the prophetic and healing was exceptional. We held special meetings at times for speakers from Israel and also from the International Christian Embassy of Jerusalem, opening up God's eternal plan for this ancient country and our connection as the church. We hired the local RSL hall for this occasion and in full view of the town and all those passing through on the highway, we displayed the Australian and Israeli flags.

At that time we were still just a small, on-fire group with large connections in Australia and internationally. Our connections with the Indonesian church and my brother, Matthew, led us to Jakarta to the World Prayer Assembly in 2012. Once again, I was with thousands of prayer warriors from around the globe—from the east to the west, north to south. 9,000 delegates from different tribes and tongues, in unity with the Holy Spirit, came together to pray for their own nation and the nations of the world. There were hundreds of child delegates at the conference as well and they had an input in all that was happening. They were given the opportunity to mingle among the adults and pray for them and we in turn laid hands on them and blessed them in their journey with God. On one of the evenings we spent hours in the largest sporting arena in Jakarta. Thousands kept flocking in. 120,000 children from the International Children's Prayer Network filed in and took up a large portion of the stadium. It was an amazing event with all the global, well-known people in prayer and prophecy speaking and leading prayer.

On the last day of the conference I felt to change my seating from the section assigned to those from English speaking countries to sit closer to the South Koreans. I do not know why I did this. Again it was God. He wanted me to hear what the Indian pastor, I sat with, had to say that encouraged me in the ministry of prayer. This lady and her husband were pastors in India where it was not so strict with women in ministry. They had a move of God in their area and had just baptised about 200 people. I was excited hearing that and told her of our exploits in India including the incident in the Bihar State of releasing the women in prayer. I also mentioned what I had read in the newsletter that a women's prayer network in this state had grown to 300 praying people. She was thrilled to tell me that the same prayer network had grown to tens of thousands of praying people by 2012!

We laughed at the places where God had taken us during this time. As a small group of intercessors, in a small country town, God sent us out like a fire wheel into the thick of what He was doing around the world. We did not have social media like we have today, but we knew what was happening, and used to arrive at places at the right time. Obeying God brings blessings.

We tend to see things from our human perspective but God wants to take us up into His heights of glory to see what He sees and hear what He is hearing. I love to spend early mornings with the Lord but one day I felt compelled to turn on the Television. The program was set in Dubai and hundreds of people were flocking to the front of the auditorium to receive Christ during an evangelistic, healing crusade held by a well-known evangelist. I was elated and began to thank the Lord for His workers in the field. Suddenly I had a feeling in my spirit which was familiar to me and I heard the Holy Spirit speak. *Tell your prayer groups that what I am doing* in Dubai and the Middle East is the result of their prayers. Encourage them in this. I was flabbergasted yet answered: "I don't think I had ever prayed for Dubai." The answer came to me as quick as a flash. When praying in tongues we are covering a lot of ground. God takes us around the world during these hours. We are communicating with Him but also interceding on behalf of others.

No matter where we are, or who we are, God looks at our hearts and they that humble themselves He lifts, entrusting them with His vision for the world—to establish His kingdom on the earth as it is in heaven.

God can use the sick, lonely, deaf, blind, aged, young, isolated, depressed and persecuted to accomplish His will on earth. Prayer and thankfulness is the foundation stone of all ministry. Not all of us are called to be out on the field and do seemingly amazing things, but all of us have access to the very throne room of God if we surrender to Him. He shares His will for what He is doing on the earth and gives us insight into how to pray.

To him who overcomes

Revelation 2:26-28;3:12;21 says: (paraphrased) *'He who overcomes, and keeps My works until the end, to him I will give power over the nations ... I give him the hidden manna. I will make him a pillar in the temple of My God ... to him who overcomes I will grant to sit with Me on My throne, as I also overcame and sat down with My Father on His throne.' (NKJV)*

What earned Jesus that right to sit on His Father's throne. Sacrifice and death. Not greatness: not power while on earth but giving up His life. Through this act of obedience, millions around the world have come to know the salvation of God.

Many times our lives seem nothing but struggle and heartache. Even getting out of bed in the morning takes a tremendous step of faith, while others seem to prosper in perfect health, wonderful productive lives and ministries. The key to success in God's sight, is not what we achieve for Him but what we overcome to survive in Him—never denying His name before men; never giving up. Using every measure of God-given faith to the fullest, although it seems God has withheld His grace. THIS IS SPIRITUAL WARFARE! Without a struggle, there is no victory.

So many prayer warrior's lives are traumatic. Constantly ill; children gone astray; persecuted and financially struggling. That is why they pray and intercede for others. They have had to tolerate words of condemnation thrown at them like—"Just have faith;" "Where is your faith?" Faith *is* their lifestyle compared to those living without trauma. Like Job, despite all the attacks of Satan, they love the Lord and rely on Him for every need. The devil hates them and wants them to lose heart and curse God.

Sometimes the army of God is the only army that shoots its wounded. It is easier to be critical than to suffer with them. Please pray for the overcomers who struggle emotionally and physically. God highly favours them and gives them the right to sit with him upon the throne and also gives them power over the nations. It takes sacrifice and death many times over, so that others are set free by this kind of spiritual warfare.

Many of our favourite prophets in the Bible were disheartened. Elijah had just performed a great miracle before the prophets of Baal—fire came down from heaven and consumed the sacrifice, the altar and water around it, (1 Kings 18:20-40). Then he prayed for rain, tucked up his cloak and ran all the way to Jezreel passing Ahab and his horses. The rain pelted down. Afterwards when he fled into the desert in fear for his life, he was exhausted, discouraged, lonely and wanted to die. God showed His loving heart by tenderly ministering to his physical and emotional needs. After forty days, he came to Horeb and hid in a cave. God came to him in a still small voice, rather than a boisterous wind, earthquake and fire. Elijah knew the power of God but also his own human weakness and needed the soft, caring touch of the Lord, (Chapter 19). God did not judge him, but ministered to him where he was at.

There is a time and season for everything. I thank God for family and friends who have prayed for me while suffering themselves. They have rejoiced in my healing, yet still live with their own pain. It is not only the great faith preachers that the public sees, but the quiet overcomers who are preparing the way of the Lord by removing the stumbling stones out of the way of God's people. God sees them, and the faith it takes to battle on. Thank you Lord for the battlers who seek your face day and night, sacrificing in their own discomfit, for the sake of building Your kingdom.

CHAPTER 16

The Watchman

Psalm 127:1 says: *'Unless the LORD builds the house, its builders labour in vain. Unless the LORD watches over the city, the watchman stand guard in vain.'*

What is a Watchman?

A watchman is someone who is on the lookout for any danger and brings a warning to those concerned; or reports good news of what they witness to those who need to be involved. Another word used in a spiritual sense is an *intercessor*—someone who pleads with God on behalf of someone else. In other words, they stand in the gap and pray for others, or for anything that God puts on their heart besides their own need. In Genesis 18:16-33, we read how Abraham pleads for Sodom.

When we walk in this lifestyle of prayer, the need to pray for ourselves becomes less and less. We become more sensitive to the will of God and know beyond doubt God's will for our own lives in decision making and involvement in ministry.

It is having confidence in God knowing that He is in control of our lives. In this security of our relationship with the Lord we do not have to plead, beg, or ask because there is a deep knowing God is working on our behalf. We need to have a thankful heart and thank Him for His answers to our prayers.

As the whole body of Christ we have a responsibility to watch over our local church, city, institutions, nation and international affairs. This is for every disciple of Jesus. That is when we stand in the gap and become an intercessor if something is not right.

I remember Christmas day 2004. I was celebrating with family but all day I was heavy in my spirit. It was like having depression but I just knew I needed to pray before it would lift. At the end of the day, when I was home alone, I was able to travail in prayer. I did not know what I was praying for. The next morning it was on the news. There had been a massive earthquake off the west coast of Northern Sumatra causing a huge tsunami with waves up to 30 metres to sweep Indonesia and Sri Lanka. Over 200,000 people died as the result.

I may have questioned why God had me to pray when it was to happen anyway? But I have learned not to question Him. I pray in tongues, groan or travail in my spirit and leave the results to Him. God's ways are not to be analysed but obeyed. During every disaster, lives have been spared through miraculous intervention of God. The testimonies come later.

God often speaks to us in dreams or gives us visions which launches us into specific prayer. Sometimes you are the only one in the group who sees or knows something is not right. One night in September 2001, before the infamous disaster of the twin towers, a friend rang to tell me about a dream she had. She was very emotional and it was hard to understand what she was saying. God had used her so many times like this: you would either listen or think—here she goes again. She was so desperate to find out if anyone else had the same dream or was picking up something in their spirit.

No one had, even other prayer networks nationally. There was no one able to support her. She took on the burden alone although some of us prayed with her but not so intensely. She was still seeing with her spiritual eyes the burning towers with people jumping out of the windows. Then it happened. She rang me early in the morning to turn on the television and I saw it happen just as she described in her dream days before. It was a horrendous scene on September 11th 2001. Terrorist pilots had flown into the twin towers in Manhattan on a suicide mission. Thousands were killed. Yet after the catastrophe, story after story of miracles became known where God had intervened and spared lives. I have been asked by people why God had not stopped it. God is sovereign but disasters do happen as the result of sin in the Garden of Eden. However, during times of mass destruction, God hears the heart-felt prayers of the saints and saves individuals from being destroyed. Satan is out to destroy and block our prayers so we need to break through the barriers.

Why do we pray?

2 Corinthians 4:4 says: *'The god of this age has blinded the minds of unbelievers, so that they cannot see the light of the gospel of the glory of Christ, who is the image of God.'*

God wants *us* to get involved in what He is doing on the earth. As I have said in chapter 8, He has a plan for every person, church, town, community, nation and so much more. Satan also has a plan to destroy or thwart God's plans. Prayer is active, not dull and boring as many are led to believe. If only Christians would leave the four walls of the church building to pray they would become active in what they see around them. We are the living church as believers, not the man made building we worship in. The Amplified Bible says in James 5:16b:'... *The heartfelt and persistent prayer of a righteous man (believer) can accomplish much (when put into action and made effective by God—it is dynamic and can have tremendous power.)*'

The above scripture has proven to be like dynamite in my own life at times. It is like an explosion of indignation that stands up against the powers of the devil. At the right moment when we walk closely with Jesus, He gives us that gift of faith when needed. And with that kind of faith we see miracles happen. An example of this is a message and a testimony I had written in my journal many years ago:

'As a watchman over a city or area, the need is so great to be vigilant and sensitive to the Holy Spirit. God uses any means to get our attention. Recently, as I was preparing the December message for our monthly news letter, I suddenly had a nagging sense of hunger. It was still early morning and I realised it was time for breakfast. I was so enthralled with the revelation of God's word, time was slipping by. Nothing in the fridge tempted me. I had cereal but no milk: butter but no bread. I decided to pop out to the local store at Branxton, two minutes away. I had not as yet had a shower but that did not worry me as I expected to be back home within 15 minutes, maximum.

Four hours later, unkempt and reeking of smoke, I wearily staggered into my home and flopped on the lounge. I had been out on the battle field. The enemy was fire! I did not get to the store. Instead I felt compelled to head towards Cessnock—a town twenty two kilometres away although the fuel gauge of my car registered empty.

The reason for the change of plan soon became evident. In the distance, ominous black smoke billowed from the back of Cessnock. As if a magnetic force was drawing me, I kept driving. I had no idea where I was going and why. God led me to confront a fiery furnace bent on devouring everything in its path. I had driven fires back before by crying out to God in fervent prayer. This was different. The whole community was at stake. The hot gusty winds added to the fury of the moment. It was like pushing back the gates of hell.

I had never felt such panic as I stood with raised hands in the midst of onlookers and property owners. I cried out loudly to God. The wind abated and so did the fire. The whole street was spared. God led me from one lookout to the next to pray against the fires that day. Before I had been called out to the area fourteen homes were lost and one man lost his life trapped in his car. I believed there would have been so many more casualties if I had not obeyed the call of God. The communities below every lookout where I prayed were spared.'

One area I stopped to pray was at a cricket ground where the game was in full swing. The players seemed oblivious to the wall of fire behind them. They must finish the game. It reminded me of the people of the world oblivious to the flames of hell as they are so wrapped up in the things of this life not realising what awaits those who do not repent. I was there before the local newspaper reporters and photographers, because when the article had been printed, the photo on the front page of the newspaper showed that the cricketers were winding up the game. The same scene is also painted as a huge mural on a building in a local town.

How did I pray against the fires. I travailed in the spirit through the Holy Spirit. It is like a wailing sound coming from deep within my being. The Apostle Paul likens travailing to labour pains in Galations 4:19. As labour pains open the birth canal of a woman to give birth to a child this type of prayer breaks opens the heavens giving birth to the answer to prayer. In my case the answer was to command the wind to cease and the fire to die in the name of Jesus. It did, and I was able to minister to an elderly lady who stood with me. She witnessed first hand the intervention of God. A few minutes before she was terrified of the fire roaring towards a paddock where horses were enclosed. She did not know who owned the horses and she could not find the gate to set them free. I had told her I could not help her but we will cry out to God for help. The results were amazing. The owners of the horses had no idea what this poor neighbour had gone through.

Fire is always expected with Australia's hot, dry seasons, so it is always good to be alert and pray against them. Fire emergency crews face horrendous challenges and are always needing our prayers for safety.

Another time when a fire was raging in the same area as I mentioned above, our prayer team headed towards the direction from where the smoke was coming. It was not long before we came to a road block with police manning it. We used to have magnetic letters forming, 'Prayermobile' attached on the bonnet of our cars which made them look official. The police asked why we were there and we said to pray. To our surprise they let us through with the advice of where to stop. The fire front was raging towards the vineyards and tourist areas of the Hunter Valley. When we arrived it was almost at the arts and craft galleries. We did not let up with our fervour in prayer although the police and other vehicles began to park near us. The fire fighters were able to contain the fire and the community was spared. We spent some time worshipping the Lord before heading for the next place of call.

This time it was a lookout bordering a golf resort and villas surrounded by bush. Again, the fire had almost reached its boundaries. In the name of Jesus we commanded the wind to change and instantly it did and the fire went backwards into where it came from and fizzled out. The resort was spared. We went home to relax. The evening news announced the miracle of the wind changing at the right moment to spare the galleries and the golf resort from burning to the ground. Thank you Lord. You get all the glory!

The reason God takes us out of our homes to pray is because our prayers are more fervent on site where we can see the gravity of the situation. Prayer is also a witness to bystanders to what God does through prayer. You may say, *but the scripture says to go into your prayer closet and shut the door to pray.* Yes, especially for our private seeking of God. It was an attitude of the heart Jesus was addressing and praying with a public display to show off our piety was not God's idea of humility before him.

Fire is a community issue and needs public prayer to incite others watching to seek God. At times though, we have stayed at home and prayed half the night for communities in the line of fire until safety was restored for them. When, or not to go out is entirely how God leads you. I have always found that the safest place to be is in the will of God. Being led by the Holy Spirit is the only way to go out into the great outdoors to do warfare. All else will fail.

How do we know what God's will is? By walking humbly and closely with Him. Reading the word of God is vital as it is full of His wisdom and direction. Psalm 119:105 says: *'Your word is a lamp to my feet, a light for my path.'*

If you ask anyone to describe the feeling of being thirsty, hungry, itchy, need to use the bathroom, it is hard to describe. No one can talk you out of these feelings because you know beyond doubt that is how you feel. Reactions to these feelings is automatic to satisfy or bring relief to whatever the need is. With maturity in walking with God, comes knowing without doubt what He desires for us to do. When we first surrender our lives to the Lord we know beyond doubt we are saved. There is an inward knowing we cannot describe that we are saved. This is because the Holy Spirit comes to dwell within us. As we become in tune with the Holy Spirit, we can hear His voice, just as a small voice coming from our own spirit. He guides us in what to do and where to go. Sometimes His voice comes as just an impression that we should do something: other times there is an urgency to act. Many times I do things not realising I am directed by the Lord until the reason is apparent.

Like I have said before, walking with the Lord is exciting and so our prayer life should be. When we walk in the Spirit of the Lord we just know His will. When we are young, we know what our parents require of us and what pleases them. We do not ask can we go places that they will disapprove of, because they will say no.

When we walk with God, we already know by His word what we are to do and not to do. We are friends, brothers or sisters of Jesus and God is our Father. He gives us freedom to make decisions that will not harm ourselves and others. We all have had other people trying to rope us into their interests, or ministry in life. As good and enticing they seem, this may not be what God wants for *our* life. When you are young in your spiritual growth it is normal to say yes to everything. It is like—bring it on, I will do anything, Lord. As you mature in Christ and your calling and gifts from God are obvious, you know God's will for your life. And outside of that nothing else sits right with you. Often, even when someone tells me to pray about it when they have asked me to be involved in something, I do not need to pray because, on the spot my answer is either yes or no. If I am in doubt and have to pray about it, the answer should be no. God will impress upon my heart if I need to change my mind.

Do we make mistakes? Yes, unfortunately. We are still living in the natural and influenced by what goes on around us. Some of our mistakes can endanger our lives. God is so gracious and even when we do not listen, or obey His voice, He always has a way of rescuing us.

Jonah

A good example of this in scripture is when Jonah, a prophet, disobeyed God's call to preach to the city of Ninevah. He ended up on a ship sailing in the wrong direction. A storm came up and they were in dire straits. The captain and crew wondered why this was happening to them and they cried out to their own gods which of course did not help. They took up lots to find out who was the cause of this dilemma. The lot fell to Jonah and he confessed he was running away from God and convinced the crew to throw him overboard. When they heard he was a Hebrew and disobeying his God, they were horrified. This led to them worship the true God and offer up sacrifices to Him.

Even in Jonah's disobedient state, God used the situation to turn the crew to Him even if it was out of fear. They threw Jonah overboard and a big fish swallowed him. Then after three days he prayed to the Lord and offered up sacrifices of praise to him. After Jonah cried out to God, the fish vomited him onto dry land. He then headed towards Ninevah, preached repentance and had tremendous results. What an amazing preacher! Even though he knew God was going to relent from destroying the city, he preached a convincing message to be believed and not scorned. As a result, a whole city was spared of the judgement of God.

CHAPTER 17

The Prayer of Faith

Hallelujah! God still works like that in this day and age! I should imagine we have all had experiences where God has come in and rescued us in our mistakes and poor decision making. My brother Matthew included.

Dad, Mum and I were up at our prayer mountain staying for a few weeks. We had been there a few days and expecting to be joined by Matthew at the weekend. He was going to come up after work with a packed trailer on the back of his car, and an esky full of food to add to our supplies. He was due to arrive before sundown. Previously, there had been a heavy storm which is always a major concern due to water crossings and bad, muddy roads. Matthew was only young and those days there was no way to warn him not to come. We had to trust God that he had the common sense not to do anything reckless. It had grown dark and there was not much to do so we went to bed early, relieved Matthew had not taken the risk on the roads—so we thought.

Little did we know that Matthew had no idea there had been a cloudburst in the mountains above us and the usual, peaceful, flowing stream was running rampant. As the weather cleared and the sun was shining, he headed out on his journey. There were many water courses to cross that were just flowing at their usual levels. All was well on the steep climb into the mountains and he merrily went on his way through the forest. It was dark by this time and he turned on his headlights. The road began to slope downwards so he changed to a lower gear to tackle the winding road leading towards the brook. He could see that it had been raining but he was quite unperturbed. He approached the water crossing and noticed the water level was a lot higher. That also did not faze him too much as he was used to driving through deep water. He took the risk and drove ahead.

Matthew soon regretted his decision. The water lifted his car off the bed of the brook. He was adrift and had lost control of the car. In his panic Matthew was going to climb through the window to escape the car. He heard a voice loud and clear, say — "NO! WAIT!" Sudden peace clothed him like a blanket. He obeyed God's voice clinging to the useless steering wheel while the car was swept away with the rushing water. The steep, craggy sides of the mountain gully were closing in on him. A massive rock loomed in front of the car. He felt a jolt as his car was caught on the rock and began to tilt onto its side. Miraculously the car went over the rock and landed the right way up. The rapids hurtled the car around the bend and swept him along for about another two hundred metres. Matthew suddenly had the urge to get out of the car. He had no second thoughts or doubts. It was now or never! As quick as a flash he wound down the window, somehow slid through and landed in the water. To his relief the current swept him to safety on the embankment. The car rushed on with the rapids and disappeared out of sight.

It was pitch black. There was no moon. He was without a torch. All his gear was lost including his new, expensive tool kit. His car and trailer were gone. He still had his life and he belonged to the Lord who took care of him.

Matthew felt around until he found some flat ground away from rocks. He was amazed to find a track in the midst of the rough terrain. He had a fair idea which direction to take and was able to struggle upstream until meeting the road that would take him to our property. He had several kilometres to walk and many times bending over to feel the ground to make sure he was still on the road. Finally, we were stunned to hear his voice call out. He was shocked and cold, and when asked where the car and trailer were, he said he didn't have a clue.

Praise the Lord! He looked after Matthew that night. The next day we drove down to where he was swept away. After parking the car we scrambled downstream looking for what we expected, a badly beaten up car. Fortunately the water had receded and we had more level places to walk. We found the trailer first which was badly damaged and under water. Finally, after rounding a few sharp bends there was his car! We could not believe what we saw. It was above the water and safely placed in a place where it could easily be towed away. Not only that, the damage to the car was nothing to what we had expected. Amazingly, a track led upwards away from the area to someone's property! If that was not divine planning, what was it?

We could always wonder what would have happened if Matthew had not obeyed the voice of God.

The property owner offered to tow his car out with his tractor and Matthew left it at the man's place to dry out. We did not retrieve the trailer and the farmer salvaged what was left of it, getting it to a workable state, so we told him to keep it. A week later the car purred like a kitten and Matthew was able to drive it back home. That was a hard lesson to learn, of hearing and obeying the voice of the Lord—first the Lord spoke audibly and loudly; the next time he just knew beyond doubt he had to get out of the car, and instantly he obeyed at the right moment.

It was worth it for Matthew. He learned to know the goodness and grace of God on his life. This was his training ground for what God had planned for him to do in the future many years later. In our training as a watchman of the Lord and missionaries, we need to learn many hard lessons which cannot be learned through head knowledge, but through knowing the voice of the Lord.

God is faithful to His promises that He will not leave or forsake us, nor let us stumble to the point of destruction. Imagine how busy the angels were that night in protecting Matthew in the ominous blackness of the rushing water intent on sending him to his death. We heard later that an army truck going through the same brook in flood, a few years earlier, had tipped over and three soldiers were drowned. A gentle flowing stream can become rushing, perilous waters in flood time.

Many years later, God had taken Matthew on extraordinary places to preach the gospel. Through the jungles of Indonesia, Malaysian-Borneo where head-hunters used to grab their victims, and black magic and witchcraft is still rampant. He was in a four wheel drive bus crossing over the mountain on a steep, winding and slippery road in Nepal when many of the passengers had gotten out of the vehicle on a hair-raising section of the road. Matthew stayed in the bus. The driver crept along standing up so he could see, to make sure the front wheels would not slip over the edge and hurtle them to their death. They had seen the results in another area where a bus had gone over 200 meters below.

The world does not acknowledge or realise the restraining hand of God. In other words, they do not know what goes on behind the scenes when the people of God cry out to him. Prayer summons the power of God and activates the warring angels to come to the rescue on our behalf. Satan has his cohorts who are out to challenge the power of God. They have power but no authority because they were stripped of that. We have the authority of God most High through the cleansing blood of Jesus and when combined with His power we can do tremendous things.

Matthew has had Animists turn up to his gospel meetings to test out his power a few times at the darkest places in Central Kalimantan and West Sulawesi. He also has healed and delivered witch doctors in the name of Jesus. After repenting of their sins and surrendering to the Lord they have burned all their paraphernalia.

Matthew's experience in the mountains had been preparing him for physically tough times ahead. His fervency to serve God deepened as he grew older. He spent many hours in prayer over the years up at Mount Sugarloaf, another high place near where he and his family lived. Late at night he would be up there singing and praying. One night he interrupted a witches gathering. They also frequented high places, and this time they had ladders and paraphernalia festooning the trees, apparently to do with their demonic rituals. Matthew began to pray out loud to the Lord some distance from them but it disturbed their style. They quickly gathered their paraphernalia and vacated the area post haste. Many times other Christians would join him and the glory of God would fall. There is something about high places and lookouts over a city to stimulate active prayer. The Church is the watchman on a high place as we worship God.

Matthew's ministry in South East Asia began to unfold after God placed on his heart the persecuted churches of Indonesia. He finally bought a video camera and flew to interview pastors in need. From this developed a ministry of preaching and moving in the power of God, majoring in deliverance ministry. This ministry was vital so as to combat black magic and witchcraft in some very dark places.

During these seasons of ministry Matthew never neglected building himself up in the Lord through worship and prayer. When at home in Australia, he would go up to Mount Shammah to pray and fast for up to forty days. I would drop him off in my four-wheel drive vehicle, leave him without a phone—as there is no mobile reception, and pick him up later at the arranged date.

Once when I was due to pick him up after a long fast, my car needed repairs and I failed to arrive on the due day. He had finished his fast and lacked food but had plenty of water. A neighbour came by and threw him a loaf of bread from the trailer load he was bringing for his horses. The bread was an unwrapped loaf and fell on the ground. Matthew flicked the dust off and was thankful for his feast of bread and water.

Matthew's ministry overseas began to broaden to other south-east Asian countries. Instead of just preaching in church and ministry at the altar calls, he had a passion for street evangelism in obedience to Jesus' command to go out and make disciples by healing the sick, casting out demons, baptising the new believers and of course preaching the gospel. He was finding that in the Church as a whole, everyone was enjoying ministry, as it can be very demonstrative, but the next time he visited the same churches there was no real change in people's lives. There was no passion for the lost in order to go out into the market places to reap the harvest field which is already waiting. Social media had its benefits and soon he began to train groups of disciples in how to make disciples for the kingdom of God. Invitations for his teaching seminars began to flow from Indonesia, Malaysia and Malaysian-Borneo, Brazil, Chile, India, Nepal, Philippines, Dubai and France and of course in his home country Australia—Newcastle, Maitland and Goondiwindi in recent years, until Covid 19 restricted him. Below I have written passages from some of his emails sent to me.

Matthew's testimony dated, 18/8/2016: "Today my friend and I went to a market place in Sorong, West Papua, to buy fruit. As we always do, we look for opportunities to pray healing over those who are sick. After a short time we had that opportunity, and two ladies we had met, were instantly healed of back and joint pain.

After that, what we experienced was incredible and unexpected. For word had spread like wild fire of the healing, and people came from everywhere. Over the next two hours, the sick were lined up within that market place. We must have prayed for over one hundred people and all testified that they were healed. Many Muslims also approached us and they were healed.

There was much joy and excitement in that place and at one stage people burst out in songs of praise. I also preached Jesus to the gathered crowd several times, with loud shouts of amen as people responded."

24/10/2016: "I had the privilege in the last two weeks of being the first ever to bring healing and deliverance to a predominately Christian village of the central, northern, district region of Nepal. It involved a trek of over three days and during that time I proceeded to teach and demonstrate to my young co-worker and guide him on how to heal the sick and preach the gospel. As we passed through many Buddhist villages, we had a great opportunity to demonstrate the power of God to the local tribal people. It was most exciting to see them have that encounter and what unfolded over the next week or so, undoubtedly reminds me of something straight from the Gospels.

Upon arrival at our village destination of Lapa, within the Dhading District, we were set to work immediately. The sick came continually to us. At times we could not sneak through the village at night, for they would hear us and invite us to their homes, pleading for us to bless them. For word had got around that the blind were seeing, the lame were walking and the deaf were hearing. Much joy and excitement then unfolded.

On Saturday I was scheduled to preach in the local church where approximately 250-300 assembled. It was powerful and at one stage many people started calling out in repentance of sin. There were weeping and spontaneous falling down under God's presence, my camera man included. Upon an invitation for prayer to be healed, over two thirds of the people responded.

My assistant and I divided the crowd into two groups and we both proceeded to work our way through each group individually. I was assisted by a young man who spoke some English. He too caught on and started healing the sick in Jesus' name with some effect.

However, what transpired next is what surprised me. For the crowd sitting on the floor rose to their feet and thronged around me, tugging at my clothes and pulling on my arms. Such was the desperation, mixed with emotional excitement from the people. For a few minutes we could not proceed until the crowd was subdued by the leaders. Incidentally it was a 5-6 hour meeting and most people had walked away healed.

Next morning we were scheduled to leave early for a long trek out but people were waiting outside the door for prayer. With some fanfare we departed—somewhat late I might add. However, we were still chased an hour later up a mountain by people wanting healing."

Matthew held seminars in Newcastle, Maitland and Goodiwindi of which I was involved. What a tremendous time we had as we went into the streets healing the sick, casting out devils, and sharing the good news of Jesus. There were singing and rejoicing as many were baptised in the Hunter River both in Newcastle and Maitland. Healing the sick brings so much liberty to share the gospel when people are healed. Their hearts respond to the goodness of God.

Matthew was interviewed by a local radio station presenter and his response to questions raised were: "Great is the need. Jesus said the fields are ripe for harvest and he also declared the labourers are few. This goes for wherever I travel including my own nation of Australia. For people are dead in their sin and going to a lost eternity and most of us are just letting it happen. Sitting in church week after week, year after year.

For I am convinced more than ever that most of us do not know how to: heal the sick; share the gospel; cast out demons; baptise someone in the Holy Spirit and baptise in water. For we as disciples of Jesus are commanded to make disciples. To go and carry on the work that He started."

A very challenging message from someone who loves the Lord and wants to serve him while he still is able. In the emails above Matthew just centred on the healing side of miracles. Other emails he tells of, not only healing the sick in hospitals, but outside of hospitals and afterwards, the people had no need to go to see the doctors because of being healed or delivered of demons beforehand. At another hospital, his cousin cleared a hospital ward of sick people and was thanked by the doctors. Others on the street were delivered of addictions. Hundreds of schoolchildren were delivered of demons because of practising black magic, voodoo and casting spells. The teachers of the school had called the team in to minister.

We pray and pray for revival year after year but see little results. The harvest is out there but the labourers are unwilling. The Church is here for the healing of the nations. Most people are waiting for God to do something dramatic but Jesus has done it on the cross, and He has given us the Holy Spirit for us to obey. Receiving the Holy Spirit in our lives is the most dramatic thing that can happen to us. Jesus says in John 14:15- 24: *'If you love Me keep My commandments.'* In other words, if we truly love and worship Jesus we will obey Him.

Jesus has given *us* the authority to heal the sick so there is no need to pray: "Jesus you heal so and so." He will say *you do it in my name*. He has done the healing on the cross: *'By His stripes we are healed.'* In other words, we are ambassadors on His behalf. Through the power of the Holy Spirit we can do all things through Christ who strengthens us. We only need to speak to sickness and disease to go.

The Church needs the breakthrough. We have the tools. We are filled with power: Power to preach the kingdom of God. Power to heal the sick. Power to cast out devils. Power to speak with boldness and all that Jesus teaches us through His word.

It is time to hear the breaking of chains as God releases His people to go out with His eternal power, demonstrating in signs and wonders, performing miracles, speaking to the elements, driving out the powers of darkness and dragging out the lost from the dungeons of iniquity. We are not a voiceless Church! It is beginning to happen around the world as God is visiting His people like a raging fire. We are living in days of preparation. We are voices of ones crying in the wilderness. A united force not to be meddled with. Jesus commanded in Matthew 28 to make disciples.

Disciples are people who follow Jesus. They speak as He spoke, walk as He walked and does what He had done. There are 20 references to a disciple in the New Testament. Unfortunately we are stuck with the term 'Christian' which is only mentioned 3 times in scripture. It was used as a nick-name to describe the followers of Jesus.

Every disciple is a Christian but not all Christians are disciples. It is not good enough just to believe in Jesus—even the devil believes in Jesus. It is not good enough to claim Christianity as a religion just because we were brought up as one. It is not good enough to be just christened a Christian as a baby for salvation. It is not good enough to be confirmed without repentance from the heart.

Many people on the street we meet up with say they are a Christian but not really into it, or they do not read the Bible, and at least of all, do not go to church and fellowship. In today's society a Christian can be anyone who goes to church on a Sunday and sit in a pew and do nothing. That is not the sign of a glorious and prepared church that Jesus is coming back for. A person calling himself a Christian can get away with slackness because he is neither hot nor cold. The devil wants them to stay that way. But God has no interest in them as He said in Revelation 3:16, *'I will spew you out of My mouth.'*

A disciple is a person who has repented of their sin, has been baptised, and on fire for the kingdom of God. They are constantly watching for signs of the coming of the Lord. They are constantly interceding for the church and community. They are constantly sharing the gospel with whoever they meet; constantly healing the sick and setting the captives free. They are totally surrendered to Jesus and walk humbly before Him. Often we want the power but we are not prepared to humble ourselves.

God said to Daniel, *'Since the first day that you set your mind to gain understanding and to humble yourself before your God, your words were heard, and I have come in response to them,'* (Daniel 10:12).

The scripture says in 2 Chronicles 7:14: *'If [My] people who are called by [My] name will humble themselves and pray and seek [My] face and turn from their wicked ways I will hear from heaven, and I will forgive their sin and will heal their land.'*

There are so many scriptures instructing us to walk humbly before the Lord. We are not above our Master. He walked in obedience to His Father even to dying on the cross. The key to answered prayer is humility which is from the heart out of love for God. Recognising He is the One and Only who can bring us into the fullness of life.

To walk in revival is to keep a life of devotion serving the Lord and the lamp of God's presence burning in our heart. It does not die out. In times of heart-break, hardship and devastation it only shines brighter and faith rises higher. When God pours out a spirit of repentance and supplication on His people He will cleanse them from their sin. This is the revival fire that sweeps through His church. This is an act of God's grace and when we are walking in purity we will truly see God.

> *'Blessed are the pure in heart for they will see God.'*
> Matthew 5:8

When we see God we become like Him. Our compassion for the lost will be so much greater than our fear of man. With this grace and supplication we will see an outpouring of His love like we have never seen before. It is this love that will draw the whole body of Christ together to work together, to sing the same song *"O give thanks to the Lord for His love endures forever!"* The power of those words of love will break down barriers; push back the darkness; perform mighty miracles; move in signs and wonders—bringing the lost into the kingdom of God. It will be like the vision I saw of a river flowing through the towns as the singing army of God swept people along with it when they were touched by God.

Jesus paid the price for His beloved church. We are so precious in His sight. He is not concerned by doctrinal differences or division because He can change us all with the a twinkling of an eye. What God did in one day at Pentecost, He will do it again and again but with more passion as the battle against His people intensifies. Jesus has begun a perfect work in His church and He will complete it!

We often carry burdens for the church that are too great for us, forgetting that God will do what He promises.

The Apostle Paul said in Philippians 1:6, *'Being confident of this, that [He] who began a good work in you will carry it on to completion until the day of Christ Jesus.'*

'Now unto [Him] who is able, to do immeasurably more than all we ask or imagine, according to [His] power that is at work within us,' (Ephesians 3:20).

CHAPTER 18

Power of Unity

In chapter eight we studied a little of the heavenly or spiritual realm—the second heaven where there is a lot of activity going on with the unseen, opposing forces.

As Christians, all this action affects our daily lives and we are heavily involved, whether we want to be or not. We need to have our spiritual weapons sharpened and ready to defend or fight according to how God leads us.

What are our spiritual weapons? The primary ones are: repentance, the blood of Jesus, the word of God the name of Jesus and our witness.

Without repenting first of our sins the cleansing blood of Jesus has no effect on us. Without the blood of Jesus we have no power to stand. Without the word of God working within our lives we also have no power to operate. Without the name of Jesus on our lips we are vulnerable to the enemy's attacks. Without being a witness for Jesus we do not reproduce.

Another great weapon against the evil one is UNITY. Jesus prayed to the Father for His disciples in John 17:11b: '*... that they may be one as [You] and I are one.*' This unity that Jesus is longing for is not only a physical unity of coming together to fellowship but one of the heart in loving relationship with Him and our heavenly Father. A unity that can bring a united purpose in serving God and reaching out to each other, and the lost, in love.

Ephesians 4:2,3 says: *'Be completely humble and gentle; be patient bearing with one another in love. Make every effort to keep the unity of the Spirit through the bond of peace.'*

There are also many examples in Scripture that we read where great results occurred when the people of God came together in unity. After Jesus rose from the grave believers gathered together continually to pray. Unity in prayer precedes an outpouring of God's Spirit.

There is so much power released when we are united in heart and soul. And as we praise God together it becomes another weapon against the enemy as we saw in Chapter one, (2 Chronicles 20).

Unity in worship releases the hand of God to bring victory over the enemy.

We also read in 2 Chronicles 5:11-14: *'The trumpeters and singers joined in unison, as with one voice, to give praise and thanks to the Lord. Accompanied by trumpets, cymbals and other instruments, they raised their voices in praise to the Lord and sang; "He is good; [His] love endures forever." Then the temple of the Lord was filled with a cloud, and the priests could not perform their service because of the cloud, for the glory of the Lord filled the temple of God.'*

The glory comes when we are united with one purpose, with one heart and with one voice. Preceding this event was the consecration of all the priests in office. God will interrupt our order of things or service and reveal

His presence if our hearts are open, humble, expectant and united in worship to Him.

Another example in the Old Testament where unity was required was in Jonah 4. Jonah brought a stern message of judgement. *All* of Ninevah came together in unity at the command of the king, to fast and repent of their evil, and call out to Jonah's God. What a powerful response to the message God had given Jonah. The Ninevites' response to God caused Him to relent from bringing His judgement on that city showing His love, compassion and mercy.

It takes a city-wide effort of repentance to move the hand of God

Joel 1:14 says: *'Declare a holy fast; call a sacred assembly. Summon the elders and all who live in the land to the house of the Lord your God and cry out to the Lord.'*

Judges 20:1 says: *'Then all the Israelites from Dan to Beer Sheba and from the land of Gilead came out as one man and assembled before the Lord in Mizpah.'* The tribes of Israel were scattered throughout the areas but they came together during worship and war.

If only the Body of Christ could grasp how important it is to come together in unity for worship and war on a regular basis, to bring God's powerful and loving response to our city.

Galations 3:26-28, and Colossians 3:11 says: *'There is neither Jew nor Greek, slave nor free, male nor female, for you are all one in Christ Jesus. If you belong to Christ then you are Abraham's seed and heirs according to the promise.'*

As we have seen before, God does not live in houses made by men but He lives within the lives of living stones which are *'being built into a spiri-*

tual house to be a holy priesthood, offering spiritual sacrifices acceptable to God through Jesus Christ,' (1 Peter 2:5).

The body of Christ is not a product of one particular denomination country or tribe, but one global, holy nation—making up one house—THE HOUSE OF THE LORD!

The Church—believing Jews and Gentiles, are living stones formed by working together. We are built upon the Living Stone, Jesus Christ. We read earlier how the foundation stone on which the ark of the covenant stood, was sprinkled with blood of animals as the mercy seat also was not recovered. The Holy of Holies without the Ark and mercy seat, was without the glory of God. The rock, or what it is referred as 'the temple mount' was a substitute for God's manifest presence. This rock was a foreshadow of a future rock—Jesus and the Church!

It is written in Ephesians 2:19-22: *'Consequently, you are no longer foreigners and aliens, but fellow citizens with God's people and members of God's household, built on the foundation of the apostles and prophets, with Christ Jesus [Himself] as the chief cornerstone. In [Him] the whole building is joined together and rises to become a holy temple in the Lord. And in [Him] you are built together to become a dwelling in which God lives by [His] Spirit.'*

1 Peter 2:4-5 says: *'You have come to [Him], the living Stone—rejected by men but chosen by God and precious to [Him]—you also, like living stones, are being built into a spiritual house to be a holy priesthood, offering spiritual sacrifices acceptable to God through Jesus Christ.'*

Why are we stones and not referred to as bricks? Because we are all in different sizes and shapes. None of us are alike. We are all unique and our lives are shaped by our nature, nurture and experiences of our journey in life.

My sister Lorraine had taken up lapidary when she was young. There are many processes to go through to make a rough-looking stone into a beautiful, shining gem. First of all the stone needs to be cut into a workable size with a smooth flat base. It is then stuck on to a stick called a dop. It is done by heating wax, dipping the dop into the wax and then pressing the stone onto it and letting it cool.

The next step is to grind away with fine sandpaper and water to smooth the rough edges. It takes many hours and patience to form the desired shape before the polishing process begins. Another way of polishing river stones is to use a tumble machine. Multiple stones tumbling over and over together soon come out smooth in the hand.

It is amazing how we could overlook a dirty, dull-looking stone thinking it has no value, but when cutting it in halves the inside beauty is exposed. God sees that potential in us but, it takes some patient grinding in His hand, and like the tumbled stones, working shoulder to shoulder with each other we come out radiant with the glory of God.

2 Corinthians 3:18 says: *'And we, who with unveiled faces all reflect the Lords' glory, and being transformed into [His] likeness with ever- increasing glory, which comes from the Lord, who is the Spirit.'* When we seek God and feast on His word we take on His divine nature and are transformed by the renewing of our minds.

John 2:19 says: *'Destroy this temple and I will raise it up in three days.'* Jesus was referring to His own body and His resurrection after three days in the grave, (1 Corinthians 6:19). Followers of Jesus are referred to as 'temples of the Holy Spirit'. Houses where the Holy Spirit dwells. We cannot work alone in God's kingdom because we are responsible to function in the gifts that God has poured out on us. We are fitting in together to make a firm house. If we take one stone out and the whole house can crumble.

1 Peter 4:10 says: *'Each one should use whatever he has received to serve others, faithfully administering God's grace in various forms.'*

We are there for each other, to protect and build up. If one hurts we all hurt and are there to support.

Several years ago something extraordinary happened within the animal kingdom that I was a witness to. Where we live on a cattle farm overlooking the paddocks, we can usually see the cows grazing peacefully.

One day the peace was shattered by the arrival of a dog from a neighbouring property. A little calf had just been born and a dog was coming in to kill it. Mother cow was distraught and cried out but in her panic she accidentally trod on her baby. Hearing the fracas, cows from all over the vast area began to come to the rescue. Many grouped around mother and baby for protection but the majority seemed to form ranks to counter-attack the enemy. The dog was determined and tried to outsmart them. The cows seemed to be ready for every trick and with heads down they charged at it. Finally the dog, seeing that it was a losing battle took off toward the nearest fence while it was still in front. But that was not the end of the story. Horses from a distant property also had come galloping down the hill to witness what was going on and were ready for the dog when it crossed over into their territory. They reared up with the intention of stamping on him. The dog by now had lost interest and was only out to preserve it's own skin. It dived through another boundary fence as a way of escape from the horses. It was not so simple. Two other dogs were there ready to defend their territory and drove him out of the region.

It was an incredible sight and an example of every animal pulling together to oppose the attacking force within its boundaries. All had different ways of using their weapons. The cows used their heads to butt and hooves to kick; the horses reared up on their hind legs to stamp on the dog with their forelegs, and the other two dogs their teeth. We can learn from this as the body of Christ. We are all called to function together in protecting, defending and fighting off the enemy when our brothers and sisters are under attack.

Unity in prayer

We come together to pray because we need to. Prayer cannot only be a wonderful time of seeking God but exciting. What are we expecting when we pray? We are expecting God to move on our behalf in the fulfilment of our prayers. There are many keys in succeeding in prayer as a group, but unity is important to take note of.

It is in the heart of God that his people will live and work together in unity. Psalm 133:1-3 says: *'How good and pleasant it is when brothers live together in unity. It is like precious oil poured on the head, running down on Aaron's beard, down upon the collar of his robes. It is as if the dew of Hermon were falling on Mount Zion. For there the Lord bestows [His] blessing and life for evermore.'*

Mount Zion represents the highest place where we can go to meet with God. That is why it is brought out in Hebrews 12:22-24:

'But you have come to Mount Zion, to the heavenly Jerusalem, the city of the Living God. You have come to thousands upon thousands of angels in joyful assembly, to the church of the firstborn, whose names are written in heaven. You have come to God, the judge of all men, to the spirits of righteous men made perfect, to Jesus the mediator of a new covenant, and to the sprinkled blood that speaks a better word than the blood of Abel ...' It is in the plan of God for a body of people who have one mind and one purpose in serving Him. We see that in Jesus' prayer in John 17:23 *'May they be brought into complete unity to let the world know that [You] sent [Me] and have loved them even as [You] have loved [Me].'*

Matthew 18:19-20: *'I tell you that if two of you on earth agree about anything you ask for, it will be done for you by my Father in heaven. For where two or three come together in [My] name, there am I with them.'*

Ephesians 4:2 *'Be completely humble and gentle; be patient, bearing with one another in love. Make every effort to keep the unity of the Spirit through the bond of peace.'*

Unity in a prayer group brings the anointing oil of the Holy Spirit. It brings a blessing and refreshment. We learn to work together. As we follow the flow of the Holy Spirit we begin to understand each other's strengths and weaknesses. We grow to know what burdens each carry, and where their heart is in prayer—what concerns them, and we support in prayer. It is wonderful and brings peace and assurance.

A popular example from the old testament, is preceding Solomon's prayer of dedication of the temple of the Lord. When the ark of the covenant was brought into the temple, it was representing the glory of the Lord's presence. Where God's presence is, there is always music and singing.

The musicians and singers sang in unison. Unison is where harmonies come together and make one sound. God's presence always comes. There is power in this. When you hear an orchestra tuning their instruments together something stirs within your spirit: that sense of expectancy—something is about to happen. Or at a tense moment in a movie and the sound backing prolongs the music in unison. We all have a voice and when we come together in one accord to worship God and pray, God is here among us.

To be in **one voice** means unity; unison, one accord; concord (agreement). At times it is not easy to come into agreement in prayer and settle for a style that suits all. We have come from so many diverse backgrounds and ministry experiences. That is why it is so good to attend combined prayer meetings with other denominations if God leads us that way. God will answer *believing* prayer if it is done in faith regardless of how we pray.

I have always liked to flow with as many styles as possible to keep the unity of the occasion. Some intercessors, as a group, like to sit quietly and wait for a word or a picture from the Lord and then compare notes on what God is saying and pray into the outcome. It is like putting the pieces of a puzzle together. It is quite exciting and intriguing how God uses this kind of intercession.

One day our team joined an International Children's Prayer Network conference which was held a couple of hours drive from where we lived. It was a stimulating experience to see so many children from different nations, as young as five or six years-old, praying without restraint.

The worship service was led by young people and the presence of God was so strong that many children were lying on the floor weeping before God. There was one method of connecting in prayer that caught my attention. A huge map of the world was laid in the middle of the floor and we all stood around the perimeter of it. Strips of paper were handed to each child, adult or parent if the child was too young to read. On the strips were written prayers for different nations. We all prayed out loud at the one time for the nation on the strip we held. Then when we had finished that prayer we handed it on to the person next to us. There was a continuous flow and we all had a chance to pray for each nation. It was a very good way to draw out the shy person or beginner of prayer, I thought.

Other people must use a list when praying or even read their prayers. They are methodical people and everything must be done in order. Whichever way we pray is acceptable to God if coming from a pure heart and according to His will, believing God will hear and answer.

When there is no specific agenda for a regular prayer meeting, I tend to sing a song to the Lord which draws others into the flow of unity. From that God begins to impress upon the hearts of everyone gathered what His will is for that particular time and they either pray or sing accordingly. This method draws out worship continuously and prayer grows stronger and we never run dry of issues to seek God for, or thank Him for the amazing things He has done.

Other Christians prefer to declare God's will into being by using multiple scriptures. Whichever way the Holy Spirit directs is good and will accomplish great things for His kingdom if done with an attitude of humility and submission to one another. God is so diverse and has made His people that way. As long as we are eager to respect one another's uniqueness and allow each other to enter in and express themselves.

There is another kind of intercessor who has been praying in tongues half the night. They are on a high. They come to the prayer meeting exploding with the results of their praying in tongues. What are they supposed to do with that?

What about the prayer warrior who had been battling half the night praying in the Spirit about war or calamity in another country, or commanding life into a dying person. They arrive at the morning prayer meeting all battle-scarred and exhausted. What are they supposed to do with that? It takes a lot of sensitivity to quieten down and submit to what God is saying to the whole group when you have been on a roll, or a high since before dawn. I know—I have been there also.

There are times we need to let the army of the Lord rise up and take up their weapons. That is when we hear the roar of the Lion of the tribe of Judah in our meetings. When we feel the trembling of the place where we are standing and hear the cracking of the walls of resistance as they topple before us. This can only come with unity of purpose; unity of heart and unity of mind. We all know the story of the Israelites possessing the city of Jericho.

POWER OF UNITY

Joshua 6:4-5 says: *"Have the seven priests carry trumpets of rams' horns in front of the ark. On the seventh day, march around the city seven times, with the priests blowing the trumpets. When you hear them sound a long blast on the trumpets, have all the people give a loud shout, then the wall of the city will collapse and the people will go up every man straight in."* v.16: *"The seventh time around, when the priests sounded the trumpet blast, Joshua commanded the people, "Shout! For the Lord has given you the city! The city and all that is in it are to be devoted to the Lord.""*

In 1990, God stirred up every church in Maitland, a town in the Hunter Valley, to pray. It made the news when twelve ministers joined forces with one purpose and marched around the city for seven days each carrying a trumpet. The purpose was unity of heart working together. They marched in silence without speaking to anyone on the way.

In the natural there is a powerful reaction through a resonating sound of a certain pitch. It is a proven fact that an opera singer can crack a mirror when he or she reaches a certain high note. God has given us the ability to do damage to the enemy's schemes with just our voices. It was on the news once that an opera singer living alone heard someone break into her home. She used her God-given weapon and sang a high prolonged note. The burglar could not take off fast enough. How much more damage can we do to Satan's kingdom if we come with one heart and mind. Unity is a powerful weapon. Father, Son and Holy Spirit are one—perfect unity.

Back to chapter one again which is based on 2 Chronicles 20 and is a good example of where the unity of the singers and army went into battle singing:

"O gives thanks to the Lord for [His] love endures forever"

There is power in that. I have mentioned in an earlier chapter that we can picture scenes from old movies set in Medieval times. Enemies would break down the heavy gates of cities or castles by using a long heavy pole and with united momentum and lots of noise they would smash through the barriers.

In spiritual warfare we do the same thing. It can be loud, forceful and prolonged, until we know beyond doubt we have had a breakthrough in the Spirit. Most times we give up before the victory.

Often we need to raise our voices together in tongues as there is so much to pray for and limited time. Often there is one strong voice leading throughout the lengthy duration. This is the usual way when prayer meetings are attended by thousands. It is like being carried along in a swift, river of prayer. There is no listening to each other's prayers because we are praying as ONE VOICE—a universal language of heaven. The atmosphere becomes electric.

I have been in meetings like this. People are crying out, wailing and beating their breasts in repentance. It sounds like thunderous rushing water. An incredible sound. After three hours building up momentum it is deafening, but you leave a changed person knowing that you have prayed. I believe God wants to take us there during combined prayer meetings. Do not be afraid of noise. There is continuous sound in heaven— worship around the throne of God; sound of rushing water; God's voice like thunder to a back drop of lightning flashes.

Jesus prayed in John 17: 22-23: *'I have given them the glory that [You] gave [Me], that they many be one as [We] are one—I in them and [You] in [Me]—so that they may be brought to complete unity. Then the world will know that [You] sent [Me] and have loved them even as [You] have loved [Me].'*

The key to unity is humility and love. Love is so much more impressive to those out in the world where love has grown cold. We can do the right things, but without the love of God for each other, we are just like clanging cymbals.

One day in the Maitland mall where we usually share the gospel, another Christian group was there before us witnessing for Jesus. A brother in Christ was singing songs of God's love and sharing the gospel between songs. It was coming across loud and clear and the atmosphere was beautiful. I did not know these people as they were from Sydney and teamed up with a local Pastor who was carrying a cross. The joy I felt was overwhelming, I could not help but join in with the flow of what the Holy Spirit was doing. That was the unity of the Spirit. Their approach to the public was different to how we do things but the atmosphere they had created activated me to pray for someone in need of healing, both physically and emotionally.

CHAPTER 19

The Coming of the King

'How beautiful on the mountains are the feet of those who bring good news, who proclaim peace, who bring good tidings, who proclaim salvation, who say to Zion, "Your God reigns!" Listen your watchmen lift up their voices; together they shout for joy. When the Lord returns to Zion, they will see it with their own eyes; Burst into songs of joy together, you ruins of Jerusalem, for the Lord has comforted [His] people, [He] has redeemed Jerusalem. The Lord will lay bare [His] holy arm in the sight of all the nations, and all the ends of the earth will see the salvation of our God.' Isaiah 52:7-10.

 The prophet Isaiah saw the restoration of David's throne, the temple of the Lord in Jerusalem. When the kingdom of this world has become the kingdom of our God. He shall reign for ever and ever. God has planted His watchmen around the world who are looking for the signs of His coming in the Middle East.

Before His return the gospel will be preached throughout all the world. Time on earth is growing short as we know by what is happening in all the world affairs. We have been in birth pangs for many years: wars and rumours of wars; famines; earthquakes; the love of God growing cold. During these dark times the Church of Jesus Christ needs to shine brighter and stand firm. We need an outpouring of His Holy Spirit as we worship Him; more manifestations of His working in our ministry. This can only come through yielded, holy, obedient and worshipful vessels so He can freely flow through us.

Jesus is coming again in clouds of heavenly glory! The scripture says in 1 Thessalonians 4:16-17:

"For the Lord [Himself] will come down from heaven, with a loud command, with the voice of the archangel and with the trumpet call of God, and the dead in Christ will rise first. After that, we who are still alive and are left will be caught up together with them in the clouds to meet the Lord in the air. And so we will be with the Lord forever.'

Jesus says in Matthew 24:31 *'And [He] will send [His] angels with a loud trumpet call, and they will gather [His] elect from the four winds, from one end of the heavens to the other.'*

The graves will open and those believers in Christ who are already dead over the years will rise first. You may ask, if they are already in heaven why would they need to rise? Because they are coming back to the earth to live. Their spiritual bodies will be transformed like Jesus' body so they can pass to and fro from heaven and earth. Those saints still living on earth when Jesus comes will be gathered into glory with them. Their whole beings will also be glorified so they will be able to live on earth as well as in heaven. Our old corruptible bodies will not be needed anymore. But we will still need an earthen body and a spiritual body to live on the earth as well as in heaven.

We will be like Jesus and will be able to move freely from place to place. Nothing will be able to obstruct us. As Jesus just appeared in a room with His disciples, so we will be able to pass through walls and arrive wherever we need to go. There will be no more pain, disease, tears, trauma or death. All things will become new. We will be able to pass from one dimension to another.

The sons of God will be transformed and revealed to all of creation. Every eye will see Jesus and the whole earth will rejoice because of the wonderful restoration and healing of the earth. All of creation has waited in eager expectation. Earth will once again become like the garden of Eden. In the beginning of creation God had seen His handiwork as good. As the Prince of Peace takes the government of the Kingdom upon His shoulders peace will be restored. It is hard to imagine living in peace and safety for a thousand years. The scripture says in Isaiah 11:6-10, that the wolf will live with the lamb; the leopard will lie down with the goat; the calf and the lion and the yearling together, and a little child will lead them. The cow will feed with the bear, their young will lie down together. Even the cobra or viper and young children will be playmates. There will be no violence, brutality or killing. Total harmony will be on the earth. Animals will have no need to attack for food as the ox and the lion will eat straw together. There will be tremendous respect for each other, animal, plant and human as God's creation co-exists. There will be a universal language of earth and heaven that communication barriers will be non-existent. All creation has suffered through the sin of man. The healing comes when the children of God come into their divine fullness and purposes of God, (Romans 8:19).

Isaiah 51:3 says: *'The Lord will surely comfort Zion and will look with compassion on all her ruins; [He] will make her deserts like Eden, her waste-*

lands like the garden of the Lord. Joy and gladness will be found in her, thanksgiving and the sound of singing.'

There will be no more droughts, floods and no more destructive elements. No such thing as climate change. Why will this be? Because Yeshua Hamashiach will rule and reign with perfection along with His saints. He will reign in holiness, truth and wisdom, righteousness and justice. There will be no need for democracy as the King will reign with a rod of iron—unbending and uncompromising. There will be no room for rebellion during this one thousand years reign of Christ and [His] bride. Instead, the glory of the Lord shall fill all the earth as the waters cover the sea. Habakkuk 2:14 says:

'For the earth will be filled with the knowledge of the glory of the Lord as the waters cover the sea.'

The earth will be in a state of perfection! All of our questions and prayers will be answered. Not only will our bodies be redeemed but also our brains. We will know all things without going into overload. There will be no sin in our lives to block out the voice of the Lord. Our ears will hear clearly and our eyes will see with ultimate clarity. We will finally be able to achieve the excellence and fulfilment we so strive for on earth. Our music and our voices will be refined to produce sounds we could never attain to while in our mortal bodies. If you considered that you were left behind when God gave music and singing gifts to others; never fret because throughout eternity you will be able to express so much melodious beauty as you are caught up into the love song of the bride of Christ. You will not be disappointed with what God has planned for you. We will be moving into the realm beyond the music—the back stage scenes will not be veiled from our eyes any more. We will be living them.

If we think that we are just going to laze around and retire, its going to be far from that. We are going to come back to rule and reign with Christ from [His] temple in Jerusalem. Jesus is going to empower us to rule people groups, rural areas, villages, towns, large cities and nations according to what the Lord has trained and equipped us as individuals to do.

The nations will be nothing like they are today. Every eye will see Him and every nation and ruler will bow before Him. No more will there be a separation between heaven and earth. The two will become one kingdom—the Kingdom of God.

Revelation 11:15-17 says: *'The seventh angel sounded his trumpet, and there were loud voices in heaven, which said: "The kingdom of the world has become the kingdom of our Lord and of [His] Christ and [He] will reign for ever and ever." And the twenty four elders, who were seated on their thrones before God, fell on their faces and worshipped God, saying: "We give you thanks Lord God Almighty, the One who is and who was, because [You] have taken [Your] great power and have begun to reign."'*

We are going to be present at this glorious proclamation of the Kingdom of God. It will be announced by the sound of a trumpet and loud voices. There will be a new song in heaven! No more will there be need of singing about the sorrows of life and being stained with sin, because the song of the redeemed will be about the glories of Christ and His Kingdom. It will be a new sound that heaven and the earth have never heard before. A song of unity in harmony with all of creation—every created thing on earth, under the sea, in heaven and the redeemed, as we acknowledge the Lamb of God who sits upon the throne. This kingdom is an everlasting kingdom and will not divide, weaken or die. It will be all power, love and devotion to its King.

Revelation 5:9-13 says: *'And they sang a new song saying: "You are worthy to take the scroll and to open its seals, because [You] were slain, and with [Your] blood [You] purchased men for God from every tribe and language and people and nation. You have made them to be a kingdom and priests to serve our God and they will reign on the earth." Then I looked and heard the voice of many angels, numbering thousands upon thousands, and ten thousand times ten thousand. They encircled the throne and the living creatures and the elders. In a loud voice they sang: "Worthy is the Lamb, who was slain, to receive power and wealth and wisdom and strength and honour and glory and praise!"*

Then I heard every creature in heaven and on earth and under the earth and on the sea, and all that is in them, singing: "To [Him] who sits on the throne and to the Lamb be praise and honour and glory and power, for ever and ever!"

The prayer of Jesus in John 17 will be fulfilled. The saints will be glorified and become one in all things. The prayer of the disciples that Jesus taught in: *"Thy kingdom come, Thy will on earth be done as it is in heaven,"* will happen as it has been declared for over two thousands years for many generations throughout all Christian denominations. Many times it had become a ritual but nevertheless declared to the heavenly realm of the kingdom of God to come. There will be no need to ask for daily bread; prayers to keep us from temptation or deliver us from evil as the tempter, the devil, will be bound for a thousand years. At the end of the disciple's prayer—*For Thine is the kingdom and the power and the glory forever, Amen!* is the finale throughout eternity. Hallelujah!

In an earlier chapter I had mentioned George Frederick Handel. He had the revelation of the awesome and glorious reign of the King of kings as he expressed in his writing of the oratorio, the *"Messiah"*. We will be singing the *"Hallelujah Chorus"* for ever and ever, except it will be thousands of times more glorious with all of heaven involved as *"He shall reign for ever and ever!"* There will be such magnificent freedom of celebration!

This is our hope! This is our future! Why would we want to miss out on such a glorious future?

All that Jesus has promised us will be fulfilled!

2 Timothy 2:12 says: *'If we died with Him, we will also live with Him; If we endure, we will also reign with Him.'* As we were baptised into His death we died to our sins, our own desires and yielded our lives to Him. We have become one with Him sealing, our marriage to Him as the bride of Christ. We have been made worthy through His blood to reign with Him for eternity.

Zechariah 14:9 says: *'The Lord will be king over the whole earth. On that day there will be one Lord, and His name the only name.'*

You may be asking when will these things happen? The disciples asked the same question? What do we do in the meantime? The beginning of this chapter started with *"How beautiful on the mountain are they that brings good news."* We have good news! We have a responsibility until the end of this age on earth to proclaim the good news of the kingdom of God. These are the days of our preparation and separation from the ties of this world.

It is time for the church to rise up and to possess the kingdom of God—to carry on the works of Jesus in overcoming the deeds of the evil one, (1 John 3:8). The Church is here to clean up the carnage in the wake of the devil's destruction. We are here to bring healing to people's lives. Yes, Jesus has defeated the devil on the cross. In other words, robbed him of his authority over mankind. Instead Jesus has empowered His church, with the authority to continue in the work He started.

The book of Daniel tells of what is to come—the rise of an antichrist, global power which will war against the saints of God and for a season its seems he wins. But in Chapter 7:22-27 it says:

'... until the Ancient of Days came and pronounced judgement in favour of the saints of the Most High, and the time came when they possessed the kingdom ... He (antichrist) *will speak against the Most High and oppress [His] saints and try to change the set times and the laws. The saints will be handed over to him for a time, times and half a time. 'But the court will sit, and his power will*

be taken away and completely destroyed forever. Then the sovereignty, power and greatness of all kingdoms under heaven will be handed over to the saints, the people of the Most High. His kingdom will be an everlasting kingdom, and all rulers will worship and obey [Him].'

Watchmen! What of the night! The world is under the dominion of Satan's workers and for a short season the Antichrist will rule from the third temple in Jerusalem and defile it .

The preparations for this temple is underway, which is a sign that it is closer to the Lord's return to take over the earth.

Coming, ready or not!

I guess we all can remember the hide-and-seek game we used to play as children and have passed it on to our children. One person would be the seeker and the rest of the group would hide. The point of the game was that the seeker would hide his or her face and count to twenty or more, whatever was the set rule for the game according to the setting. When finished counting the seeker would call out, "Coming, ready or not!" Then he would go about snooping for the hidden playmates. The one found first became the next seeker.

Jesus is coming back for a bride who has made herself ready, (Revelation 19:7). She is without spot or wrinkle, and is waiting for His return, (Ephesians 5:26-27).

Revelation 21:9-13 says: *"...Come, I will show you the bride, the wife of the Lamb. And he carried me away in the Spirit to a mountain great and high, and showed me the Holy City, Jerusalem, coming down out of heaven from God. It shone with the glory of God, and its brilliance was like that of a very precious jewel, like a jasper, clear as crystal. It had a great, high wall with twelve gates, and with twelve angels at the gates. On the gates were written the* names of the twelve tribes of Israel. There were three gates on the east, three gates on the north, three gates on the south, and three gates on the west."

We read the story of the ten virgins in Matthew 25:1-13 who went out to meet the bridegroom. Five were wise and planned ahead in preparation for the groom to come for them. They had bought enough oil to keep their lamps burning until he arrived. They trimmed the wicks of their lamps to keep them burning.

They had no idea when he was coming, because in Jewish customs of marriage ceremonies, only the father of the groom sets the day and the time when his son is ready to take his bride home. The groom also has to prepare a house for his bride. Just like Jesus said in John 14:2 *'In my father's house there are many mansions. I go to prepare a place for you.'* Jesus is preparing a place for us in His Father's house. The bride is waiting. Who is the bride of Christ? Those who are ready and alert. They are the ones who have trimmed their lamps—trimmed off the charred, frayed and useless bits in their lives that hinder the oil of the Holy Spirit from getting to the wick. Instead it dulls their light from shining brightly. The foolish virgins are the ones whose lamps once shone brightly, but were deceived by thinking the groom was never going to come. They were tired of waiting and grew slack in their preparations. They were not ready when the groom did come but were asleep. They let their lamps run out of oil and wanted to borrow from the wise virgins who had prepared. It is like some Christians who rely on others to feed them spiritually and do not worship and seek God for themselves. What a burden they are for those around them. We need to be ready and watchful for the Lord Jesus Christ coming for His bride. The count down has started for His return. The clock is ticking loudly. Then we will hear the final shout. "Coming, ready or not!"

Matthew 24:44 says: *'So you must be ready, because the Son of Man will come at an hour when you do not expect Him.'*

I love to look out at the stars and the moon. One night I sat staring out of the window. The full moon was bright and shining and the scripture came to mind: *'like a bride adorned for her husband ... dressed in fine linen.'* She was pure, innocent and dignified. The moon receives her splendour and light from the sun. It is eternal. It is symbolic of the church who receives her light and glory from the Son of Righteousness.

Psalm 89 :35-37 says: *'Once for all, I have sworn by my holiness— and I will not lie to David—that his line will continue forever and his throne endure before [Me] like the sun; It will be established forever like moon, the faithful witness in the sky.'*

The church, the temple of the Holy Spirit is the faithful witness of the glory of God—to be always on the watch for signs of the coming of the Lord. While looking up at the stars, multitudes of clouds passed over the moon like masses of shadows. But the moon still shone brightly and each cloud was etched with its brilliance radiating far and wide across the darkened sky. The clouds passed on and the moon seemed to shine even brighter. Then other clouds came. A wide ring of rainbow-like colours of refracted light enclosed around it. Even as the moon has eclipses and times when it is in darkness, so the church also has times when she seems to have periods of darkness, clouds of troubles, problems and disobedience block out her purity and glory.

Daniel 12:3 says: *'Those who are wise will shine like the brightness of the heavens, and those who lead many to righteousness, like the stars for ever and ever.'*

My thoughts have just wandered to another game we used to play which relates to the above. It was:

Starlight, moonlight the wolf is not out tonight

This game is played outside at night when the moon is full so you can see. It is similar to hide-and-seek, except the seeker—the wolf, decides how long to count, then he suddenly shouts: "Starlight, moonlight, the wolf is not out tonight!" He was a liar and a deceiver. He was out alright and ready to pounce on anyone who was too slow to hide. A scary game when you are a child and you take it seriously. Jesus likens wolves to false prophets and warns us in, Matthew 7:15:

'Beware of the false prophets. They come to you in sheep's clothing, but inwardly they are in wolves clothing.' (NKJV)

Referring back to the game above. The last time I played the game was several years ago with lots of relatives' children. It was fun yet chaotic. I had my lovable dog, Candy, with me. She loved the game but had entirely missed the point of it. She would expose the ones who were hiding by running up to them wagging her tail and barking. She did the same to the wolf. She loved it too. Candy was innocent of the rules and a people- pleaser. We can liken her to Christians who put their willingness to serve others before God himself. They do not know the rules of worship to God because they are not diligent in prayer and reading the scriptures. They are loving and accommodating, accepting everything they hear as truth. Unfortunately, they are easily deceived. Then we can also liken Candy to the person who likes to be at the centre of attention, and hurt others to get it by exposing them to gossips. Again, she could be like the ones who change the rules to suit themselves, manipulating the scriptures to a point of even deceiving themselves.

1 Peter 5:8 says: *'Be self-controlled and alert. Your enemy the devil prowls around like a roaring lion, looking for someone to devour.'*

Proverbs 28:1 says: *'The wicked flee though no one pursues, but the righteous are as bold as a lion.'*

We hear of great men and women of prayer who were heaven and earth shakers. John Knox was a great prayer warrior who cried out to God: "**Give me Scotland or I die!**" It was said that Mary, queen of the Scots, was more afraid of John Knox prayers than all the armies of England. Reinhard Bonnke prayed by asking God for Africa in the same way, and at the age of nineteen asked: "**Lord, I also want to be a man of faith.**" He led about 79 million people to the Lord. We all hear of the massive revivals wherever Charles Finney went, even as he travelled through towns, the whole towns would repent. But behind the scenes, a forerunner, Daniel Nash, went before Finney and travailed in prayer. Susanna Wesley bore nineteen children, yet spent two solid hours a day in prayer.

There are so many more. We all desire a mighty outpouring of the Spirit of God. Now is the time to cry out and to receive all He has for His church. Throw off all the ties, and desires of the world, that keep back the move of God's Spirit. His habitation is in the midst of the hungry people of God.

It is in human nature to be always looking for something bigger and better—house, job, car, boat or whatever we fancy. No one can really be satisfied with what they have. But of course this earth is not big enough for what we really need because our vision is so small. That of course does not make sense. The point is what we think we need, God has something better. God is big and extravagant! After living 1,000 years during the millennium, Satan will be loosed but will be overcome by the Lord and His saints then thrown into the lake of fire along with his followers. This will be the final battle that we will ever be a part of. This wonderful earth that was so amazingly restored, will be destroyed so no taint of sin remains in existence between earth, heaven and the universe. John the apostle describes what he saw through the Spirit in Revelation 21:2-3:

'Then I saw a new heaven and a new earth, for the first heaven and the first earth had passed away and there was no longer any sea. I saw the Holy City, New Jerusalem, coming down out of heaven from God, prepared as a bride adorned for her husband ... And I heard a loud voice from heaven saying, "Behold, the tabernacle of God is with men, and He will dwell with them, and they shall be His people, and God Himself will be with them and be their God."' (NKJV)

This is our future. This is our final destination. This is what we have invested in! It is debt free—no house repayments, rent, land rates, water rates, taxes, power and gas bills. God is our power source, the living waters never run dry. Jesus is our light and we reflect His light. Until these wonderful things happen let us live the rest of our lives as people with a hope and a future knowing we are sons and daughters of the King who has paid the price with His blood.

Abraham saw this city with spiritual eyes and he longed for it as we read in Hebrews 11:10:

'For he was looking forward to the city with foundations, whose architect and builder is God.'

I could understand that more clearly while staying at a Christian holiday resort in Israel. It was in the mountains and the views surrounding were beautiful. Way below I could see a village and children were playing on the street with what seemed to be a go-cart. Like children everywhere they were having fun and squealing with delight. On the other side of the ridge the scenery changed into natural forested hills and rural areas in valleys. Between tall trees was an opening that I could see through, far into the distance. There appeared to be miles of open flat land which was a little hazy with the early morning sun. When I checked the images on my camera I realised that something was out there—way in the distance beyond the haze, but I could not see with my naked eye. I zoomed in with telescopic lens on my camera. There it was glistening in the early morning sun—a large city! I was so excited about that. It reminded me of Abraham seeing the city which has foundations, whose builder and maker is God!

The city Abraham saw was thousands times more brilliant, glistening with the light of God.

The first time of entering into the city of Jerusalem was late afternoon and its magnificent, limestone walls shone golden in the glowing sunlight. It was an amazing introduction to this wonderful city where our Lord and Saviour is coming back to rule and reign. We all cheered with thanksgiving as the bus pulled in.

Isaiah 62:6-7 says: *'I have posted watchmen on your walls, Jerusalem; they will never be silent day or night. You who call on the Lord, give yourselves no rest, and give [Him] no rest till [He] establishes Jerusalem and makes her the praise of the earth.'*

On those stone walls the watchmen are alert, and waiting for the restoration of Zion for thousands of years. Let us be a part of the global song on the walls of Jerusalem. We are coming into a new era of kingdom worship where we go beyond the music of the earth and transition into the harmonies of heaven. God is already birthing in our spirit a song of melodies and harmonies beyond our mortal comprehension. It is conceived by our love and devotion to our Saviour and a desire for more of Him. The song of the Spirit and the Bride of the Lamb of God is growing louder and stronger until our cries will break open the heavens and the Lord Himself will descend with a shout and the sound of the trumpet!

MARANTHA!

COME LORD JESUS

And the watchmen on the walls of Jerusalem will lift their eyes and burst into song together, with those waiting on His Holy Mountain:

"BARUCH HA BA B'SHEM ADONAI!
BLESSED IS HE WHO COMES IN THE NAME OF THE LORD!"

ABOUT THE AUTHOR

Margaret Pickstone-Dark was born in the Hunter Valley, Australia, in 1949. She grew up in a hard-line religious sect until the age of 18. After she was released from this group, she studied music, which led into teaching piano and singing for 40 years. Besides teaching and directing music, choirs, drama and worship in Pentecostal churches, Margaret had been active in caring for the sick, counselling, street ministry and leading prayer groups in isolated country towns.

Her music ministry was launched in Auckland, New Zealand in the early 1970's and prayer ministry in South Korea in 1987. Her involvement with different prayer networks and evangelism has taken her around Australia, Philippines, India, Turkey, Indonesia and Israel. She is also an artist and author of six books. Margaret married for the first time in October 2020 to Peter Dark. They are presently living in the Hunter Valley and passionate about serving God together wherever He leads.

www.ingramcontent.com/pod-product-compliance
Lightning Source LLC
Chambersburg PA
CBHW060459090426
42735CB00011B/2035